Writer
to
Writer

Writer to Writer

Arthur W. Biddle

University of Vermont

McGRAW-HILL BOOK COMPANY

New York   St. Louis   San Francisco   Auckland   Bogotá
Hamburg   Johannesburg   London   Madrid   Mexico
Montreal   New Delhi   Panama   Paris
São Paulo   Singapore   Sydney   Tokyo   Toronto

WRITER TO WRITER

1 2 3 4 5 6 7 8 9 0 DOCDOC 8 9 8 7 6 5 4

See Acknowledgments on pages 233–237. Copyrights
included on this page by reference.

ISBN 0-07-005213-1

This book was set in Weiss by Better Graphics.
The editors were Stephanie K. Happer and Barry Benjamin;
the designer was Anne Canevari Green;
the production supervisor was Charles Hess.
The drawings were done by Danmark & Michaels, Inc.
R. R. Donnelley & Sons Company was printer and binder.

Library of Congress Cataloging in Publication Data

Biddle, Arthur W.
    Writer to writer.

    Includes index.
    1. English language—Rhetoric. I. Title.
PE1408.B4935 1985   808'.042   84-11298
ISBN 0-07-005213-1

FOR CARTER, ELLEN, AND JENNIE

Contents

STAGE II
THE WRITER EXPLAINS AND PERSUADES

STAGE III
THE WRITER REVISES

Preface

THE AIM OF THE PREFACE IS TO ESTABLISH THE PURPOSE AND SCOPE OF
YOUR BOOK

The McGraw-Hill Author's Book

TO THE STUDENT

Describing this book in a few words figures as one of the most challenging writing assignments I've been given in a long time—and I've been handed some tough ones. From the beginning, two principles have guided me. The first is suggested by the title, *Writer to Writer*. This book was written from one writer (me) to another writer (you). Like you, I struggle with getting started and with meeting deadlines, with finding just the right word and with that paragraph that simply won't come together. You know, the world is not made up of WRITERS (like Shakespeare, Dickens, Hemingway) and writers (like you and me). Instead, we are each somewhere on a spectrum of skill and experience. At one end of that spectrum, the kindergartner struggles to form the letter A, while at the other end the most accomplished stylists and master storytellers gnash their teeth and swear at their typewriters. Yet we are all engaged in the same activity. Where you are on the spectrum now matters less than where you find yourself at the end of this course. Along the way you'll produce a lot of solid writing and even occasional passages of brilliance. It's true—I've seen it happen just about every time. With determination and a good writing teacher, you can learn to write confidently and well. The purpose of this book is to give you the knowledge and the practice to achieve that end.

You'll progress further faster if you work on your writing one stage at a time. This second principle, called "writing as process," focuses first on discovering what you know and what you need to say, then on getting it into the most appropriate form for your purpose and audience. Each chapter's topics are arranged to help you move through the process from the germ of an idea to the finished piece.

These principles, like the advice and the writing assignments that follow, have been tested with hundreds of students for more than 10 years. They work for students in first-year English and for upperclass students in more advanced courses. They'll work for you.

TO THE INSTRUCTOR

The instructor will find *Writer to Writer* a text that most students enjoy reading, perhaps because the approach is pragmatic, not dogmatic. Just as there are many ways of teaching a writing course, so there are many ways of composing an essay, many processes. At each stage the student-writer is shown several methods and techniques and encouraged to experiment to find which is most helpful. Topics and assignments are carefully sequenced to allow each student to develop expository skills. Other features of the book are:

Purposive writing that explains a process, analyzes a problem, makes a decision, convinces a skeptic, gets action.

Audience-directed writing that stresses the needs of the reader.

Writing assignments, of which there are more than eighty to provide flexibility for classes of differing experience.

Handbook elements, only the most necessary, presented at the point of need: outlining in a prewriting chapter; paragraph generation, sentence structure, and punctuation in revising chapter; documentation in research chapter.

Style explained throughout in treatments of purpose, voice, audience, subject, revision.

Writer's protocol showing a writing process from choice of topic, listing of ideas and development of a plan through drafting and revising stages and accompanied by student writer's comments.

Writer to Writer offers a richness of resources that allows instructors to tailor the materials to their own classes and institutions.

ACKNOWLEDGMENTS

Acknowledging the assistance of others in the long process of writing this book is a pleasure. To my classes, past and present, my thanks for your patience and good sense. And for what you've taught me. Many of the writing samples in this book came out of those classes. I'm grateful to the authors for permission to use their work.

A number of friends and colleagues have also helped with this book. At the University of Vermont, Mary Jane Dickerson, Frieda Gardner, and Sidney Poger have been especially supportive. John Clarke, David Huddle, and Tony Magistrale have let me borrow ideas and writing activities. From neighboring St. Michael's College, Jennie Stoler has assisted with several chapters and cast the objective eye of the economist at several more. Writing teachers at other colleges and universities have read large parts of the manuscript and offered valued suggestions: John J. Clayton, The University of Massachusetts, Amherst; Edward Corbett, Ohio State University; John Ferré, University of Illinois-Urbana; Lynn Garrett, Louisiana State University; Thomas H. Miles, West Virginia University; Elaine M. Miller; Robert Perrin, Indiana State University; Maurice Scharton, Illinois State University; Richard M. Verrill, Boston University; Suzanne Wolkenfeld; William Woods, Wichita State University; and Ruth L. Wright, Auburn University. Through it all, I've been very fortunate to have a talented, long-suffering typist like Diann Varricchione to make even my worst prose look elegant.

Finally, I want to acknowledge my debt to two men whose examples as writing teachers have influenced my work. Indeed, the humanity and wisdom of Ken Macrorie and Donald Murray have enriched our entire profession.

Arthur W. Biddle

Stage I
The Writer Prepares

WRITING IS EASY. ALL YOU DO IS STARE
AT A BLANK SHEET OF PAPER UNTIL DROPS
OF BLOOD FORM ON YOUR FOREHEAD.
—*Gene Fowler*

Maybe writing has never come easily to you. It doesn't to most of us. And if we don't sweat blood, well, we do suffer a lot, especially at the beginning of a piece of work.

The first section of this book will help you get started. Step by step you'll discover how to tap the ideas and knowledge you already have, then how to increase and organize that knowledge. In Chapter 1 you'll try some stretching exercises for loosening up and building confidence. In Chapter 2 you'll learn proven ways of finding subjects to write about—subjects that interest you as well as your readers. You'll also see how to organize your material. Your work in Chapter 3 will teach you how to identify your audience and how to clarify your purpose.

My purpose in these chapters is to assist you through the first stage of the writing process. Good writer or shaky one, no matter what your ability at the beginning of this course, take heart. This section and the rest of the book that follows will give you the confidence and many of the skills to meet the challenges that lie ahead.

Chapter One
You and the writing process

*T*his book is about writing. It's probably not the sort of book you would hunt down in a bookstore and willingly lay out 10 or 12 dollars for. I understand that. If at the end of the course you still feel the same way, we, this book of mine and I, will have failed. And that would bother me. You see, the idea behind this book is that one of the two or three most important intellectual skills that you can learn in college is to write effectively. I teach writing because I know that people can learn to write—and I can see every day how important that is to them.

Let me tell you a story. Some time ago I read a paper by a student in the modern American novel course I teach. As a reader, the student seemed to have a good insight into the book he was discussing. But, as a writer, he just couldn't put it across. He wasn't making the connections clear between his ideas. Although the evidence he had selected from the novel was potentially good, he didn't know how to use it. He couldn't show cause and effect relationships—"because of this, therefore that." When he came in for a conference, he was concerned not so much because the paper had gotten a poor grade but because he knew that the comments I had written on his paper were true, true not only of this essay but of most of what he had written in college. I tried to describe to him what I saw: a fairly bright college student who had grown intellectually in the last couple of years (he is a junior) but whose writing ability had not developed much at all. Here were the perceptions and insights of a college junior handcuffed to the writing skills of a tenth or eleventh grader. Ken shook his head glumly in agreement. I wish I could tell you that the story had a happy ending, but I can't. It isn't over yet. I do have the feeling, though, that next semester Ken will take the writing course I suggested to him. Then, perhaps, I can add, "And he lived happily ever after."

The point of the story is that writing well matters. Writing well matters not only in this course—just one of forty or so you'll take in your 4 years of college—but also in the control that ability gives you over ideas and situations, in the confidence that skill gives you to confront new experiences, and in the power that proficiency gives you to develop and shape your ideas. This control, this confidence, this power can be yours if you want and if you work at it.

SO DON'T BELIEVE ME

Last year I took an adult education course in yoga and meditation. Not knowing much about these subjects or the cultures that gave birth to them, I was curious yet a bit skeptical. But the instructor had the perfect defense against any doubts that I or other students might harbor. Whenever he introduced a new concept or made a claim that a particular kind of exercise would relieve tension, for example, he would add, "I don't expect you to believe me. Just try it, test this exercise, and see if it works for you." He had discovered the only way of teaching his subject to people trained to be suspicious. He didn't demand acceptance of an alien culture or faith in his wisdom as a teacher. Instead, he invited his students to apply the American principle of pragmatism: Does it work? Then let's use it! Judging by this standard, I found much of what he taught us to be true or valid or workable.

Many students complain that writing is not their strength. They never expect to feel comfortable about writing. Perhaps you have heard it said that you can't teach anyone to write. Not true. You can learn to write effective prose—prose that informs and persuades with clarity and grace—and feel confident about your ability to compose whenever the need is there. I know you can because I've seen students master the intellectual and technical skills necessary to that end semester after semester. Never have I had a student who worked faithfully on his writing fail. In fact, I offer my students a "money-back guarantee," and only half in jest. I tell them what my yoga teacher told us and what I now tell you: "I don't expect you to believe me. Just try it and see if it works for you."

Approach the suggestions made in this book with the attitude of the experimenter. Please don't accept them on blind faith just because you see them in print. Many falsehoods, half-truths, and just plain silly ideas are to be found in books. The funny thing is that they look so respectable when they are set in type. Readers need to learn that and to exercise independent judgment about what they read. So don't believe any idea or suggestion you find in these pages. Test it. Apply it to your own writing. Then decide if it is true. No teacher should ask for more—or hope for less.

APPLY YOURSELF 1. "Why Johnny Can't Write." They began about 10 years ago—the complaints that Johnny can't write. Parents held emergency meetings and demanded action from the schools. Employers complained that job seekers couldn't even fill out application forms. *Newsweek* ran a cover story revealing just how serious and widespread the problem was becoming. Letters to the editor poured into newspaper offices. An entire nation, it seems, was concerned that its future voters and leaders wouldn't be able to string a dozen words together in a coherent sentence.

You've probably heard and read some discussion of this problem. List the causes that you're familiar with and tell whether, in your experience and observation, they hold true. Then describe your own situation and needs. What are your strengths and weaknesses as a writer? What do you hope to learn from this course?

THE WRITING PROCESS

Back when I took freshman composition, the routine in the course went something like this: The instructor would assign a 500-word theme, due in a week. We might have to define *democracy* or argue against capital punishment. While we were agonizing over that outside of class, in class we would deal with some matters of language, perhaps discuss kinds of propaganda or examine magazine ads for effective techniques of persuasion, maybe do an exercise with adverb clauses. When the theme was due, we turned it in. A week later it came back with several errors marked, usually a word or two of encouragement, and a letter grade. The end.

During the years since then, writing teachers have learned a good deal about the nature of the writing process. As a result, most freshman comp classes aren't like the one I had many years ago. What we writing teachers have learned is what I want to pass on to you, first in condensed form in this chapter and then in very practical ways throughout this book.

The most effective way to learn to write is to go at it as a process. You will probably have to learn a number of processes this semester. In your political science course, for instance, you may study the way a president is elected: petition drives, state primaries, party conventions, national elections, electoral college. In zoology the process might be the developmental stages of a butterfly: egg, larva, pupa, adult. Like these, writing is a process. The stages are prewriting, drafting, revising. We teach writing this way because people seem to make the greatest improvement when they learn it this way and because most writers compose this way.

PREWRITING

The word "prewriting" has come to stand for all the preparations the writer makes before beginning to draft or write. This stage includes, but is not limited to, perceiving a subject, determining a point of view toward that subject, defining the purpose and the audience, gathering information, and choosing the best form. Some of these are activities of the head, others of the hand and pen.

> *Writing is like pulling the trigger of a gun; if you are not loaded, nothing happens.*
> Henry Seidel Canby

Prewriting is the loading of the gun.

In the next chapter, we will look at the many faces of prewriting, beginning with finding something to write about. You will learn how to load the gun so that when you pull the trigger, something happens. The purpose of this chapter, though, is to introduce the stages of the writing process and to get you loosened up.

FREE WRITING

Sprinters warm up by stretching their muscles and practicing getting off the starting blocks. Pianists run over scales and chords to limber their fingers and their ears. Writers, too, need to warm up sometimes. Free writing is one such practice. Rapidly and without judgment or revision, you write absolutely anything that comes to mind. Simply record your thoughts.

How do you get started? Sit down with some paper and a pen or pencil. Set a time limit of 5 or 10 minutes and begin writing. Write your thoughts as fast as you can. You won't be able to get them all down because the mind works much faster than the hand, but you will catch many of them. When your mind goes blank (and it will), write "I can't think of anything to write" or something like that. Keep writing "I can't think of anything to write" until you do have another thought. The point is not to think of something to write about, but to write what you are thinking.

> It's Sunday, April 4, and it's snowing. Enough. It's not supposed to snow on April 4. I've had enough of a harvest I *never* desired (apologies to Robert Frost). Weekdays are always sunny and warm—well, that's not true. But most of the sunny, warm days are during the week. Weekends are always dreary, it seems. That's probably for the best anyway. Do you really think you'd be inside working on your book right now if it were about 60 degrees and sunny? Who are you kidding?

Sometimes your free writing will yield an idea that you can develop into an essay. As I did that chunk of free writing just now, I was sitting between my windows on one side and my desk on the other. Reflecting on the passage and my present situation, I realize that the windows and the desk represent the conflicting attractions of two worlds—play or recreation (the windows) and work or responsibilities (the desk). That's a conflict we all struggle with many times a day. And it's an idea that could be the germ of an interesting essay.

The discovery of ideas is just one of the results of free writing. Another is the gradual removal of inhibitions toward writing that have become ingrained by a dozen years of schooling. In free writing, you don't have to worry about spelling, punctuation, sentence structure, or anything else. None of that matters. When and if you decide to use an idea or passage, only then need you revise. Free writing is truly free of restrictions. Still one more outcome of free writing can be the development of an authentic voice—a voice that sounds like you. If you are like most college students, nearly everything you have ever composed has been for teachers. That means that you've developed a voice and a style that you believe is what the teacher wants to read. Chances are good that that voice and style are cautious, dull, and pseudoscholarly. If they gave Academy Awards for bad writing, the academic variety would be nominated for an Oscar every time. Your free writing session is an ideal occasion to begin breaking out of that mold of lifeless pedantry.

APPLY YOURSELF 2. Free writing. I've shown you mine, now you show me yours. You can do this in class or out: Write steadily for 5 minutes. Put down whatever comes into your head. Do this every day for a week, perhaps trying a 10-minute session once or twice. Then look over what you've written. Do you see any changes in style or tone? In subject? Do you sometimes stick to one idea for the entire session? Are there any passages worth saving? Any ideas worth developing? Do you think it would help you to continue free writing for another week?

THE JOURNAL

Keeping a journal can change your life, at least that's what some of my students tell me. While I won't go so far as to push that claim, I will assert that regular work in a journal can help to make your writing better and possibly even easier. It can also aid you in finding something to write about in this course.

A journal is a notebook in which you regularly write your thoughts. In the nineteenth century, it seems that every literate American kept one—not just political leaders and generals but farmers and shopkeepers too. Ordinary people recorded such diverse matters as the weather, the death of Uncle Joe's horse, the reports from Civil War battlefields, and the news of relatives moved West or left behind in the East. They must have felt that keeping a journal somehow gave order to their lives and preserved their thoughts and feelings for their descendents. One 23-year-old made this entry in the early pages of his journal:

> November 3, 1874.
> . . . Why do I keep this voluminous journal? I can hardly tell. Partly because life appears to me such a curious and wonderful thing that it almost seems a pity that even such a humble and uneventful life such as mine should pass altogether away without some such record as this, and partly too because I think the record may amuse and interest some who come after me.
>
> *Francis Kilvert*

Some of these old diaries make fascinating reading today. Your college library probably has a number of manuscript journals written by local people in the last century. Perhaps an older member of your family has squirreled away somewhere the journal of an ancestor of yours. Material like this could easily become the basis of a research project.

In our time writers keep journals for many of the same reasons their great-grandparents did. And for other reasons as well. The journal becomes a place to work out their thoughts and to record their ideas for future use, kind of a savings bank.

As a developing writer, you too can profit by keeping a journal, a practice I require of all my students. Your journal may be personal, but it should not be private. It is not intended to be a diary. Buy a stitch-bound (not a loose-leaf or spiral wire) book measuring about 8 by 10 inches, and you'll have a permanent repository for your thoughts, responses, and experiences with the world. Make a habit of writing in it every day.

As your journal is intended primarily for your own eyes and use, don't be overly judgmental about what you put in it. Some students write nothing but complete little essays, carefully proofread. I don't think they are writing for themselves. If that's what they want, I suppose it's all right. But I suggest you use your journal more adventurously. Sometimes you will want to be serious. At other times you can have fun. Play with words, with sentences. Play with images and metaphors. Yesterday I came across a magazine advertisement for Hellman's mayonnaise. Above the picture of a huge bowl heaped with salad was the lead: "Salad time and the dressing is easy!" Does that ring a bell? The copywriter was playing with the line from the *Porgy and Bess* song "Summertime and the Livin' Is Easy." Your journal should be a place for playful as well as serious thoughts.

A DOZEN IDEAS FOR YOUR JOURNAL

1. Copy clever graffiti. One of my favorites was a collaboration. The first scribbler wrote, "God is dead!" and signed it, "Nietzsche." Someone came along later and scrawled beneath it, "Nietzsche is dead! God." "Graffiti," by the way, is plural. Do you know what the singular is?

2. Copy effective advertising slogans—from radio, TV, magazines. See how they work. Or look for dishonesty in ads, manipulations of language that distort the truth in an attempt to mislead consumers.

3. Talk back to lecturers, respond to reading assignments.

4. Transcribe passages from your reading that strike you as superbly written.

5. Imitate those passages—that is, try to reproduce the sentence structure and style—but use your own words and ideas.

6. Anticipate the essay topic on an upcoming exam and draft a trial essay.

7. Copy words that fascinate you for their sound, their spelling—words you want to remember.

8. Explore the meaning of something that happened to you recently.

9. Recollect an event in your past, perhaps your earliest childhood memory.

10. Plan your future.

11. Jot down ideas for stories, poems, articles.

12. Write freely—just begin to write, putting down anything that comes into your mind. Sometimes this "unconscious" writing will turn up good ideas that you can develop into a "conscious" essay.

APPLY YOURSELF 3. Starting a journal. While I was in the library last week, I came across the journal kept by a student at my university over a hundred years ago. Here is the way he began it:

> Oct. 20th 1848.
>   Some great man has said that it is a good thing to keep a journal. It teaches one to write and leads him to review his actions during the past day or week as the case may be. Considering these things I have begun.
>   I suppose it would be well enough in the beginning to make a statement of my own affairs, describe the place I dwell in, and give a short account of my companions. . . .
>   So you see (for I am writing this to whoever reads it first: I must have an auditor or I cannot write, and the one that is so fortunate to first lay his or her hands upon this may consider himself or herself the one addressed), well, as I

was saying, . . . [The writer tells about his senior class and the reasons such as "drunkenness, laziness, hornblowing" that they now number only fifteen.]

Now for myself. You must have noticed before this that I am rather vain, self-conceited, egotistical, or whatever you choose to call it. Well I intend to be as everyone must, when writing such a thing as this, in some degree; but I mean to have *myself* stick out as plain as the nose on your face. . . .

I hardly know how to begin such a description. I am five feet eleven inches. . . . Perhaps you can get a better idea of me from a drawing. Well here I am, so you can consider yourself perfectly acquainted and take what I say as gospel.

Begin your journal as Roswell Farnham did in 1848: Make a statement of your affairs, describe the place you dwell in, and give an account of your companions.

APPLY YOURSELF 4. Keeping a journal. Keep a journal as suggested in this chapter. Let it reflect you, but try to vary the entries. Don't let them all become summaries of "What I did today." Use some of the suggestions in "A Dozen Ideas for Your Journal." Looking through half a dozen student journals, I came across the following entries.

About roommates:

> She makes me nervous because when she heard that if your roommate dies you get a 4.0, she got this horrible glint in her eyes. Well, if I die, and there's any suspicion about my death, here's the evidence.
>
> *Lisa Wright*

Favorite words:

> pleonasm, snaffle, nugatory, fusilade, paroxysm, insipid, redolent, mantissa, interdict
>
> *Ross Nayduch*

About human nature:

> Here's a classic. You walk by a store window and you always have to check and make sure you look cool.
>
> *Michael Mathews*

About a lecture:

> Tonight I went to listen to the Reverend Ralph Abernathy speak on Civil rights and the Black Freedom Movement. . . . Much of what he said reminded me of Ralph Nader's address in the fall. They both attended to the need to change the apathetic feelings of college students and how in the sixties people were so much more involved than today. But what these speakers fail to realize is that it is much more difficult for the majority of students to go to college today. Many need jobs to afford the rising prices. Who has time to go to classes, then a job, do homework and then write a letter to a senator or congressman? Some may say this is a copout but for others it is a very real problem.
>
> *Danielle Moran*

Life of a first-year student:

> Having problems with my schedule, many problems. Finally did laundry and found nine unmatched socks. How the hell could I have lost nine socks? Got robbed by the University store, four English books and a notebook for $38.
>
> *Ross Nayduch*

TWO CRAZY IDEAS THAT JUST MIGHT WORK

In her superb little book, *Becoming a Writer*, Dorothea Brande claims that the *psychology* of the developing writer is as important as any of the traditional skills of paragraph development or use of specifics. Like athletes who need to psyche themselves into long, boring, and sometimes painful practice, writers must learn to confront and then overcome their inner resistance and laziness. Writers (and writing teachers) who ignore this need overlook a fact of human nature. To help the developing writer get started and learn to write on demand, Brande offers two exercises: waking-up writing and writing by prearrangement.

Waking-up writing may seem strange at the beginning, but it is helpful to some. You write first thing in the morning, every morning. Set your alarm to go off half an hour earlier than usual. Then, before you have that first cup of coffee or glance at the newspaper or wake your roommate, write. Write anything—limericks, your recollection of that horrible dream, or just free write. *What* you produce is far less important than *that* you write and do it before you are truly awake. Keep at it for 15 to 30 minutes. Brande's notion is that in this state between sleep and wakefulness your unconscious is in the "ascendant" and that before long the words will come easily. Here's one student's waking-up writing, as he recorded it in his journal:

> The dream was so vivid, the picture was so clear. Last night I travelled back at least a hundred years in time.
>
> They were bringing the railroad to town. They were going to build it right up Ryan's Hill, however steep it was. First came the loggers, with horses, crosscut saws, axes, hundreds of them. The work progressed rapidly. There were people working everywhere. Some were wheeling crushed stone, others were setting down ties, still others driving in the spikes. They set off right up that hill carving their way through the wilderness. The view was tremendous. The sky was blue. There seemed to be more mountains in the distance. It was quite a sight, all the people working, the mountains, everything else.
>
> Then I was in a newly built house half way up the hill. You know the way dreams eliminate the transition part, one minute you're here, then you are there. Someone told us there was trouble following this railroad. From up the line, and down, came workers to build a large fence between the house and the railroad.
>
> Then there were all these people in and out of the house. It was nighttime, I think. Someone had gotten stuck in the snow, I don't remember with what. Then everyone was gone.
>
> Then I turned to someone, as we reached the top of Ryan's Hill, to talk about a huge eagle that sat in a huge nest on top of the highest tree. I said something about how that eagle probably wouldn't be coming here much longer with the railroad coming through. It was quite a sight to see all those people working away, the men with their suspenders and beards.
>
> *Harry Miller*

Maintain this practice for several days; then increase you output by a few sentences, a paragraph, another page. You may be surprised to find that the work becomes easier and that you can produce at will. When you have reached this stage, you are ready for the second exercise.

The purpose of this second practice is to teach yourself to write whenever you have to, whether you feel like it or not. Brande calls it "writing by prearrangement." It works like this: In the morning after you have dressed and perhaps eaten breakfast, select a time later in the day when you expect to have 15 minutes free for writing. It might be during that hour between classes that you usually kill by talking to friends in the library. Or the time you waste after your last class while you wait for the dining hall to open. You choose the time and make an appointment with your journal. Then keep that appointment. Regardless of what happens, you will write from 5:15 to 5:30, say. Again, what you write doesn't matter all that much. Overcoming your resistance and laziness is what counts. Believe me, I know. I can think of more reasons than you can to avoid writing—painful hangnail, lost my favorite pen, horoscope is unfavorable. Let's face it, for most of us writing is hard work. And solitary. No one is ever around to help or even to shout encouragement. It's just not the same kind of fun that a pick-up game of basketball is. The pleasure that we do gain from writing comes as a quiet sort of satisfaction at having said something and said it well. As you practice writing by prearrangement, you will probably find your reward. Choose a different time each day and keep at it for a week or two until you can overcome obstacles like friends' dropping in unexpectedly. Either chase them away or make them comfortable, then excuse yourself and go into the kitchen or the bathroom and write. These 15 minutes are sacred to you. Day by day you should find it becoming easier to keep your contract with yourself.

APPLY YOURSELF 5. Waking-up writing. For a week practice waking-up writing in your journal. Then, after rereading your entries, write an assessment of the value of the practice for you. Decide whether you should continue this kind of writing or move on to writing by prearrangement.

APPLY YOURSELF 6. Writing by prearrangement. To see if this approach works for you, try it for a week, then write a response to the experiment. What was unexpectedly hard or easy for you? Describe the circumstances in which you did your best work. Did you discover anything new about your attitude toward writing? At that point, you can decide if you want to continue to write by prearrangement.

A LOOK AHEAD

If you've done several of the assignments in this chapter, by now you ought to be writing a little more easily and freely. Perhaps you're beginning to feel that you're not such a klutz with a pen or typewriter. That's good. It's an important first step in your development in this course. The other purpose of this first chapter has been to introduce the concept of writing as process. Most of these activities—free writing, journal keeping, waking-up writing—are varieties of unstructured prewriting.

The next two chapters treat aspects of prewriting that point more directly toward a product, an essay. In Chapter 2 you will learn several ways to find something to write about when you are not given a topic and several other ways to find something to say when the topic is assigned. You will also see how to plan an essay. Chapter 3 lets you in on some decisions the writer needs to make, consciously or otherwise, in the early stages, decisions about purpose and audience that lead to more choices about style and tone.

Stage II of this book takes you through the drafting stage. Each chapter is concerned with one of the modes of explaining or persuading: definition, the how to, classification, comparison and contrast, several kinds of analysis, argumentation and persuasion, and, finally, research. The last part of the book, Stage III, is about the third stage of the writing process, that is, revising or rewriting or editing. This is the phase most often neglected by developing writers, yet revision and editing make all the difference between a raw outpouring and a smooth, impressive performance.

Can you make a commitment to yourself and keep it? You want to be able to organize your knowledge and present it convincingly, to express yourself clearly and perhaps even with grace. This is the time, and here in this class is the place. You, your instructor, and this book are the ingredients. It's up to you.

Chapter Two
In the beginning . . .

HE HAS HALF THE DEED DONE,
WHO HAS MADE A BEGINNING.
—*Horace*

*T*he opening verses of Genesis report that in the beginning the earth was without form and void. Although we may find it difficult to grasp that cosmic chaos, as writers we often experience our very own varieties. The emptiness or void engulfs us when the command comes to write and we haven't the least glimmer of what to write about. Or when we have a subject but don't know what to say about it. Those obstacles surmounted, topic and lots of information in hand, there remains the second quality of chaos—it is without form.

Every writer faces these problems with regularity. Not knowing what to write about. Not knowing what to write when we have a subject. And, even after these two difficulties are overcome, not knowing how to organize our information. In this chapter, you will learn some solutions to these problems. Perhaps it's unfortunate, but no single approach to composition has yet been found that works for all writers in all situations. Instead, research and teaching experience have yielded a number of methods, each with its uses. Study the prewriting strategies presented in this chapter, try them out, and note the value of each for you.

THE ACTS OF PREWRITING

The acts of prewriting, easy enough to list, are much more difficult to describe. Partly, that's because so many of them take place behind closed

CHECKLIST FOR ACTION

by Carol Cartaino and Howard Wells

OK, YOU'VE ALREADY

—cleaned your glasses

—reset your watch

—trimmed your nails

—washed your hands again

—brushed your teeth, put the cap back on the tube, rolled the tube up neatly

—cleaned your comb and brush

—fed the dog

—made a snack

—looked out the window

—eaten your snack

—checked the fish tank

—brought in the paper

—made coffee

—poured coffee

—read the cereal box again

—weighed yourself

—cleaned the light switch

—adjusted the lamp

—cleaned your typewriter keys

—changed the typewriter ribbon

—emptied the ashtray

—picked paperclips out of the rug

—sharpened your pencils

—emptied the pencil sharpener

—selected an FM station

—alphabetized your record collection

—done your sit-ups

—looked through the junk mail

—balanced your checkbook

—matched all your socks

—put all the hangers in the closet facing the same way

NOW: THERE'S NOTHING LEFT TO DO BUT WRITE!

Adapted from Writer's Digest

APPLY YOURSELF 1. Checklist for action. Make your own "Checklist for Action," things you might do to avoid the hard work of writing. Or make a different kind of humorous list: Things I'd Rather Do Than Take Chemistry (or Go to the Dentist or Spend Summer Vacation Living at Home).

doors—in the writer's head. The subconscious. Intuition. The flash of insight. Don't think I'm getting mystical—that's just the way it is. But some aspects of this process can be put into words, can be taught and learned and even internalized.

The steps are listed below in a rational sequence. You should realize that it would be unusual to follow these steps sequentially every time you plan a piece of writing. Often you'll begin with step 1, then work on 2, 3, and 4 simultaneously, and finish with 5, 6, and 7 in order. But all sorts of variations keep cropping up.

1. Finding a subject
2. Defining an audience
3. Determining a purpose
4. Selecting a point of view
5. Choosing an appropriate form
6. Collecting specifics
7. Making a plan

1. Finding a Subject

One of the acts of prewriting that gets easier as you gain experience is finding a subject. Maybe it's the practice, maybe that your knowledge has increased, maybe it's just growing older. People who have an insatiable interest in the world around them, a curiosity about life, seem never at a loss for something to write about. A good friend of mine who does a lot of free-lance writing published feature articles on the following subjects over a 2-month period: Dungeons and Dragons, mid-Eastern cooking, fat and obesity, and winter picnics. She finds these subjects all around her. You can too.

How do you go about finding a subject when there are no guidelines and no restrictions? You're already familiar with two techniques described earlier: free writing and journal keeping. In the next section of this chapter we'll look at several more.

Even when the subject is given, it will surely need to be refined. You will need to decide what aspects to treat. One student in a special education course was directed to write a ten- to fifteen-page paper on the history of special education in the United States or on mainstreaming. Although the subject was "given," I think you can see the problem that remained: what to *do* with the subject. My student, choosing the history of special education, had still to claim it as her own, to decide on a treatment that would distinguish her essay from thirty-five others in the class. And, since a thorough examination of this subject would require five hundred to one thousand pages, not the ten to fifteen she was allotted, she had to limit the subject. To limit is to reduce the scope of a subject so that you can cover it in some depth. The alternative is to skim the surface as you did in sixth or seventh grade when you wrote a five-page report on Brazil or aviation or the Renaissance. Much student writing suffers from the affliction of super-ficiality. You can avoid that disability by limiting.

So even with a subject in hand, you still need to know how to proceed. An entire field of research has developed that deals with just that problem. Later in this chapter, you will find four procedures that will help you move from a broad subject to a focused approach to the task.

2.   Defining an Audience
Sometimes inexperienced writers forget this step. Don't. Who are you writing this for? What do they already know about this subject? What do they want or need to learn from you? You must answer these questions to communicate effectively. Defining an audience is treated in Chapter 3.

3.   Determining a Purpose
Why are you writing this? The answer is not "Because my English (or psych or history) professor told me to." That may be the cause, but you have to supply your own reason for writing this particular piece about this subject. If you're composing a response to an exam question, the first of your purposes will be to demonstrate your knowledge of the subject. Subordinate purposes will relate to the question and help you decide on an appropriate form: compare and contrast Carter's and Reagan's foreign policies or define *main-streaming*. Some other large purposes are to inform, to entertain, to change behavior. More about determining a purpose in Chapter 3.

4.   Selecting a Point of View
In its broadest interpretation this is a complex act, for it relates to several others on this list. Point of view means the set of attitudes expressed by a writer toward subject, audience, and self. Attitude toward subject includes the point you wish to make about your subject as well as the distance you establish between you and that subject. The tone, as in tone of voice, relates to both your treatment of subject and your perception of your audience (friendly or hostile? formal or informal? personal or objective?) Tone also is a result of decisions you make about the authorial voice (self) that you will project in this piece of writing. Don't worry unduly if you're confused about point of view; we'll get into these issues in a much more helpful way in the next chapter.

5. Choosing an Appropriate Form

Sometimes the form chooses you, as in the assignment *"Analyze the functions* of the kidney" or *"Explain the causes* of the decline and fall of Rome." When the form doesn't choose you, your choice will depend in large part on the decisions you have made in the preceding four acts of prewriting: finding a subject, defining an audience, determining a purpose, and selecting a point of view. Oftentimes the experienced writer is not conscious of choosing a form; the form seems somehow to be an intimate part of his or her perception of the subject. Stage II of this book, The Writer Explains and Persuades, treats the basic forms or modes of nonfictional prose: definition, the how to, classification, comparison and contrast, analysis, and argumentation.

6. Collecting Specifics

Usually, you collect specifics and gather information after completing the preceding acts of prewriting. Only then do you know what kinds of details and data you will need. In many instances, the needed information is already in your head—you merely have to drag it out. List making and brainstorming are two methods of doing that. Huddle's questionnaire later in this chapter is another. In other cases you must find the details outside yourself, in your observations of your environment, in the conduct of an experiment or an interview, in library research. You'll learn how to find these specifics later in this chapter and in Chapter 10, "Search and Research."

7. Making a Plan

You can write without a plan. Many writers do. But planning has at least two advantages that I can think of. First, the written plan helps the writer see in tangible form the parts of the whole and thus perceive relationships and weaknesses in the structure. Second, it is infinitely easier and faster to rearrange subtopics, to add or delete items, or to ditch the whole scheme and start over in the planning stage than it is to make comparable changes in a draft. The plan is the place to pull together all the other acts of prewriting. Your plan may be as simple as listing the four steps of photosynthesis or as complex as constructing a formal outline for a twenty-page research essay. This subject is treated in detail in the last section of this chapter, "The Written Plan."

FINDING A SUBJECT WHEN YOU HAVE NONE

Your instructor—like most English professors I know—is probably going to ask you to write every week. And you—like most English students I know—

are probably going to run out of ideas very quickly. There is a way out, and it's legal.

Quotations

The main street in the town where I live is dominated by the 150-year-old Unitarian church. On the lawn in front of the church is one of those glassed-in bulletin boards that features a thought for the week, a short, provocative quotation. Sometimes the passage has no effect on me at all, but often it starts me thinking and leads me in surprising directions. If you've ever read a sentence in a book, heard a line in a song, or come across a verse of poetry that set you thinking, you know what I mean. A passage like this can become the departure point for an interesting essay, especially if it enables you to write about matters that matter to you.

Unfortunately, striking quotations just never seem to be around when you need them most, that is, when you're looking for a paper topic. One solution is to jot them down in your journal, whenever you come across them. Then they're yours and available for future use. Another way is to go to a book of quotations. Two standard collections are *The Oxford Dictionary of Quotations* and Bartlett's *Familiar Quotations*. One is arranged alphabetically and the other chronologically by author, but they have topic indexes so you can look up *wine* or *love* or *gardens* or whatever interests you. Whether you browse through the book or use the index, you're certain to come across a passage that moves or angers you, and, we hope, provides you with a subject for an essay. Here are some new (to me) quotations that I found by flipping pages.

> We are always getting ready to live, but never living.
> > *Ralph Waldo Emerson*

> Every man loves what he is good at.
> > *Thomas Shadwell*

> Of making many books there is no end; and much study is a weariness of the flesh.
> > *Ecclesiastes*

> The idiot who praises, with enthusiastic tone,
> All centuries but this, and every country but his own.
> > *William S. Gilbert*

> It is not the consciousness of men that determines their existence, but on the contrary their social existence determines their consciousness.
> > *Karl Marx*

Education . . . is hanging around until you've caught on.

Robert Frost

The end of man is an action, and not a thought, though it were the noblest.

Thomas Carlyle

APPLY YOURSELF 2. Quotable quotes. Spend 15 minutes with a collection of quotations, copying half a dozen that you find of interest. Hold on to your list—you might need it later. Better yet, copy it in your journal.

Daily Newspapers

For 30 cents you can buy one of the world's best aids to invention—today's newspaper. If you page through the paper in a receptive frame of mind, you can find a dozen ideas for essays. Read the headlines, look at the ads. You don't need the Washington *Post* or the St. Louis *Post-Dispatch*. The list of ideas below came from our local paper, circulation 51,329.

1. Section (of the paper): Front page and main news section
    Item: Israeli ambassador shot
    Idea (for essay): Ethical versus political issues of terrorism

2. Section: Front page and main news section
    Item: Historic county courthouse to be torn down
    Ideas: Architectural and historic story of the courthouse
        How do you tear down a courthouse?
        Desire for historic preservation versus needs of present

3. Section: Front page and main news section
    Item: Michigan school to flunk 22 percent of students in kindergarten
        and first and second grades because they didn't pass basic compe-
        tency tests
    Ideas: Your experiences with basic competency testing
        How about basic competency tests for teachers?
        Argument: basic competency testing wastes everyone's time

4. Section: Features
    Item: Daily horoscope
    Idea: Astrology—hoax or help?

5. Section: Entertainment
    Item: Review of a new film
    Ideas: Write your own film (record, play, concert, restaurant) review
        Write a review of a course you're taking

6.   Section: Comics
      Item: Your favorite comic strip
      Idea: An analysis of "Doonesbury," "Peanuts," whatever
7.   Section: Features
      Item: Columnist Erma Bombeck satirizes her college student son
      Idea: Write your own satire of the parents of a college student

And on and on. This list doesn't touch the sports section, display ads, the editorial page, or the classifieds (sometimes the most interesting of all). A newspaper will give you a lot of value for your money.

APPLY YOURSELF 3. What did you expect? Get a newspaper and make a list like the one above. Save it—you might be desperate for a topic someday.

Discovery, or Zero, Drafts

One way of meeting a writing assignment or need is to do a discovery, or zero, draft. You identify your subject and just plunge in and begin to write. You keep on drafting—exploring the subject, your knowledge about it, and your attitudes toward it. Two very accomplished writers and teachers of writing, Karen Burke LeFevre and Mary Jane Dickerson, explain:

> Writing serves not only as a way by which we communicate meaning to others, but also as a process by which we discover and make meanings for ourselves. We want to find out how we think and feel, what we know and what we need to learn. When we write, we do not simply record thoughts that we have already had. We can write to discover connections, make new meanings, and articulate understandings we may have been only vaguely aware of before we started writing.
>
> *Until I See What I Say: Teaching Writing in All Disciplines*

THE VALUES OF A DISCOVERY DRAFT

1.   To find out what you think about a subject. "How do I know what I think about something before I've written about it?" is a common answer students give when asked to tell what their paper will be. A zero draft is a good way to explore your attitudes.
2.   To find out what you know about a subject. When a zero draft contains an inventory of your knowledge on a subject, you learn where your strengths lie and can then channel your plans in that direction.
3.   To find out what you don't know about a subject. You may discover

through the zero draft that your knowledge is so limited that you would be better off choosing a different subject. More likely, you will see gaps in your knowledge, gaps that can then be filled through research, interviews, observation, or some other means.

I have used the names "discovery draft" and "zero draft" interchangeably. They both convey the notion, I hope, that this kind of writing is preliminary, really a variety of prewriting. This is important. If you come to think of your zero draft as a *first* draft, you're headed for trouble. This is not just a case of another English teacher playing with words. The discovery draft is intended to help you make a preliminary survey of the territory—the subject and your mind. It is not meant to yield a piece of writing that needs only a little attention to mechanics and a retyping job before it is turned in. I've seen a lot of students stalled in their writing progress over this point. With little or no planning, they launch into a draft. Having finished, they tinker a little here and there, check the spelling, and consider the job done. That's not the way it works, at least not for most of us most of the time.

If you are going to use the discovery draft approach, acknowledge it frankly as part of prewriting. When you step back and look at this draft, you should be able to see what you need to do before you are ready to write a first draft: further narrowing of the subject, research of one sort or another, finding a different approach, and so on. Don't mistake the relief you feel at having put some words on paper for satisfaction at having written your essay. And beware of another hidden danger of the zero draft: too early a commitment to a draft. The resulting essay is too often thin, short of information, lacking in detail. You'll have two and one-half pages when you need four; so you'll try to expand it, stretch it, pad it. And that just doesn't work.

If, on the other hand, you employ the discovery draft as a step in the prewriting process, you may find it a useful technique.

Focused Free Writing

In the last chapter I described free writing as a means of warming up and becoming more relaxed about your work. You probably tried the exercise in class or in your journal. A variation on this is focused free writing, which can be a kind of discovery draft. All the rules are the same—write rapidly and without judgment or revision—except one. In unstructured free writing, you write anything that comes to mind; in focused free writing, you stick to a single subject. It is fine to let your mind roam the territory of that subject, exploring its limits, coming at it from different angles, making lists, narrowing to subtopics. Just stay on the subject.

APPLY YOURSELF 4. Focused free writing. Choose one of these methods for selecting a subject. Then do a focused free writing for 10 to 20 minutes or until you've exhausted the subject.

A.   Use the topic already assigned for a course you're taking, perhaps a paper you have to write or an exam you're studying for.
B.   Choose a subject arbitrarily from your life, something related to school, friends, current events.
C.   Do a 5- to 10-minute unstructured free writing first, then look it over to find a subject that interests you. That subject becomes the center of the focused free writing.

THE 2-MINUTE LIMIT

Teaching an intermediate writing course several years ago, I invited as a guest speaker a man who earns his living by writing. Like the students in that class, he has regular deadlines to meet. He can't wait for the muse of poetry to whisper in his ear. Nor can he afford to sit around until the mood strikes him. He has to produce on demand, day after day. What he said that morning has remained with me ever since. "Before I sit down to write, I check my watch," he began, "and then think of what I have to do and ways I might do it. Sometimes I'll come up with a catchy opening or some other bit of inspired thinking. But more often I sit and look at the blank page that mirrors the blankness of my mind." My students smiled to hear that someone else, a professional writer no less, had the same problems getting started that they had. "If at the end of 2 minutes," he continued, "I still can't think of a good way to begin, I start to write anyway. Something about the subject, it hardly matters what. The important point is not to allow myself to become immobilized by the blank page. Once I've written a few sentences, perhaps more, I'm over that initial paralysis and I can keep going. Then I can see what I need to do."

Student writers who have tried this 2-minute limit report that it does help them overcome that far too common inability to get started. Sometimes they will continue, writing an entire zero draft. At other times they will realize that this was a false start, but in that realization comes the intuition of where they actually need to begin.

If you have encountered the "terror of the blank page," you might just try this treatment the next time it hits.

TECHNIQUES FOR INVENTION

The Romans called it *inventio*, the Greeks *heuresis*. Both are terms for the process of discovering something to argue or write about, seen as the first of five steps in the preparation and delivery of an oration or speech. Twenty-five hundred years later, teachers of rhetoric still begin with invention, or heuristics as it is sometimes called. What has changed is the variety of approaches to teaching the subject that has developed in the last decade or two. So far in this chapter, we have already discussed several of the more informal techniques of invention: the discovery draft, focused free writing, quotations, and the newspapers. These activities help you find something to write about and aid you in discovering an approach to your subject once you have found it. The following techniques for invention are somewhat more structured and sharply focused. They are most useful after you have found or been given a subject.

Starting with Specifics

This approach to writing a description will challenge your understanding of the acts of prewriting and your growing skills as a writer. In the three related assignments that follow, you are asked to work through all the steps of the writing process—prewriting, drafting, and revising.

APPLY YOURSELF 5. Gathering specifics. Choose a place to describe. Find one that is rich in sensory details of sight, sound, smell, touch, and possibly taste. It should not be a place you know so well that you'll have trouble "seeing" it. Go there and soak it up. While you're on the scene, make a list of at least fifty specific details; these will be the raw material of the next assignment. But for now don't worry too much about how you'll use these specifics. Just get them on paper. Here's an example of the kind of list you might make:

RAINBOW LAUNDROMAT

1. The stinging smell of Clorox
2. Loudspeaker throbbing with hard rock
3. Layers of sounds
4. Water gushing into washing machine
5. Steady whirr of driers
6. Buttons banging in a drier drum
7. Whines and whistles, bleeps and blasts from Galaxian video game
8. Air from the driers—soft warm damp linty
9. Three cocky 17-year-old guys, working over the pinball machine
10. One of them blowing cool smoke rings
11. Ten-speed bike with trailer filled with laundry
12. Amber lights signal "washer in use"

13. Red lights signal "drier in use"
14. Joe the proprietor with a six pack of Michelob
15. Wisk
16. Clorox 2
17. Lite
18. Coke
19. Shout
20. Tide
21. Orange Crush
22. Bounce
23. Guy in midtwenties eating a Reese's peanut butter cup and carving a 3-foot totem pole
24. Old movie posters: Caddyshack, Flash Gordon, Popeye, Blue Lagoon
25. Twenty-four washers
26. Sixteen driers
27. Rubbermaid laundry basket
28. Gold backpack
29. Garbage bag
30. Tape-reinforced cardboard box
31. Duffel bag
32. Wicker laundry basket
33. Haze of smoke around ceiling lights
34. Six unmated socks in the lost and found box
35. Yesterday's newspapers litter the folding tables
36. Last October's *Computer Decisions* magazine
37. Notice on bulletin board: "Roommate wanted—Call Steve"
38. Middle-aged man in ratty sweatsuit, probably last clean clothes
39. Fifty-ish woman in bright green knee-length coat
40. She carefully measures a capful of Downy
41. She slugs her Lite, drags on a cigarette, and sits down to work on her latch-hook rug kit
42. Pretty young woman, early twenties, smiles softly to herself as she folds her nightgown
43. Wooden sign shows open mouth with teeth: "U R WAT U EAT"
44. Cracked but clean concrete floor
45. Lids up on some washers, down on others

46. Machines: detergent and bleach, soda, candy, cigarette, dollar bill changer, pinball, video game, coin phone, coffee and soup, regular washers, supersize washers, driers, drycleaning
47. Grimy, factorylike windows keep out more light than they let in
48. Fourteen-year-old girl, hair in latest style, eyes 17-year-old boys
49. Sneakers, clogs, hiking boots, bare feet, thongs, sandals
50. Vibrations from out-of-balance washer

APPLY YOURSELF 6. Drafting a description. Fascinating to me about this assignment in description is that three or four writers can go to the same place at the same time, yet come away with very different impressions. As important as the place are the writer's perceptions of the place. Now turn loose your imagination and your memory. What are your perceptions of your place? Were you left with a single dominant impression? Do you sense a pattern in your list of specific details? Is there a point that you want to make about that place or, through that place, about human behavior? By answering these questions, you will come to your true subject, not the Rainbow Laundromat, but something about the Rainbow Laundromat. You probably will discover your purpose as well. Write a statement of true subject and purpose.

Next, with that statement in mind, select those details from your list that are of your subject and purpose, the details that will bring out your perception. Then beneath this statement, list the relevant details.

The third step of this assignment is to write a draft description. Let your true subject and purpose control the draft. The length, too, should be determined by these factors, although for our needs one-half to a full typed page will probably be fine. If you don't have a particular audience in mind, think of your English class, students and instructor, as your readers.

Here is the opening of one student's description of McDonald's:

MCDONALDLAND

McDonald's is the epitome of the sterile, efficient world of the future which the human race has created and many artists have satirized. It is the image of the mechanical world conjured by the phrase "Space Age" or "Computer Age." The fast-food restaurants, or stores as they are called by McDonald's employees, are popping up like zits on the face of the earth, infecting the consciousness of the human race.

Approaching McDonald's, I passed the ubiquitous "Golden Arches" on which a bright red sign boasted the number of billions served. To my left, the manicured lawn and shrubs seemed unnatural. I thought of how easily they could be replaced by artificial turf, much like the indoor plants had been replaced by plastic replicas, or as I, a worker, might easily be replaced by a robot. A buzzing voice attracted my attention. I glanced across the lawn and noticed the metal box of the drive-thru taking an order from a voice inside an automobile.

Karen Einstein

APPLY YOURSELF 7. Revising your description. After you have finished the last assignment and have a good draft, get some feedback on it from your instructor, your workshop group, or a critical friend. When it has cooled off for a while, reread it yourself—aloud. Listen to it, really listen. Do you like the sound of it? Is it truly descriptive—have you caught some good details? Does it do what you had planned—make a point, give a single overall impression, express a perception? Next, look at your sentences. Should any of them be combined? Split? Any unnecessary words? If you want additional guidance in revising, turn to Chapter 11, "Revision." Revise your description until you feel that it is as good as you can make it right now. Before you begin, though, you might compare Karen Einstein's revised description of McDonald's, as follows, to the earlier draft.

MCDONALDLAND

McDonald's—the epitome of the sterile, super-efficient world of the future. The perfect image of the computer age. These fast-food restaurants, or *stores* as they are called by McDonald's employees, pop up like zits on the face of the earth. On the ubiquitous Golden Arches a bright red sign boasts the number of billions served. The manicured lawn and shrubs seem unnatural. How easily they could be replaced by artificial turf, much as the indoor plants have been replaced by plastic replicas, or as I, a worker, might easily be replaced by a robot. Across the lawn a mechanical buzz intones, "Welcome to McDonald's." The metal box of the drive-thru takes an order from a voice inside an automobile.

Autobiographical Questionnaire

At the beginning of each summer an extraordinary course is offered at my university. Called simply Writers' Workshop, it's more like a Marine Corps boot camp for writers of poetry and fiction. For 4½ hours every morning for 2 weeks and again for a couple of hours in the evening, they meet to read their work aloud to each other and to listen to professional writers read from their work. In between, they write and write, the sole respite a traditional lunchtime volleyball game. At the heart of the workshop is the "only" assignment for the first week, responding in writing to an eighty-five-item autobiographical questionnaire. David Huddle, author of the questionnaire and one of the teachers of the workshop, tells me that students produce from fifty to a hundred pages of prose in response to the assignment. They then find raw material in this response for poems, short stories, or chapters of novels. The questionnaire functions as an extended prewriting activity, helping writers explore the subject they know best—themselves.

The following questionnaire has been adapted and condensed for use in this chapter.

QUESTIONNAIRE FOR AN AUTOBIOGRAPHICAL PORTRAIT

David Huddle

INSTRUCTIONS

You are to write an autobiographical portrait of yourself in the third person. Use "he" or "she" instead of "I." Using the third person ought to allow you to make a sort of character of yourself and to give you a certain amount of freedom to write as honestly as possible. Your portrait should read as an independent piece of writing; thus a reader should not have to depend on the questionnaire to understand what you are writing about. You will be asked to read much of your portrait aloud in class. However, you will not be required to read in class anything that could cause you embarrassment. You are encouraged to write through those questions that might cause you to reveal information that is personal and sensitive to you, but you are not required to open that writing either to the class or to the instructors. You should take this assignment as seriously as you possibly can; put as much work into it as you possibly can. Be concrete. Be honest. Be certain that you are trying to write about things that are important to you.

QUESTIONS

1. Describe subject physically: face, hair, hands, feet, body, gestures, way of walking, voice, clothes, etc. What are subject's most pleasing physical characteristics? Most displeasing?

2. What are subject's habits? What patterns are there in subject's life?

3. Describe the place or places where subject grew up and spent most of his or her time. Be particular about this; use small areas such as city blocks or apartment buildings, or neighborhoods, or the geography of

a farm. The rule here would be to use only that area with which subject was thoroughly familiar.

4. Describe subject's attitudes toward the places that have had the most effect on his or her life. Use concrete details here as much as possible.

5. Describe subject's father (as in question 1). Provide at least three visual scenes of subject's father.

6. Describe subject's mother (as in question 1). Provide at least three visual scenes here, too.

7. What details of the senses does subject associate with his or her parents? What physical objects (such as a scarf, a knife, a tree, an ironing board, a bottle) would subject associate with his or her parents?

8. Provide conversations between subject and each of his or her parents.

9. Describe at least one (and more if possible) dream that subject has had of each of his or her parents.

10. What is subject's earliest recollection? Be as detailed as possible.

11. What are other early recollections?

12. Describe what subject remembers of his or her childhood prior to beginning school. Try to include at least three events that were of particular importance to subject's life. Remember to be especially concrete here; render scenes as vividly as possible.

13. Describe at least three events that were of particular importance to subject's life during his or her elementary education. Include as much general description of subject's life at that time as is appropriate.

14. Describe subject's passing from childhood into adulthood. Include events that were of particular importance.

15. Describe the circumstances in which subject feels most ill at ease, discontent, unhappy.

16. Describe things that subject has done in his or her adult life that have required the most profound seriousness.

17. What are subject's attitudes toward money?

18. The opposite sex?

19. Love?

20. Insanity?

21. Suicide?

22. Violence?

23. Family life?

24. What aspects of subject's own character and personality is subject most at odds with? How do these affect subject's life?

25. What are the motivating forces in subject's life? What are the things that cause subject to do what he or she does?

26. Describe the one person of the opposite sex (other than a parent) about whom subject has cared most. Give careful attention to physical description, places and events subject shared with this person. Describe changes in subject's attitudes toward this person.

27. Describe the one person of the same sex as subject about whom subject has cared most (other than parent).

28. Describe subject's behavior and thinking when alone, with no possibility of any kind of companionship.

29. In a strange city.

30. At a wedding.

31. In the immediate presence of death.

32. In games.

33. In awkward situations.

34. When affectionate.

35. When confronted with hostility.

36. When offered affection.

37. In the presence of children.

38. Describe subject's major difficulties in dealing with other people, giving specific examples and attempting to track down reasons for these difficulties.

39. What burdens does subject carry, and how does subject feel about them?

40. What insults would strike subject most deeply?

41. What flattery would subject respond to most strongly? Why?

42. Describe how subject would choose to die.

APPLY YOURSELF 8. Autobiographical portrait. Write your responses to several of the items on Huddle's "Autobiographical Questionnaire," following his directions. Your draft should be five to ten pages long. Although this is a prewriting assignment, you may want to follow through by selecting something from your response to rework into a finished piece, perhaps a narrative showing characters in opposition.

Common Topics

The common topics of invention have been with us for a long time. Because they are so useful as an aid to discovery, they are likely to be around a good deal longer. Like the other procedures explained in this chapter, the common topics provide you with a method of systematic inquiry: a number of questions to ask about your subject and a means of obtaining information about that subject. Their use can take you from a general sense of subject to an understanding of what you have to say.

The purpose of any system of invention is, in the words of Richard L. Larson, "to help students see what is of interest and value in their experiences, to enable them to recognize when something they see or read or feel warrants a response from them, in other words to stimulate active inquiry into what is happening around them. . . . " By asking the following questions of the topic, you will be seeking to uncover not merely an approach to a subject but an idea or insight that moves you to write about that subject.

1. What is it? **Definition**
   What are its characteristics or qualities?
   What are its limits?
2. What is it like? **Comparison**
   In what ways?
3. What is it different from? **Contrast**
   How does it differ from things it may otherwise resemble?
   Is this a difference of degree or of kind?
4. What are its parts? **Division and analysis**
   What goes to make it up?
5. To what larger structure or class does it belong? **Classification**
6. How does it work? **Functional analysis**
7. What causes it? **Causal analysis**
   What conditions are necessary for its existence?
8. What are its effects? **Effect analysis**
   What results might be anticipated from its existence?
   What purpose does it serve?
9. What is the value of it?
   What are its advantages?
   What are its disadvantages?
10. What do others say about it?

One of the best ways to understand how to use the common topics is in a group brainstorming session. The group could be your entire writing class or a smaller workshop section of that class. Failing that, you could get together with three or four other students from the class and try this on your own. A technique for fostering creativity, brainstorming is used by executives in business, government, education, and the military to "loosen" the thinking of the participants as well as to find unconventional solutions to problems. When the session begins, a time limit is set, the problem described, and people begin to throw out ideas. One member of the group records the suggestions. The rules are few and simple:

1. No evaluation of suggestions allowed. No comments like "that's dumb" or even "great idea." Evaluation stifles the flow. Save it for after the brainstorming.
2. Wild and wacky ideas welcome. Sometimes the zaniest solution proves the most workable.
3. Piggybacking encouraged. *Piggybacking* is modifying or building on someone else's idea. Brainstorming is cooperative, not competitive.

So, try to arrange or take part in a brainstorming session using the common topics to approach a problem. If you can't, you can hold your own private session, following the same rules.

Becoming adept at using the questions requires a little practice, but fairly soon you may be able to internalize the process, applying it with little effort. The first few times, though, you should jot down the questions, worded to fit your subject. Don't hesitate to modify the question. Results are what count. Then, beneath each question, write your response. Some questions may not pertain to your topic; move on to the next. Sometimes lightning will strike as you are thinking about one of the questions or your answers; you'll perceive what you want to say in a flash of insight. At other times you'll have to go through all the questions, write the responses, and study those responses, before you find the organizing principle that you've sought.

As an example of the way the common topics may be used, the following list describes the results of a brainstorming session on the subject "the protest movement of the 1960s." Three friends and I sat around a table and answered the questions, as suggested earlier. Here is what came out of that 10-minute session.

1. **What is it?** We began with this question and immediately raised another question: "Was the protest movement of the 1960s one movement or several?" The answer to that question may belong here or may better fit under topic 4, "what are its parts?" That doesn't really matter. We did determine that we meant by "the protest movement" the following elements: antiwar, anti-nuclear power, and rights movements by women, blacks, gays, and students. We would need to

stipulate definition, then. Perhaps related to these phenomena was the counterculture of hippies and flower children. It was a movement characterized by civil disobedience and political involvement. It had a counterpart in France, Germany, and England. It was sometimes characterized by violence.

2. **What is it like?** In one aspect or another the protest movement of the 1960s resembled:

> The march on Washington, D.C., in 1932 by thousands of unemployed workers
> The American Revolution
> The Russian Revolution
> Union organizing efforts
> Popular movements in Europe in the mid-1800s

3. **What is it different from?** We agreed that the protest movement of the 1960s was different from these earlier movements in many respects. It was beginning to look like a comparison/contrast essay might be one interesting way of treating this subject.

4. **What are its parts?** One way of looking at this question would give as answers the elements listed in topic 1, like the antiwar protester and the black civil rights force. Looked at another way, we came up with marches, journalistic propaganda, campus strikes, sit-ins, draft resistance, flag burning.

5. **To what larger structure or class does it belong?** One answer is that the protest movement was part of a broader raising of political and social consciousness. It was suggested too that it was part of a larger, worldwide leftist movement.

6. **How does it work?** One answer to this question would yield a chronological history of the movement, surely the subject for a book-length treatment. Another answer was a study of the process of a single event, one campus demonstration, for instance.

7. **What caused it?** Many answers: It started at Columbia University, John F. Kennedy, liberal trends in education, reaction to the somnolence of the 1950s, Martin Luther King, Jerry Rubin, Abbie Hoffman, Betty Friedan, other individual leaders, the Supreme Court decision in 1954 in the case of *Brown v. Board of Education*, the Voting Rights Act of 1965, disenchantment with the perceived materialism of American society.

8. **What are its effects?** Short-term: the publicity surrounding the events

at the Democratic Convention in Chicago in 1968, the presidential candidacy of George McGovern and George Wallace, the election of Richard Nixon in 1968, Lyndon Johnson driven out of the presidency, emigration to Canada of draft resistors, terrorism, the events at Kent State University. Longer-range effects might be: the liberalization of college curricula and rules, the ending of the draft, the ending of the Vietnamese war, greater rights for some minorities, the broadening of the drug culture.

9. **What is the value of it?** Stopped Vietnamese war, led to Voting Rights Act of 1965 and other civil rights acts, increased general interest and participation in the political process.

10. **What have others said?** We didn't pursue this one. We might look at newspapers from the period or research books that have been written since then.

As a group, I think we were surprised at the great number and variety of ideas that came out of this 10-minute session. Some specific topics for essays that were suggested follow:

1. Which part of the movement I would join
2. Effects of the movement on today's society
3. How anti-Vietnam-war movement affected the political situation between 1964 and 1968 (comparing President Johnson's policies of 1964 to the campaign of 1968)
4. Relation between the antiwar movement and race riots in a number of American cities between 1964 and 1968
5. Changes in rules of the Democratic party after the convention of 1968

APPLY YOURSELF 9. The common topics. Choose a subject and apply the common topics. List your responses beneath each question. Then list at least three possible limited approaches to your topic that you might use as the basis of an essay.

THE WRITTEN PLAN

A writer's written plans may take many shapes, ranging from a few words scribbled on a bar napkin to a fully developed outline with roman and arabic numerals, capital and small letters. Probably those who use a written plan aim for something in between these extremes most of the time. As a writer, I find my own practices vary. If I know the subject very well and the piece will be short (a memo or a letter, say), I will probably just begin writing, with only a mental plan. For a longer piece that might require greater control (like a book chapter or an article), I will jot down the points in the order in which they will be covered or with indications of relationships such as topics and subtopics. For an example of this kind of plan and the essay that was written from it, see Chapter 5, "How To." After I had written that plan, the article almost wrote itself. Five typed pages in less than 2 hours.

Sometimes, though, even if you're certain about purpose, audience, voice, and context, you may be unsure of exactly how the essay should develop. Writing down ideas and examples helps, but the order and emphasis will be determined only during the drafting. That's the way I wrote the section on the journal that appears in Chapter 1. Here is my plan, such as it was.

> *Journal*
> > Kinds of entries
> > > Trial essay exam topics & responses
> > > Commentary (not notes) on lectures, reading assignments
> > > Graffiti
> > > Ad lines
> > > Passages from reading
> > > Imitation of a passage
> > > Words that fascinate you—that you like the sound of, etc.
> > > Ideas for stories, poems, essays
> > > Recollections of your past
> > > Plans for your future
> > > Free writing
> > > The meaning of something that happened to you
> > Daily writing
> > Nonjudgmental
> > Bound volume
> > Journal, not a diary,
> > Personal, but not private
> > The idea of *play*
> > Source of ideas for future essays
> > "Salad time and the dressing is easy!"—mag ad for Hellman's mayonnaise
> > Ex of play: taken from song, "Summertime and the living is easy!"
> > Ex "Winter time and the sledding is easy"

Brainstorming the list of things to put in a journal was easy. So was coming up with the other ideas. I'd been making these points to students for years. The "salad time" line I found a couple of days ago and copied it into my journal. But I just couldn't get any further with the plan. Stumped, I decided to begin a zero draft. As it was just a few hours ago, I can recall very clearly not knowing when I started drafting what shape that little essay was going to take, what the order of points would be, or where the list of things to put into your journal belonged. I had to discover solutions to those problems during the draft. The written plan did tell me what information to include, and with that in hand I was on my way—slowly, very slowly. About 2 hours of very hard writing for a page and a half. Many writers develop sketchy plans like this on occasion, surveying the territory they expect to explore. As drafting progresses, they may return to the plan and modify it or even leave it behind altogether.

Which of these methods of planning is best for you—the mental plan, the written notes, the formal outline? That's not a question that can be answered simply. Your personality, the topic itself, the length and kind of treatment are all elements that affect planning decisions. There's no single best way. Experiment to find which method works in the situation. And if you feel most comfortable with every detail plotted before you begin to write, study the following section on the outline and apply it when you write your next essay.

The Outline

What is supposed to happen when you study your informal notes is that you begin to see patterns emerge. Often relationships between ideas leap out at you; you understand which points are of similar importance or are in opposition to each other or make the three reasons for something. But sometimes you study and study your notes and your brain refuses to function. That's what happened to me as I was planning this chapter.

Reproduced below are the very rough notes I made. As I studied them to figure out where to begin, my head literally hurt. I felt stupid: I couldn't make any sense of them. My next approach was to use colored pencils, underlining in red all those notes that dealt with finding something to write about, blue for a second topic. That didn't work either. So I wrote each item on a small slip of paper. That gave me a sense of accomplishment, at least. Furthermore, I could spread the slips out on the floor and rearrange them until a pattern began to take shape. Then putting the slips into piles (subtopics) came easily. That was the first step in preparing an outline, which seemed necessary given the difficulties I'd been having.

Outlining is a method of organizing your ideas according to your insights about their relationships. It enables you to perceive and express the

Chapter 2   In the Beginning... ✳

Prewriting
    general
    discovery / invention
1. finding something (topic or subject) to write about.
2. finding something to say about it — what <u>you</u> want to say.

    <u>discovery draft</u>

    limiting (LATER)
      (the shape of the essay (funnel or inverted pyramid))
      the written plan
      √informal
      outline
        to organize ideas, perceive relationships,
        test alternatives
        or outline <u>after</u> a draft to see if essay
        holds together.
    terror of the blank page and AY (or in Ch.1)
      (focussed free writing)

    50 specific details and AY.
    <u>2 minute limit</u>

    <u>WRITING AS DISCOVERY</u>
    zero draft
    (brainstorming

✳ He has half the deed done, who has made a beginning.
                          — Horace (Bartletts)

connections. Through an outline you can indicate which points are the main subtopics, which other subtopics should come under them, and so on. Outlining also permits you to test alternative patterns economically. Here is the first state of the outline prepared for this chapter from the preceding notes.

STATE 1 OUTLINE

Topic: Discovery/Invention (Prewriting)

I. The problem
  A. Finding something to write about
  B. Finding something to say about it
II. Writing as discovery
  A. Zero draft
  B. Discovery draft
  C. 2-minute limit
  D. Terror of the blank page
III. Techniques for invention
  A. Fifty specific details
  B. Brainstorming
  C. Limiting
  D. Autobiographical questionnaire
  E. Focused free writing
  F. Daily newspaper
  G. Tagmemics
  H. Analogies
  I. Classical invention
  J. Five ·W's
IV. Plans
  A. Informal plan
  B. Outline
  C. Shape of the essay

Getting an outline to this stage will probably help you feel a lot better about your essay-to-be. You will have begun to exercise some control over the material.

    That first outline still might not satisfy you. When you have the difficulty I had planning this chapter, you might make two or three trial outlines before you discover the organizational pattern that finally integrates the parts into the whole in the best sequence. That was my problem, so I did a second outline.

STATE 2 OUTLINE

Ch. 2 In the beginning . . .

Intro

I. Writing as discovery
  A. Discovery, or zero, draft

  B. Focused free writing
  C. Checklist for action
  D. The 2-minute limit
  E. An autobiographical portrait
 II. The acts of prewriting
  A. Finding a subject
  B. Defining an audience
  C. Determining a purpose
  D. Selecting a point of view
  E. Choosing an appropriate form
  F. Collecting specifics
  G. Making a plan
 III. Techniques for invention
  A. Brainstorming
  B. 50 specific details
  C. Five W's
  D. Daily newspaper
  E. Classical invention
  F. Tagmemics
 IV. The written plan
  A. Informal
  B. Outline
  C. The shape of the essay

This pattern felt much better. The major headings were altered, and some of the items were moved from topic III to topics I and II. At this point I began a first draft, realizing that the plan might still need to be refined.

  Usually, if you need to make an outline at all, you will include more details than I had in my state 2 outline. Each of the lettered items would have subtopics. Item III C, for instance, would appear this way:

  C. Five W's
   1. Who?
   2. What?
   3. When?
   4. Where?
   5. Why?
   6. And an H: How?

Some writers develop a progressively more detailed outline, down to complete sentences for sub-subtopics. Such a plan becomes a major part of the composing process; drafting is a relatively small step.

Rewriting the Outline

The outline complete, you begin to draft. In most cases, you'll have no big obstacles from here on. But what if you do? What if the essay just doesn't go together? You might face the difficulties I encountered as I drafted this chapter. Perhaps the problems arose because of my method of drafting a long piece like this. Even when I have an outline, I don't always start at the beginning. This time I wrote one section at a time, jumping around out of sequence. At any rate with thirty pages written of what became a forty-page chapter, I was still dissatisfied with the organization and thus the state 2 outline. Although the individual sections seemed satisfactory, the sequence and the relationships of the parts weren't clear, coherent, and easy for the student to follow. Further, I had decided to emphasize some items and drop others. Consequently, before I could finish writing the chapter, the outline needed to be revised once more, and it was in the process of that revision that I was finally able to perceive this chapter as a whole. That revision accomplished, I could complete the drafting. Of course, the parts already written had to be rearranged. A pair of scissors and a roll of tape took care of that. The following state 3 outline represents the *final* organization of this chapter.

STATE 3 OUTLINE

Ch. 2 In the beginning . . .

Checklist for Action

Introduction

I. The acts of prewriting
   A. Finding a subject
   B. Defining an audience
   C. Determining a purpose
   D. Selecting a point of view
   E. Choosing an appropriate form
   F. Collecting specifics
   G. Making a plan
II. Finding a Subject When You Have None
   A. The discovery draft
   B. Focused free writing
   C. Quotations
   D. The daily newspaper

III.   The 2-minute limit
IV.   Techniques for invention
     A.   Starting with specifics
     B.   Autobiographical questionnaire
     C.   Common topics
V.   The Written plan
     A.   Notes
     B.   The outline
VI.   The shape of the essay

The Mechanics of the Outline

The mechanics of outlining are simple and straightforward. The roman numerals stand for major topical divisions; the capital letters are used for the next smaller division. An outline of some complexity might look like this:

```
I.
    A.
        1.
            a.
                (1)
                    (a)
                    (b)
                (2)
            b.
                (1)
                (2)
        2.
    B.
    C.
II.
    A.    etc.
```

About the only rule that applies is this one: No A without a B, no 1 without a 2. If you think of A and B as divisions of I, the rule makes sense. You can't divide something into one part. The topic you put at A should either be incorporated into I or divided, yielding an A and a B.

THE SHAPE OF THE ESSAY

In attempts to describe the form or shape of an essay, writers have turned again and again to metaphor. Sometimes useful for explaining the unknown in terms of the known and the abstract in terms of the concrete, metaphor is a helpful, if inexact, tool. Thus, one textbook writer sees the shape of the essay as something like an inverted pyramid:

To another teacher of composition the form of the essay seems more like a funnel:

Just what is there about an essay that causes people to perceive it in these similar ways? What essential qualities of the essay are they trying to single out by these metaphors? Both figures start out at the top as relatively wide then taper either to a point (inverted pyramid) or a narrow tube (funnel) at the bottom. If the shape of the essay is like that, it must begin as somehow wide or broad and become narrow as it goes along.

The sense in which the essay may be called wide at the beginning is that the initial statement (the topic sentence or thesis or central idea) is relatively broad or general. In fact, by definition and agreement the sentence which states the central idea or subject or thesis of the essay is ordinarily the broadest, most general sentence in the essay. The movement of the essay from that sentence onward is toward the specific. Sentences and paragraphs that follow that thesis are narrower in scope. They are more explicit or particular developments of the broader idea. This principle can be illustrated in the paragraph that follows, taken from an essay about the rights of mental patients to refuse drug treatment:

1. Even more troublesome to patients and their advocates have been the side effects of the drugs.

2. Many patients complain that the medications cause muscle stiffness, cramping, and tremors.

3. The drugs' sedative effects may lead to drowsiness or, in the extreme, a spaced-out state in which thinking itself becomes difficult.

4. All of these side effects usually can be managed by reducing dosage or using countervailing medications.

5. Yet, in many large state hospitals, the staff has neither the time nor interest to fine-tune medication dosages, and many patients regard the troublesome side effects as an inevitable concomitant of medication.

> Paul S. Appelbaum, "Can Mental Patients
> Say No to Drugs?" The New York Times Magazine

In the sense in which we have described the metaphor of the inverted pyramid or the funnel, either of those images can be said to describe that paragraph. But that is only a paragraph, not an essay.

A more appropriate metaphor for the shape of an entire expository essay might be a spool of the sort that holds sewing thread. Like the spool the essay is broad at the beginning (the thesis statement), becomes more specific (narrower) in the body, and, as the body ends, reverses the shape of the beginning by becoming more general. The conclusion is likely to be as broad as the opening.

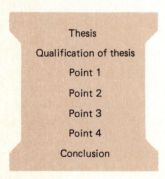

Thesis

Qualification of thesis

Point 1

Point 2

Point 3

Point 4

Conclusion

You can see an example of a student writer's use of this model in the outline on page 219.

In attempting to explain the shape of the essay in these terms, I have oversimplified for the sake of presenting a general model for your understanding. Different kinds of writing have somewhat different patterns. A passage of description will not be shaped like an extended definition. A comparison will not have the structure of a causal analysis. In Stage II of this book, The Writer Explains and Persuades, the treatment of each kind of exposition includes an explanation of its typical structure.

APPLY YOURSELF 10. Write an essay. Now it's your turn to write an essay. Review the acts of prewriting and then perform them. Use the common topics as a way to focus your subject. Make the kind of plan that is appropriate for your topic and treatment. Finally, write a draft. Good luck!

Chapter Three
Decisions, decisions

*A*s a high school senior you undoubtedly filled out a number of college admissions applications. After listing your hobbies, high school sports and activities, and likely major, you might have come upon an item like this:

> Assess your reasons for wanting to attend college. How have your previous experiences influenced your current academic and/or career plans?
>
> *Application for Admission, University of Vermont*

As you faced a request for an essay about yourself, you confronted several issues, consciously or otherwise. "What's the reason they want me to write this? Who's going to read my response? What will they be looking for? Which of the many *selves* within me should I reveal?" Then you resolved these issues as we all must whenever we need to communicate. Perhaps you've never thought much about it, but every time you write, you make decisions or accept conditions that affect the tone and style of your work.

The purpose of the first section of this chapter is to clarify these issues, then to help you make informed decisions about them.

THE WRITER'S DECISIONS

Just what are these decisions made early in the writing process? What are the conditions you must cope with? For any piece of writing you plan, four or five central questions need answers.

> What will this piece of writing be about?
>> The answer to this question clarifies your subject. *Subject* is the topic or underlying idea of a written utterance.

Why am I writing this? What do I want this to do?

The answers to these questions reveal your purpose. *Purpose* is your intent, including both the reason that moves you to write and the desired result of that effort.

Who am I writing this for?

The answer to this question identifies your audience. *Audience* is the reader or collection of readers you are addressing.

Who am I as I write this?

The answer to this question describes your voice. *Voice* is the character, personality, and attitudes you project toward your subject, toward your purpose, and toward your audience.

Subject, purpose, audience, voice—these elements are controls in the writing process. Once you arrive at decisions or accept conditions concerning their natures, the organization, the tone, and the style of the piece are governed by them. To clarify these controls, let's turn to an example. By altering slightly the questions raised earlier, we can ask them of a finished piece of writing and see the effect of the writer's decisions. The following paragraph is the first in a travel article on the Greek islands called the Cyclades.

> When Lord Byron wanted to sum up the magic of Greece he spoke of someone as "spellbound within the clustering Cyclades" and everyone knew what he meant. The Cyclades were bliss in Byron's day, and they are bliss today. They look nice, they can never be quite spoiled, and if you're not too particular about food you'll have a wonderful time.
>
> John Russell, " 'A Tumble of Tiny Specks'," *The New York Times*

Question:	*What is this piece of writing about?*	SUBJECT
Answer:	*The Greek islands known as the Cyclades from a traveler's point of view.*	
Question:	*What is this piece intended to do?*	PURPOSE
Answer:	*To inform the reader in an entertaining way. (There's more to purpose than that, but it's not apparent in this opening paragraph.)*	
Question:	*Who is this piece written for?*	AUDIENCE
Answer:	*Readers who are literate (the reference to Lord Byron would have a value), knowledgeable (would know that the Cyclades are islands in the Mediterranean Sea off the coast of Greece), and interested in travel, armchair style or otherwise ("You'll have a wonderful time" implies that the audience might consider a visit).*	

Question: *What qualities of the author are revealed in this piece?*   VOICE
Answer: *Both author and audience are literate. The author speaks forthrightly (states*
             without qualification that these islands are bliss today, look nice, and can
             never be quite spoiled). He or she addresses the reader directly (you) with a
             sense of humor ("if you're not too particular about food, you'll have a
             wonderful time").

Working backward from the finished text, then, we can see the choices the author of this paragraph made somewhere in the prewriting stage of his work.

APPLY YOURSELF 1. The writer's questions. After you've read each of the following passages, answer these questions: What is this piece of writing about (subject)? What is it intended to do (purpose)? Who is this piece written for (audience)? What qualities of the author are revealed in this piece (voice)?

A.   A Declaration by representatives of the United States of America, in Congress assembled.
          When in the course of human events it becomes necessary for one people to dissolve the political bands which have connected them with another, and to assume among the powers of the earth the separate & equal station to which the laws of nature and nature's god entitle them, a decent respect to the opinions of mankind requires that they should declare the causes which impel them to the separation.

          Thomas Jefferson, The Declaration of Independence

B.   Just as it takes practice to pitch a curve or ride a bicycle, so it takes practice to gain skill with a butterfly net. In the movies, butterfly collectors always dash madly across a meadow flailing the air with their nets. In real life, the skillful insect-hunter stalks his prey and uses his brains instead of his feet.

          Edwin Way Teale, The Junior Book of Insects

C.   Most people who bother with the matter at all would admit that the English language is in a bad way, but it is generally assumed that we cannot by conscious action do anything about it. Our civilization is decadent and our language—so the argument runs—must inevitably share in the general collapse. It follows that any struggle against the abuse of language is a sentimental archaism, like preferring candles to electric light or hansom cabs to aeroplanes. Underneath this lies the half-conscious belief that language is a natural growth and not an instrument which we shape for our own purposes.

          George Orwell, "Politics and the English Language"

SEPARATE YET DEPENDENT

The writer's attitudes toward subject, purpose, audience, and voice are at once separate yet dependent. By "separate" I mean that we can define and identify each one. By "dependent" I mean that your decision about voice, let's say, is affected in critical ways by decisions about audience, purpose, and your view of the subject. We'll deal first with this dependence, then return to a more satisfactory explanation of each of the elements separately.

The following diagram shows the relationships that exist between these elements. At the core of the large triangle is *subject,* the central concern of any piece of writing. The broken lines suggest the influence that subject has on purpose, audience, and voice, as well as the bearing they have on each other.

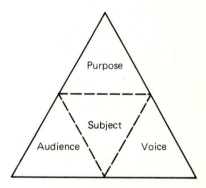

APPLY YOURSELF 2. Stephany for mayor. When I offered my support to a mayoral candidate in my city, I was asked to help by writing some radio commercials for her campaign. Some of these commercials, or "spots," focused on a single issue—roads, taxes, schools, the arts, crime, jobs, and so on. In planning to write a spot, then, I needed to know the issue and the candidate's stand on that issue (together these make up the subject); why we targeted this issue and what outcome is desired (purpose); which specific segment of the population—jobless, elderly, women—the issue most concerns (audience); and the tone and point of view of the spot (voice). Here is the text of one 30-second commercial that we did. Study it and identify the subject, purpose, audience, and voice. Then explain how these elements are related.

> The Burlington Police Department is the same size today that it was ten years ago. Yet now it must respond to 10,000 more calls a year. Ten thousand more

calls. As mayor, Judy Stephany has pledged to hire five more officers for more responsive patrols in our neighborhoods. Judy knows that one of the best ways to cut crime is to make it more likely that criminals get caught. For more police officers and safer neighborhoods, elect Judy Stephany mayor.

APPLY YOURSELF 3. Vote for. . . . Choose an office holder or candidate in your own community or state. Pick a single issue and list your decisions about the four elements of subject, purpose, audience, and voice. Write a 30-second radio commercial.

THE WRITER'S SUBJECT: DECISION 1

The process of finding a subject, then sharpening that subject as you learn more about it, and finally making a written plan is the focus of the preceding chapter. That process is decision 1. Little remains for me to add here except

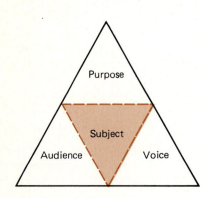

to remind you of the relatedness of subject, purpose, audience, and voice. In selecting a subject, you consider the needs of your audience. In sharpening your subject and making a written plan, you define and respond to your purpose. In determining your attitude toward your subject, you decide on one element of voice.

Subject, then, is the first of the prewriting decisions you must make. The rest follow from that.

THE WRITER'S PURPOSE: DECISION 2

> THE SECRET OF SUCCESS IS CONSTANCY TO PURPOSE.
>
> *Benjamin Disraeli*

Purpose is your intent, including both the reason that moves you to write and the desired result of that effort. If you are to remain constant to your purpose, first you must understand that purpose. We're all familiar with the more general purposes of writing: to entertain, to inform, to persuade, to move, to express yourself. But these are all so broad, so overlapping as to be of little value to the writer.

One common set of distinctions may be a bit more useful.

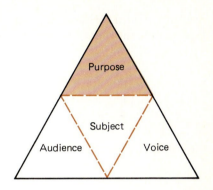

PURPOSE	METHOD
To tell a story	Narration
To describe	Description
To convince or persuade	Argumentation
To explain	Exposition

Narration

The act of telling a story probably goes back to that evening around the fire when the first cave dweller told how she had trapped a rabbit for dinner. That tale, like all other narration that followed, had one or more characters, a plot, a conflict, and a climax. Today's writer whose purpose is to tell a story might write a television script or a screenplay, a short story or a novel. Often though, narration is the primary method of biography and history, as well. And it is sometimes used to illustrate a point or make an analogy in other kinds of writing.

Description

"It was a dark and rainy night" begins many a tale. Description is the characterization of a person or a place or a thing—the way it looks, smells, feels, sounds, and perhaps even tastes. Passages of description add vitality and clarity to narration, argumentation, and exposition.

Argumentation

"Prove it!" Proving it is the purpose of argumentation. Your need to make a case for a position or persuade your readers to a course of action is met by the method of argumentation.

Exposition

The method of exposition answers the need to explain, the need or purpose that college students confront daily in written assignments, lab reports, research papers, exams. The variety of purposes served by exposition is outlined in the following section.

Purposes Classified

For many writers the classification of purposes adopted in stage II of this book makes the most sense. Related to the common topics (Chapter 2), this scheme allows the writer to begin by asking questions of the subject (invention), then to consider purpose, outlined as follows, and finally to move on to the organization of the piece (as explained in stage II).

When your need is to answer the question "What is it [your subject]?" and your purpose is to define, the mode of *definition* is the answer. See Chapter 4.

When your need is to answer the question "How do I do it?" and your purpose is to explain how to, the *how-to* form is called for. See Chapter 5.

When your need is to answer the question "What is the pattern?" and your purpose is to classify, the mode of *classification* is what you want. See Chapter 6.

When your need is to answer the question "What is it like?" and your purpose is to show similarities or differences, look to *comparison* and *contrast*. See Chapter 7.

When your need is to answer the question "How does it work?" and your purpose is to analyze structure, function, process, or cause and effect, the modes of *analysis* provide the means. See Chapter 8.

And when your need is to answer the question "Can you prove it?" and your purpose is to convince, turn to the mode of *argumentation*. See Chapter 9.

For many longer pieces of writing, you might want to combine several of these modes because your purpose will be complex or manifold. For shorter essays, however, or when the purpose is simple, choose the mode that fulfills your purpose.

THE WRITER'S AUDIENCE: DECISION 3

Have you looked over the confusing jumble of magazines in a well-stocked store lately? *The Needleworker, Golden Age of Wrestling, High Times, Modern Retirement*—each magazine produced for a specific market, that is, a readership with special interests. The editors of these magazines know their audience:

who reads their magazines and what their tastes, interests, and expectations are. They shape editorial content and advertising to that market.

As writers, you and I need to identify our audience, to decide who our readers are. Every time we write, we write for somebody. That somebody is our audience. Analyzing or selecting your audience is decision 3.

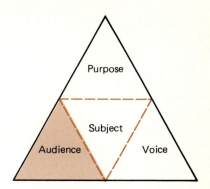

Speaking versus Writing

Why do most people find it easier to speak a thought than to write it down? One reason is that the speaker stands in a context—a definite place, time, situation, and relationship to the listener (audience). The speaker knows who this listener is and can see and hear reactions. Thus, the speaker can tailor his talk to the audience, even modifying it in progress according to the feedback he receives. The writer, in contrast, is seldom in the physical presence of the reader (audience). Often he doesn't know the reader personally. Or even know how many readers make up the audience. Seldom do readers talk back.

This contrast between the speaker-listener relationship and the writer-reader relationship points up the significance of prewriting decisions about audience. Before you begin to write, you should know who your audience is. Then as you draft and revise, keep that picture of your readers in mind.

The Unseen Audience: Building a Profile

What does the writer need to know about the unseen audience? That often depends on *purpose*, the goal of the particular piece of writing. An engineering student was asked by her dean to draft a letter to female high school seniors, pointing out the opportunities in engineering careers for women. Her purpose (providing information about career options) was a given, as was her audience (female high school seniors). Yet to get her message across, the writer needed to explore the nature of her audience further. In doing so, she might have consulted a checklist such as the one that follows, searching out those qualities of her audience that might be relevant to her subject and purpose.

AUDIENCE PROFILE

1. Age?
2. Sex?
3. Education?
4. Job?
5. Income?
6. Religion?
7. Previous knowledge of subject?
8. Likely attitude toward subject?

The letter writer knew the age, sex, and education of her audience and recognized immediately that these were important elements in her appeal. But it was only when she got to items 7 and 8 that the true value of building an audience profile occurred to her. She realized that her readers probably had little previous knowledge of the subject, careers in engineering, because that field has until recently been seen as largely closed to women. For the same reason, many of her readers would have negative attitudes toward the subject. She had to describe engineering careers clearly and overcome negative attitudes by stressing the many opportunities in a positive way. Now that the writer knew the true demands of her task, she was able to meet them successfully.

Building an audience profile by answering the questions just listed helps to assure the success of your writing. Not every question is relevant every time, but with some practice you'll find it easy to identify those audience factors that are pertinent to any particular piece of writing.

APPLY YOURSELF 4. Building an audience profile. Using the preceding questions, write a one-paragraph profile of the likely audience for each of these situations.

A. The state legislature (or the board of trustees of your college) is considering a proposal to raise tuition by 12 percent next year. You decide to write them an open letter.
B. Your reputation as an amateur bird-watcher (or cross-country skier or builder of dollhouse furniture) has spread far and wide. The features editor of your local newspaper asks you to write an article about your hobby.
C. Another situation, real or imagined, of your own devising.

APPLY YOURSELF 5. What a weekend! Explain how a report on Homecoming weekend (or Oktoberfest or Spring Fling) would be affected by the audience in each of the following situations. What topics would you emphasize for one audience and not another? What would one audience find funny and another not? Write some phrases that describe this event for different audiences.

A. A letter to your parents
B. A letter to your best friend back home
C. An article for the college paper
D. A college recruiting brochure for high school students

Don't Write for the Professor

Some of the worst writing produced since the invention of the pencil has been done by students for teachers. I know—I've written some of it myself and read a lot more. Why is that? I think that one reason is that students often don't see their professors as human beings. They misjudge their audience. Here are some hints about the audience of college papers.

Defining your audience is usually easy in a writing course like this one. Unless you have another audience in mind for a piece of writing, think of your entire class, students and professor, as your readership. Construct an audience profile based on your knowledge of these people. Many college composition courses these days are conducted as workshops. Students read their work to the rest of the class, which then responds to it. This immediate feedback gives the writer a clear sense of that audience for that essay.

Writing for some other course—history, psychology, education, literature—presents the problem of a different and somewhat unknown audience. One approach is to picture your readers as students beginning that same course but lacking your special knowledge of the subject. Your audience, then, has the same intelligence as you and similar education. It is interested in your topic but unfamiliar with it. The advantages of this approach are these: You will likely use a voice that is less stuffy and "academic" than if you were writing for the professor alone, and you will neither overlook nor belabor the elementary aspects of your subject. Treatment of the elementary aspects of your topic is relevant to our discussion of audience. Many student papers fail because their writers either overlook the obvious or beat it to death. Sometimes students strain so hard to treat the complexities of their subject that they neglect to begin at the beginning by defining their terms, citing the textual reference, showing the connections between the known and the speculative. Don't be afraid to review the basics, the common ground, before you go on to the intricacies of your presentation. This will let the professor know that *you* know. And if you do go astray later in the paper, you'll probably get credit for the earlier parts. I confess that it took me a long time as a student before I learned this lesson. I always omitted the elementary—"Why, the professor would be insulted if I treated it" was my notion. This was a hard lesson for me to learn because no one ever told me what I was doing wrong. If you think of your audience as students in your course, you're more likely to begin at the beginning, instead of trying to write the way you imagine a graduate student would write.

Notice that I said *begin* at the beginning. Some student papers not only begin there but never leave. They belabor the obvious. If you keep your readers in mind, you will meet them where they are in their knowledge of the subject and bring them along to an exploration of deeper or more complex aspects of it. For example, your poetry paper should do more than show why such and such a poem is a sonnet. It should answer the question, so what?

Professors, whatever else they may look for, usually expect two things in a paper. They want to be informed about the subject. And they want to see what you know. Focus on the question asked and its elements and implications. Your reader is someone ready to be convinced if good reasons are given but unwilling to accept unsupported assertions. By giving some thought to the needs of your audience, you can be sure that your professors get what they want.

Borrowing an Audience

Still another way to clarify your sense of audience has been suggested by Walter J. Ong, S.J. Often, he observes, the writer doesn't have an actual person as reader to whom he might legitimately "tell his story." In that case, the writer "borrows" an audience from another piece of writing with which he is familiar. "If the writer succeeds in writing, it is generally because he can fictionalize in his imagination an audience he has learned to know not from daily life but from earlier writers." Wanting to recount a childhood experience, let's say, you might be unable to visualize a reader who would be interested or suitable. One solution is to turn to the ready-made audience provided by another author—J. D. Salinger or Mark Twain, for instance. Imagine that you are writing for someone who has just finished *Catcher in the Rye* or *The Adventures of Huckleberry Finn.* The writer of a how-to article can refer to a magazine that regularly publishes pieces of that sort. The student planning a term paper for a course can read a couple of articles published in the appropriate journals for that field. A survey of journals would suggest not only an audience but also several possible voices and acceptable methods of proof. But watch out: Much academic writing is stuffy and jargon-riddled. You must be of strong moral fiber to write clearly.

THE WRITER'S VOICE: DECISION 4

I USED MY VOICE TO COLOR MY ROLES. SALOME WAS BLOOD RED. MELISANDE WAS ICE, MELTING ICE. . . .

Opera singer Mary Gardner

The writer's voice may thunder or whine, crackle or drone. The writer's voice may nag, tease, amuse, uplift, browbeat, or tickle. It may also be entirely concealed. Voice is the personality and attitudes you project toward your subject, toward your purpose, and toward your audience. Voice also reveals something about the way you perceive yourself. It's a rare person, indeed, who uses the same voice in every piece of writing.

Certainly we speak in different tones to different people in different settings. Imagine the tone of voice you would use in each of these situations:

You come back from class to find that your puppy has made a mess on the rug.

You are a mechanic telling a customer her car needs a new transmission.

Your roommate spills a mug of hot chocolate on your chemistry notes.

You are stopped by a policeman for defective brake lights.

Your history professor has miscalculated your score on an exam—you should have gotten a B, not a C.

Your best friend sent you flowers for your birthday.

Just as your speaking voice changes throughout the day, so must your writing voice change according to need. The question is not which voice is correct, but which voice is appropriate for this situation. Is it formal or informal? Should you be serious or humorous? Personal or objective? Here's an example of a clearly marked voice: Huck Finn describing one of the Widow Douglas's attempts to civilize him.

> After supper she got out her book and learned me about Moses and the Bulrushers; and I was in a sweat to find out all about him; but by-and-by she let it out that Moses had been dead a considerable long time; so then I didn't care no more about him; because I don't take no stock in dead people.
>
> Pretty soon I wanted to smoke, and asked the widow to let me. But she wouldn't. She said it was a mean practice and wasn't clean, and I must try to not do it any more. That is just the way with some people. They get down on a thing when they don't know nothing about it. Here she was a bothering about Moses, which was no kin to her, and no use to anybody, being gone, you see, yet finding a power of fault with me for doing a thing that had some good in it. And she took snuff too; of course that was all right, because she done it herself.
>
> Mark Twain, *The Adventures of Huckleberry Finn*

The voice employed here is personal, informal, naive, and uneducated. Although the reader may smile, the voice is serious. We hear Huck speaking straight-faced. He doesn't see the humor. We also perceive the voice to be colloquial, with features characterizing speech rather than writing. The voice is appropriate or "right" for a 13-year-old boy raised in Missouri in the middle of the nineteenth century. Striking just the right note in selecting a voice is seldom easy, yet nearly always crucial.

Voice in the College Paper

This problem becomes yours when you must write a paper for a college course. The uncertainties surface each time: Should I use the first person ("I think . . . ")? Should I try to be humorous? Should my voice be undetectable? Should I try to sound like an economist (or a literary critic or a sociologist)? Apply Yourself 10 at the end of this section provides one way for you to find answers to these questions, questions that many students struggle with for four years without discovering satisfactory answers. The following paragraph illustrates one student writer's choices about voice. After you've read it carefully, I'll explain why I think she found an appropriate voice for this short paper about one aspect of a short story.

> The function of setting and atmosphere is to establish the mood of the story. In "Big Two-Hearted River" Hemingway creates the relaxed mood through great detail and repetition. He begins the story with a description of a burned-over town. Immediately we are confronted with a slow pace. Nick looks around at his simple surroundings—the hillside, the railroad track

leading to the bridge over the river. The track travels out of sight. Through Nick we climb the hills, feel the heavy pack on our backs, smell the sweet fern, observe the trout, grasshoppers, and the far-stretching landscape.

Beatrice Lynch

The voice in this opening paragraph of a two-and-a-half-page paper is knowledgeable, assured, businesslike yet human. Beatrice begins by offering a general principle ("The function of setting and atmosphere . . . "), then in the second sentence relates that principle to the story under study. The third sentence gets right down to proof. What these opening sentences convey to the reader are a writer who knows the subject and what she wants to say about it, a writer who isn't going to waste the reader's time. (The voice is knowledgeable, assured, businesslike.) Notice, though, that there's no sense that the writer feels smarter than the reader or more capable. The voice is not that of someone trying to impress the reader. Then as she begins to present details of setting from the story, we sense that a human being is here, that a real person read "Big Two-Hearted River" and selected images that had meaning to her. The last sentence of the paragraph confirms this judgment: "Through Nick we climb the hills, feel the heavy pack on our backs, smell the sweet fern, observe the trout, grasshoppers, and the far-stretching landscape." This human voice is communicated through two devices: the personal pronouns and the sensory verbs. *We* and *our* suggest Beatrice's reactions to the setting and her willingness to share them with the reader. *Climb, feel, smell,* and *observe* reiterate her sensitivity to Hemingway's work and also allow the reader of the paper to share some of the feelings of the story. In this paragraph, Beatrice has managed to use a voice that is appropriately objective for a course paper, yet one that reveals human sensitivity to the piece of literature that is being explored.

Voice and Style

Several elements of the writer's style convey voice. Sentence structure is one of these. A series of short, simple declarative sentences doesn't sound the same as one lengthy, complex sentence, no matter how clear the latter is. Ernest Hemingway, for instance, is more apt to write short sentences, Henry James the long. Read a page from each and you'll see what I mean. Although Hemingway and James are novelists, writers of nonfiction also vary in their selection of sentence structure. Usually longer, more complex sentences are called for in formal situations when the ideas themselves are of some complexity.

Another stylistic choice that affects the writer's voice is the kinds and values of the words used. Even individual words may impart the message of voice. For instance, I am looking at a thesaurus or dictionary of synonyms and find listed under "convey" (a word I used in the first sentence of the last paragraph) a number of words that mean nearly the same. Not only are the meanings slightly different but each word sounds a bit different in terms of voice. Some are simple and straightforward, others seem more formal: *transmit, impart, bear, communicate, carry.* I found someone's example of this principle left on a blackboard last week: "She purveys exoskeletons at the pelagic area." The voice in that sentence is certainly different from the voice of whoever first said "She sells seashells at the seashore," even if the content is the same. Words that have come to us from Latin or Greek, like *exoskeletons* and *pelagic,* carry greater formality than words from the Anglo-Saxon source of English such as *shore* or *sells.* That's why *exoskeletons* and *pelagic* sound odd when used in a child's tongue twister—they are too fancy. Put another way, they are inappropriate for the situation.

Most native users of English intuitively resort to a somewhat different language for writing than for speaking. Poet and master of the English language T. S. Eliot observed, "The spoken and the written language must not be too near together, as they must not be too far apart." One difference is that we ordinarily exercise more care in our written utterances. Incomplete sentences are more acceptable in speech than in writing, for instance. So too are contractions, which signal a degree of informality. The distinction that Eliot points out between the spoken and the written language is complicated by a second standard, the degree of formality of the occasion or situation. A formal written utterance differs from an informal written one, just as it differs from a formal spoken utterance. The speaker/writer's effectiveness is often measured by the way he can select an *appropriate* style and thus voice, appropriate for the situation, the subject, and the purpose.

APPLY YOURSELF 6. The voice of words. Each of the following items contains several synonyms at differing levels of formality and erudition, that is, some words are high class, some are slangy. Describe the voice suggested to you by each word. Consider circumstances under which you might use each. Suggest an additional word for each list, perhaps from current slang.

A. Douse, drench, soak, saturate
B. Loathe, abhor, hate, abominate
C. Impecuniousness, poverty, indigence
D. Resign, quit, throw in the towel

APPLY YOURSELF 7. Voice. Describe the voice in each of the following passages. Point out specific aspects of style that reveal that voice.

A. In warm evenings I frequently sat in the boat playing the flute, and saw the perch, which I seem to have charmed, hovering around me, and the moon travelling over the ribbed bottom, which was strewed with the wrecks of the forest. Formerly I had come to this pond adventurously, from time to time, in dark summer nights, with a companion, and making a fire close to the water's edge, which we thought attracted the fishes, we caught pouts with a bunch of worms strung on a thread, and when we had done, far in the night, threw the burning brands high into the air like skyrockets, which, coming down into the pond, were quenched with a loud hissing, and we were suddenly groping in total darkness. Through this, whistling a tune, we took our way to the haunts of men again. But now I had made my home by the shore.

Henry David Thoreau, Walden

B. Under certain circumstances there are few hours in life more agreeable than the hour dedicated to the ceremony known as afternoon tea. There are circumstances in which, whether you partake of the tea or not—some people of course never do,—the situation is in itself delightful. Those that I have in mind in beginning to unfold this simple history offered an admirable setting to an innocent pastime. The implements of the little feast had been disposed upon the lawn of an Old English country-house, in what I should call the perfect middle of a splendid summer afternoon.

Henry James, The Portrait of a Lady

C. Changing Money Abroad. You generally get the best rate at banks, except where, as in Brazil and the Dominican Republic, there is an unofficial rate at which you can trade legally elsewhere, such as in hotels and shops. But always avoid money-changers who approach you furtively in building lobbies or on the street. Keep invoices covering all exchanges at official rates; you may need them to change money back into dollars when you leave the country.

Paul Grimes, New York Times

D. There are so many new books about dying that there are now special shelves set aside for them in bookshops, along with the health-diet and home-repair paperbacks and the sex manuals. Some of them are so packed with detailed information and step-by-step instructions for performing the function that you'd think this was a new sort of skill which all of us are now required to learn. The strongest impression the casual reader gets, leafing through, is that proper dying has become an extraordinary, even an exotic experience, something only the specially trained get to do.

Lewis Thomas, "On Natural Death"

APPLY YOURSELF 8. Space letter. When the U.S. space agency NASA sent the Pioneer 10 spacecraft toward the red star Aldebaran, light-years away, a message went along. Engraved on a gold-anodized plaque, the message is addressed to any alien civilization that encounters Pioneer in its journey. A man and a woman stand in front of a sketch of Pioneer. Other elements include the twin circles of a hydrogen atom (upper left) and our solar system (bottom). What can you determine about subject, purpose, audience, and voice of this message?

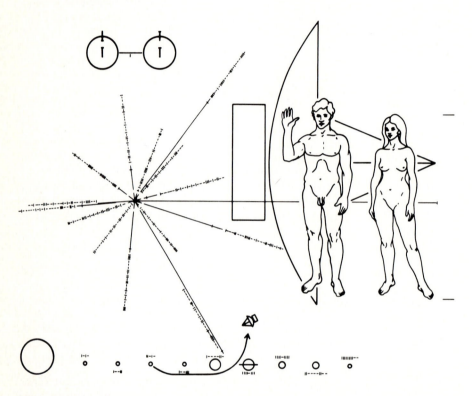

The Pioneer spacecraft carried this plaque on the journey beyond the solar system, bearing data that tell where and when the human species lived and that convey details of our biological form. When Pioneer 10 flew by Jupiter it acquired sufficient kinetic energy to carry it completely out of the solar system. Some time between one and ten billion years from now, the probe may pass through the planetary system of a remote stellar neighbor, one of whose planets may have evolved intelligent life. If the spacecraft is detected and then inspected, Pioneer's message will reach across the eons to communicate its greeting. *Source:* (David Morrison, *Voyage to Jupiter*, National Aeronautics and Space Administration, Wash. D.C., 1980.)

APPLY YOURSELF 9. Time capsule. Instead of sending a message to the universe as NASA did on Pioneer 10, write a letter to your own descendants to be opened in five hundred years. Tell your great-grandchildren's great-grandchildren about yourself, your life, and your times. Consider purpose, audience, and voice.

APPLY YOURSELF 10. Choose an article from a newsmagazine like *Time* or *Newsweek* or from some other periodical in your college library. Read the article, then write a brief description of the writer's subject, purpose, audience, and voice. Include the name of the author, the title of the article, the name of the magazine, and date of publication. Your English instructor may ask you to turn in a photocopy of the article with your description.

Stage II
The Writer Explains and Persuades

In the first three chapters of *Writer to Writer*, we explored the idea of writing as a process, a movement from prewriting through drafting to revising. Stage I deals with a number of aspects of the *prewriting* phase. State III treats *revising*, or rewriting. This section, Stage II, concerns the middle step of the process—*drafting*.

Drafting is what most people think of whenever they think about writing at all. It's getting the words down on paper. Indeed, drafting is at the heart of the whole process. The chapters that follow take up, one at a time, several kinds, or modes, of writing. Worth knowing in advance are two facts about these chapters. First, like the earlier chapters in this book, each of these teach you the needed skills step by step, with frequent opportunities for practice. When you complete each chapter, you will have mastered the basics of that mode of writing. Second, the organizing principle of this section is the common topics.

The common topics as an aid to invention were explained in Chapter 2 as a method of systematic inquiry: a number of questions to ask about your subject and a means of obtaining information about that subject. Useful to the writer who uses the common topics as an aid to invention is the connection between them and the modes of expression. Each topic is directly related to a chapter in this section. For instance, the first common topic raises the question, "What is it?" In other words, what are the characteristics or qualities of your subject? What are its limitations? If this is the topic you select, the appropriate form is *definition*. Here are the ten common topics along with the chapters in Stage II that explain them:

1. What is it? Definition   Chapter 4
2. What is it like? Comparison   Chapter 7
3. What is it different from? Contrast   Chapter 7
4. What are its parts? Analysis   Chapter 8
5. To what larger structure or class does it belong? Classification   Chapter 6
6. How does it work? Functional analysis   Chapters 5 and 8
7. What causes it? Causal analysis   Chapter 8
8. What are its effects? Effect analysis   Chapter 8
9. What is the value of it? Argumentation   Chapter 9
10. What do others say about it? Research   Chapter 10

The common topics are no more or less than the ways in which we perceive and order our world. Your work with them in this section of the book will not only improve your writing but will also strengthen your ability to perceive relationships in things and ideas.

Although this section of the book explains one mode at a time (classification, for instance), that doesn't mean that every piece of writing must be completely in one mode. When the writer's purpose is simple and single—to define a term in marketing, let's say—then the mode is simple and single as well: definition, in this case. On other occasions, however, the writer's need and purpose are more complex. An essay for a literature course giving a close reading of a poem might combine a number of modes, for example, structural analysis of its parts, definition of an unusual word, comparison to another poem, and classification as a sonnet.

Stage II concludes with chapters on argumentation and research, neither one an expository mode. They are included here for different reasons. Many of the papers you will write in college are in at least one sense arguments. Your task is to prove a point and to persuade the reader (the professor) that yours is a valid position. The skills you will learn in Chapter 9 will help. The chapter on research (Chapter 10) first explains the purposes of research, then shows you how to go about it, and concludes by telling how to use the fruits of your research in your writing.

As you work in your other courses this semester, I believe you will find this section of *Writer to Writer* continually useful. Through your study of the following chapters, you will learn how to deal with the varying writing assignments your professors make. And your understanding of the several modes of exposition will probably make you a better reader of the texts you encounter in those courses too.

Chapter Four
What is it? definition—

*T*o define is to identify or determine the essential qualities of something—its meaning. Sometimes we need to explain the commonly accepted meaning of a word we use. Before presenting an analysis of Germany's irredentist policies in the 1930s, the writer would be wise to define *irredentist*. At other times we may wish to broaden or alter slightly the common meaning of a word: "In calling contemporary American society narcissistic, I mean . . ." Although definition may be the mode of an entire piece of writing, more often it is used in combination with other expository modes. The writer establishes the meaning of a term and then proceeds to analyze, compare, or argue.

The word is not the thing. It is more like the name that parents give to a baby. Something new has come into the world, and it is assigned a name by which it becomes known, let's say *Maria*. But the girl child might have been called Carol or Holly or Francesca. Thus, the word or name affixed to the thing is arbitrary and a matter of the assent of users of the language. The baby is still the same baby, whatever her name. This fact of language shows clearly in the illustrations on page 70.

Cat   Gatto   Chat   Katze

The animal remains the same, only the word used to describe it changes. Italians have "agreed," so to speak, to call it *gatto*, Frenchmen *chat*, and Germans *Katze*. Please note that the little beast is unaffected by whatever you call it.

If we return to our first illustration, *Maria*, another valuable fact of language may be seen. As our girl grows older, some people call her different names: *Sis, honey, Mom, Grandma, Mrs. Estaban*. Like the cat, she doesn't change, but in this instance the name (word) she is called does— according to the relationship between the user of the word and Maria.

Definition is more than words, then. It is an expression of the relationship between words and the things or concepts that the words represent. This truth becomes even more important when we leave behind such concrete words as *cat* or *Maria* and turn to abstract words like *courage, beauty,* and *freedom*, each of which has a number of different meanings. When writers or speakers use one of these abstract words, they run the risk of being misunderstood without even realizing it. The word *servitude* may suggest slavery to a black, low wages to a migrant worker, and a sink full of dirty dishes to a young mother. When using such words, writers must do their best to ensure that they and their readers have the same definition in mind.

The necessity of this understanding was brought home to me twice in an American literature class I was teaching last semester. The first instance was a student paper entitled "Ritualistic Qualities of Hemingway's 'Big Two-Hearted River.'" Apart from using the word *ritualistic* in the title, the student claimed that fishing was for the central character "a kind of rite." This appeared to be his thesis. But nowhere in the essay did the writer define what were obviously key terms: *ritualistic* and *rite*. The reader, then, is uncertain of the precise way those terms are used. Worse, as it turned out, the writer didn't know exactly what the words meant either; that was obvious in the examples he had chosen. The writer's failure to define his terms meant the essay couldn't possibly succeed. The second instance occurred during a class discussion of the "innocence" of one of the characters in another Hemingway work, *The Sun Also Rises*. Two students were disagreeing rather heatedly when one realized that they each meant something different by the word *innocent*. After they defined their meanings, the discussion could move on to points of agreement and eventually yield an insight about the character and about the author's values.

Constructing a definition is often an essential element in writers' attempts to know a subject and to clarify their own thinking about it. Further, the act of defining may well be the first step toward action. When and if a college faculty can define what *educated* means, it can build a curriculum that will help develop an *educated* person.

The means of definition are many, and the trained writer becomes acquainted with them all. Sometimes the most effective way to explore and explain the meaning of a word is to come at it from several angles.

MEANS OF DEFINITION

1. Formal

This is what we usually think of as the dictionary definition. It is useful only for nouns. The word (*term*) is defined by naming the category of things to which it belongs (*class*) and the qualities that distinguish it from other members of that category (*distinction*). All three elements (*term, class, distinction*) are necessary to the formal definition.

Term		Class	Distinction
A potter	is	an artisan	who makes clayware.
A gill	is	an organ	for obtaining oxygen from water.
A beard	is	hair	that grows on a man's face.

Sometimes the distinction is placed before the class:

Term		Distinction	Class
A growl	is	a low rumbling, menacing	sound.

The test of the formal definition is the reversibility of subject and predicate. If the definition of *potter* above is a sound one, we can turn the sentence around and it will still be true.

Class	Distinction		Term
An artisan	who makes clayware	is	a potter.

Just as all potters are artisans who make clayware, so all artisans who make clayware are potters. The definition passes the test. It is sound. Now let's try another definition.

Term		Distinction	Class
A pencil	is	a writing	instrument.

That appears to be an adequate definition until you reverse it.

Distinction	Class		Term
A writing	instrument	is	a pencil.

The limitations of this definition become immediately clear. A writing instrument *may* be a pencil, but it may also be a pen, a crayon, a piece of chalk. More distinctions are called for.

Term		Distinction₁	Class	Distinction₂
A pencil	is	a writing	instrument	consisting of a

cylinder of graphite and clay embedded in a cylinder of wood.

Reversing this reveals that we now have a sound definition: A writing instrument consisting of a cylinder of graphite and clay embedded in a cylinder of wood is a pencil—and nothing else.

2. Synonym

One or two words that have the same or nearly the same meaning as the term to be defined are considered synonyms.

Term	Synonym
hostelry	inn
distant	far off
obdurate	inflexible
to speak	to talk

Because of his descent from the royal line, young Rupert was a hemophiliac, a bleeder.

A true synonym is the same part of speech as the term and may be substituted for that term in a sentence.

> The senator's *obdurate* position on the Middle East hampered the work of the Foreign Relations Committee.
> The senator's *inflexible* position on the Middle East hampered the work of the Foreign Relations Committee.

Writers who turn to a thesaurus for synonyms should realize that the words listed are rarely identical in meaning. For instance, *feeble, infirm, delicate,* and *frail* may all be listed as synonyms for *weak,* yet each has at least a slightly different value or connotation. Try matching each of those four adjectives with an appropriate noun from this list: a young woman, an invalid, an aged man, a light boat in a storm.

3. Derivation

The writer may define by revealing a term's origin or sources. Knowing where a word comes from can be interesting as well as informative.

Metropolis comes from two Greek words meaning "mother" and "city."

Laser is an acronym formed from the words light *amplification by stimulated emission of radiation.*

Drifting where the currents carry them, with no power or will to oppose that of the sea, this strange community of creatures and the marine plants that sustain them are called "plankton," a word derived from the Greek, meaning "wandering."

Rachel Carson, *The Sea Around Us*

4. Negative; Antonym

A negative definition tells what the term is *not;* an antonym gives its opposite. Obviously, both of these means of definition are limited for they fail to explain what the term *is.* Nonetheless they can be useful on occasion.

Negative: Mainstreaming is not forcing every mentally retarded child into the classroom.

The lawyer's questions were malevolent, not charitable.

Antonym: anxiety—security
courageous—cowardly

5. Example

The example points to one or more representatives, leaving the reader to discern the essential or common qualities.

Trademark—Coke, Caterpillar, Band-Aid
Conifer—pine, spruce, hemlock, yew

The examples given for *conifer* reveal a limitation of this type of definition. The reader may conclude that *conifer* means *evergreen*. It does not.

6. Context

The meaning is given indirectly by the rest of the sentence. If you look at the definition of *laser* in the discussion of derivation, you will find a contextual definition of *acronym*. We can infer that an acronym is a word formed from the initial letters of a series of words. Here is another example of a contextual definition.

> To *compensate* the woman for her injury and hospitalization, the judge awarded her $50,000.

7. Function

A functional definition tells what something does or how it works. The preceding sentence is, in fact, an example of a functional definition. Here are two more.

> A carburetor produces an explosive mixture of gasoline and air.

> Myocardial infarction, the medical term for heart attack, results when the heart's demand for oxygen exceeds the ability of the circulatory system to supply it.
>
> *Darlene A. Swan*

This method of definition is also useful for explaining concepts as the following definition of the Freudian view of the ego demonstrates.

> In the well-adjusted person the ego is the executive of the personality, *controlling and governing the id and the superego and maintaining commerce with the external world in the interest of the total personality and its far-flung needs.*
>
> *Calvin S. Hall, A Primer of Freudian Psychology*

8. Metaphor

Not a true definition, *metaphor* is an implied or direct comparison. "Happiness is a warm puppy" is one example. Practically every student of modern political theory has run into another: "Religion. . . is the opium of the people." Notice that both of these definitions are what might be called "impressionistic," that is, they suggest somewhat different meanings to different readers.

The writer can, however, control the reader's interpretation more precisely. Calvin S. Hall does just this in the functional definition of the ego in the preceding discussion of function. When Hall refers to the ego as "the executive of the personality," he is constructing a metaphoric definition. By calling up the image of an executive, he suggests all the duties of the modern business leader—planning, making decisions, directing action. The reader's response to the comparison is more tightly controlled.

APPLY YOURSELF 1. Writing definitions. You can practice what you've learned by writing two or three kinds of definition of each of the words in the following list. Try to use each of the eight means at least once.

1. Obfuscate
2. Courage
3. Heptastich
4. Maudlin
5. Tributary
6. Tool
7. Childhood
8. Diffusion
9. Sing
10. Tower

EXTENDED DEFINITION

Some words (concrete nouns like *chair* or *battle*, for instance) may be defined in a sentence or two. Other words, however, require more extensive explanation. Usually these are the names of concepts or processes (*greed*, *liberty*, *osmosis*). In fact, however, the extent of the definition may depend more on the writer's purpose and the reader's needs than on anything inherent in the term itself. Extended definition often relies on other kinds of exposition such as analysis or comparison, or even description or narration. Here is an example of a portion of an extended defintion.

> The soybean is small and glossy and spherical, the size and shape of a dried pea. In its preferred varieties, it is pale yellow, the yellow relieved of tedium by a streak of black at the bean's equator, at the site of its seed scar. Its hull is also very like a pea's, peeling off easily to release two splits, two halves, that are the reservoirs of the bean's riches. Like other peas and beans—pulses, they are collectively called—the soybean is a legume. Which means, first, that the plant fixes more nitrogen in the soil than it uses for growth—the rule of thumb among farmers is one pound of nitrogen added for each bushel of beans taken away—and second, that the soybean is proteinaceous, not starchy, and contains an average of 40 percent crude protein. Compare beef and fish at 18 percent. The soybean contains three times as much crude protein as eggs or whole wheat flour, eleven times as much as whole fresh milk. Measured against the cost of its production, its nutritional value makes it one of the cheapest foods available to mankind.
>
> *Richard Rhodes, "A Bean to Feed the World?"*
> *The Atlantic*

Interestingly, this extended definition of *soybean* employs several of the means described earlier in this chapter. Look for them. In addition, four other terms are defined. Can you find them? The purpose of Rhodes's essay is to explore the potential of the soybean to solve the world's hunger crisis. The passage is the second paragraph of a fairly lengthy article.

To define something less tangible than a soybean requires all the same skills, and then some. Here is a definition of *symbol* by the German theologian, Paul Tillich.

SYMBOLS

Symbols have one characteristic in common with signs; they point beyond themselves to something else. The red sign at the street corner points to the order to stop the movements of cars at certain intervals. A red light and the stopping of cars have essentially no relation to each other, but conventionally they are united as long as the convention lasts. The same is true of letters and numbers and partly even words. They are given this special function by convention within a nation or by international conventions, as the mathematical signs. Sometimes such signs are called symbols; but this is unfortunate because it makes the distinction between signs and symbols more difficult. Decisive is the fact that signs do not participate in the reality of that to which they point, while symbols do. Therefore, signs can be replaced for reasons of expediency or convention, while symbols cannot.

This leads to the second characteristic of the symbol: It participates in that to which it points: the flag participates in the power and dignity of the nation for which it stands. Therefore, it cannot be replaced except after an historic catastrophe that changes the reality of the nation which it symbolizes. An attack on the flag is felt as an attack on the majesty of the group in which it is acknowledged. Such an attack is considered blasphemy.

The third characteristic of a symbol is that it opens up levels of reality which otherwise are closed for us. All arts create symbols for a level of reality which cannot be reached in any other way. A picture and a poem reveal elements of reality which cannot be approached scientifically. In the creative work of art we encounter reality in a dimension which is closed for us without such works. The symbol's fourth characteristic not only opens up dimensions and elements of reality which otherwise would remain unapproachable but also unlocks dimensions and elements of our soul which correspond to the dimensions and elements of reality. A great play gives us not only a new vision of the human scene, but it opens up hidden depths of our own being. Thus we are able to receive what the play reveals to us in reality. There are within us dimensions of which we cannot become aware except through symbols, as melodies and rhythms in music.

Symbols cannot be produced intentionally—this is the fifth characteristic. They grow out of the individual or collective unconscious and cannot function without being accepted by the unconscious dimension of our being.

Symbols which have an especially social function, as political and religious symbols, are created or at least accepted by the collective unconscious of the group in which they appear.

The sixth and last characteristic of the symbol is a consequence of the fact that symbols cannot be invented. Like living beings, they grow and they die. They grow when the situation is ripe for them, and they die when the situation changes. The symbol of the "king" grew in a special period of history, and it died in most parts of the world in our period. Symbols do not grow because people are longing for them, and they do not die because of scientific or practical criticism. They die because they can no longer produce response in the group where they originally found expression.

Paul Tillich, Dynamics of Faith

APPLY YOURSELF 2. Extended definition. Now try your hand at writing an extended definition. Choose a thing or a concept that interests you or select one from the list below. Write an essay of four to six hundred words.

1.	Fitness	6.	Sloth
2.	Love	7.	Education
3.	Success	8.	Home
4.	Liberty	9.	Autism
5.	Entropy	10.	City

APPLY YOURSELF 3. Name-calling. At the beginning of this chapter, we saw how Maria might have several different names, nicknames, or labels during her lifetime: *Sis, honey, Mom, Grandma, Mrs. Estaban.* I wrote back there that "she doesn't change, but in this instance the name (word) she is called does—according to the relationship between the user of the word and Maria." That was only a half-truth. People oftentimes *do* change in their outward behavior and in their perceptions of themselves to fit the *name* that is applied to them. I've noticed that students in a class are apt to respond according to the names by which I call them. I could recognize a student as *Greg, Mr. Harris, Harris,* or merely point to him.

Write an essay in which you explore the relationship between what a person is called and the behavior and self-perceptions of that person. You might treat the cluster of names given to Maria. Or, better yet, construct a similar cluster for someone you know, yourself for instance.

APPLY YOURSELF 4. Superman, high heels, and Twinkies. A friend of mine who also teaches writing, Tony Magistrale, has dreamed up an assignment in definition that his students enjoy working with. From the list below choose one item and write an essay defining and explaining its cultural significance to a visitor from Peking or Mars. You might begin by considering what each one of these words has come to represent for you on a personal level. But eventually provide the reader with necessary background information: some related words and contexts and phenomena. How, for example, would you explain waxed paper to a rural Chinese peasant, a video game to a bushman from Africa?

Superman	Polyester	Video game
Centerfold	High heels	Peanut butter
Twinkie	Waxed paper	Tupperware party

Crucial points of consideration: (1) Some readers know more than others. Be careful to explain your cultural selection as vividly as possible, using examples and illustrations. The basic identity of a Tupperware party is there, but the attentive writer seeks to remind readers of the possible relationship between plastic objects and the individuals who attend these parties in order to fondle them.

(2) Be attentive to your reader. Think of yourself as a cultural guide, about to provide a pleasant and good-natured explanation of some of America's most prized and cherished institutions. Avoid, then, easy sarcasm and apathetic dismissals.

(3) Do not feel, on the other hand, that you have to approve of the thing or person being described. Your job is not to banish from the earth any of these words. Instead, describe one by accounting for its significance. Your perceptions will certainly involve making judgments, but do so only through discriminating intellectual observation, not mere stubborn preference.

Chapter Five
How to

A young woman put in charge of a university computer center discovers that she has to write instructions for her operators.

A nurse is directed by a surgeon to write a care plan for an elderly patient recovering from total replacement of a hip joint.

A member of an outdoor recreation club needs to provide new members with a written explanation of how to perform cardiopulmonary resuscitation (CPR) before they attend a demonstration.

On occasions like these and countless others, we frequently find ourselves with the need to write explanations of how to do something. Called the "how to," this kind of essay is one of the most useful of all the modes that are covered in this book. Nearly everyone knows how to do something exceedingly well. In fact, each semester my students surprise me with the range of their skills and knowledge: Synchronized swimming, developing black-and-white film, management by objectives, playing lacrosse, and setting up a summer ice cream business are just a few of the topics my students have written on recently.

There's an old saying, "Those who can, do; those who can't, teach." The implication is that if you can do something very well, build a stone fireplace, let's say, you do it. And if you can't do it very well, you teach others how to do it. Though there may be some truth to the saying, I encourage only those who can do something well to teach others how to do it. Writing a how to is a kind of teaching, and, to do it effectively, you must know your subject. You may, of course, add to your existing knowledge through research or interviews. Professional writers do that all the time. Whether your topic is as simple as replacing a pane of glass in a window or as complex (to me, at least) as adjusting the timing in an automobile engine, just be sure you know your stuff.

FINDING A TOPIC
AND A TREATMENT

To get an idea of the wide range of topics that can make successful how to's, see the sidebar for titles of actual articles written by students and by professionals as well. Then think about your hobbies, job, sports, college courses, travel, and any other kind of experience you've had. Undoubtedly you'll discover at least two or three processes that you are familiar with already.

We might at this point distinguish three varieties of how to. The first and most common explains how to do a very concrete process such as testing the pH of a substance or planting a tree. This chapter is itself another example of a concrete how to. The concrete how to usually consists of a series of steps presented and done in chronological order—first do this, then do that. A second variety tells how to do something more abstract, less readily reduced to a series of mechanical steps. How to meditate and how to discipline the 2- to 4-year-old are examples of this type of topic. Organization of the abstract how to is not chronological. Instead, it reflects the writer's perceptions of the subject and the parts into which he divides that subject. The third variety of how to might better be called the "how I did it." Here, you relate the steps that you took in producing a musical comedy or being chosen California's Junior Miss. Unless you are a celebrity, your readers will be more interested in the process than in you. With the "how I did it," you are actually telling a story, so this form is a kind of narrative.

To illustrate the differences between these three types of how to's, let's take a general subject and devise some appropriate topics.

> General subject: Career planning
> How to do it (concrete): Writing a résumé
> Finding the openings
> Writing a letter of application
> How to do it (abstract): Choosing a career in the health care field
> Let your interests guide you to a career
> How I did it: Getting my job as a management trainee
> How I became a TV cameraman for "American Sports-man"

Sometimes the lines between the first and second methods are blurred; the job interview might be seen as a concrete or an abstract topic. The distinctions can be helpful to you, though, in finding and sharpening your own topic. If you have a general subject in mind (such as European travel),

SAMPLE HOW-TO ARTICLES BY STUDENTS

"Getting the Job You Want"—Rachel Prentiss

"Keeping Friends with Your Family While Getting a College Degree"—Monica Rossi (a wife and mother goes back to school)

"Avoiding Fatigue on Summer Car Trips"—Keith Pierce

"Look Like a Million for Less Than a Hundred"—Becky Smith (sew your own wardrobe and save)

"Make Your Own Coffee Table"—Ginny Piper

"Don't Let Your $30,000 Decision Be a $30,000 Mistake—Debra S. Verone (choosing the right college)

"Improve Your Memory"—Alison Hill

"Management by Objectives: Solving Employee Needs"—Cindy Carrier

Sample How-To Articles in Magazines

"New Routes to Good Buys in Used Cars"—*Woman's Day*

"How to Start a Successful Small Business"—*Family Circle*

"Investing A, B, C's: Common Stocks"—*Better Homes and Gardens*

"Complaint Letters with Clout"—*Better Homes and Gardens*

"Building a Solar Collector"—*Organic Gardening*

"Biking through Mexico"—*Mother Earth News*

"Three Job-Hunting Campaigns that Worked"—*Changing Times*

"Skis: Try before You Buy"—*Ski*

"Basic Black and White Printing"—*Popular Photography*

"Hair Repair: A Hot Oil Treatment"—*McCall's*

"Build this Rugged Colonial Toy Chest"—*Popular Mechanics*

try to list one workable topic for each of the three types of how to's. Of course, a specific topic may come to you without your having to work at it. Or you may be required by a boss or a situation to write on a particular process. That's fine. But if you need help in discovering a topic, try the following approach.

APPLY YOURSELF 1. Choose a general subject about which you know quite a bit. It should be something you might like to write a how to about. Then make a list like the one below and fill in the blanks with possible topics.

> General subject: Investing in the stock market
> How to do it (concrete): Buying your first share of common stock
> How to do it (abstract): Investing in over-the-counter stocks
> How I did it: How I turned $100 into $850 in "penny" stocks

AUDIENCE AND CONTEXT

When you have chosen a topic for your how-to article, you'll need to make some decisions about your audience. For whom are you writing this essay? How much do they already know about the process? Will this audience be attracted automatically to your article because of who they are and what the subject is? You can't count on that. Even the most ardent stamp collector may not read every article in a magazine on stamp collecting.

To see the differences the answers to these questions will make in your planning, let's look at a sample topic: grafting fruit trees. By *grafting*, we mean attaching a branch or shoot to a growing plant in such a way that the shoot continues to live on the new plant. If you were taking a course in plant science, you might have to tell how to make a graft in a paper or on an exam. Your audience is presumably the professor; therefore, you can make certain assumptions about what he or she already knows as well as how deeply you should treat the subject. Or in the same course you might be called on to make a presentation on grafting techniques to other classmates. Some of the conditions are the same as in the first instance, but others have changed: Your audience is now a group of students who have some interest in the subject but not the same expertise as the professor. Still another context for a how to on this subject would be an article written for a gardening magazine. How does this audience differ from the others?

Matters of audience and context need to be settled early in the planning stage, for they determine some very basic characteristics of your essay. Your decisions about audience and context will affect your tone of voice and style, the amount of detail given, the kind of title and opening used. In the sample article at the end of this chapter, you'll see how this works.

APPLY YOURSELF 2. You can get there from here. To gain some notion of just how difficult it can be to give clear, unambiguous instructions, try this:

Write directions from your classroom through a nearby building and back again. The trip should take no more than 10 minutes. Assume that your reader has never been on campus before and is incredibly dense. Your directions should be very precise: "Take a right when you leave the room and go up one flight of stairs."

When you have finished writing these, your instructor will have you swap papers with another student and then actually follow the instructions. The success of your writing will become immediately apparent—you may never see your classmate again.

ORGANIZATION

The next step in planning is to choose a pattern of organization. Sometimes it chooses you. A how-to essay may be arranged in order of time (chronologically) or in order of the importance of the ideas. Chronological order is used in nearly all concrete how to's and in all how I did it's. The recipe for elephant stew begins, "First kill one medium elephant. . . ." "First," "then," "next," "after" and similar words are links between the steps, which are listed in the order in which they are to be done. If the how to relates a complicated process, it might be wise to subdivide the steps into logical groups. An explanation of how to paint a house might be divided into preparations, application of paint, and clean up.

Order of importance is the principle used most frequently in what I've called abstract how to's. A treatment of dealing with stress, for instance, probably wouldn't contain a list of steps that must be followed in certain sequence. More likely, the main points would be those important ways of coping—reexamine your goals, consider a change of job, get regular physical exercise—that you would arrange in descending order of importance to the process as you perceive it.

APPLY YOURSELF 3. A good way to get a sense of the range of possibilities of the how to along with a better understanding of the way it works is to read and analyze several examples. Thumb through a variety of magazines (the list on page 81 suggests some popular ones that routinely publish how to's) and find three how-to articles in three different magazines. Your selection should include both the concrete (like "Home Canning of Tomatoes") and the more abstract and complex (like "Meditation: It Can Change Your Life"). Then read each how to and complete an analysis like the one that follows which has been boxed off.

TITLE _____ MAGAZINE _____

Clip or copy the lead:

How to what?

Organizing principle or structure?

Features (sidebar, diagram, photo, etc.)?

Strengths, weaknesses, comments?

THE WRITTEN PLAN

To assure that you've included all the necessary steps, some sort of written plan is essential. In this kind of writing, careful planning is almost always more productive, I think, than doing a zero, or discovery, draft. The way that works best for me is to visualize myself doing the process, step by step, almost like watching a movie. I jot down those steps as I go along. In explaining how to finish an unfinished piece of furniture, I note the following steps as I picture doing them, numbering them for easy reference. Without thinking about it, I've chosen chronological order as the pattern of organization.

1. Sand
2. Dust
3. Apply stain
4. Wipe off stain
5. Fill all nail holes
6. Let dry
7. Apply varnish
8. Let dry
9. Sand lightly
10. Remove all sanding dust
11. Second coat of varnish
12. Let dry

Already, making the list has saved me time over the alternative method of plunging in and drafting. As I pictured wiping off the excess stain, I remembered how it often puddles in dents, scratches, and nail holes which I had forgotten to fill. The list has to be changed, and the first step becomes "fill all nail holes and cracks." Now I double-check the steps, again picturing someone doing the actual work. OK. Next it occurs to me that several of the steps call for materials that the reader should buy or gather before starting. I'll jot them down where needed.

1.	Fill all nail holes	Wood putty
2.	Sand	Sandpaper (medium, fine, extra fine)
3.	Dust	Clean cloth, tack cloth
4.	Apply stain	Stain, brush or clean cloth (rubber gloves for the tidy)
5.	Wipe off stain	Another clean cloth
6.	Let dry	
7.	Apply varnish	Varnish, clean brush
8.	Let dry	
9.	Sand lightly	Extra fine sandpaper
10.	Remove all sanding dust	Tack cloth
11.	Second coat of varnish	
12.	Let dry	

If this were a more complex process, I might divide the work into two parts: preparations (steps 1–3) and staining and varnishing (steps 4–12). In this case, however, it doesn't seem necessary to make that division. Another decision is how to treat the materials list. I could refer to the material during the explanation of each step: "Fill all nail holes with putty. Plastic Wood comes premixed in a small can. Another good brand is Rutland Vinyl Wood Putty. It comes in powder form and must be mixed with water, admittedly a nuisance, but it absorbs stain better than Plastic Wood." Or I might decide that giving that kind of information in the body of the how to is apt to distract the reader from the process. Then I would use a sidebar instead as illustrated in the boxed off text that follows.

Now I have a clear plan and a list of materials. I'm assuming that my reader knows next to nothing about the subject, so I'll be explicit in all directions. Notice in the materials list that "tack cloth" is defined, for instance. The prewriting stages are over—as is much of the work of writing the essay.

LIST OF MATERIALS

Wood putty. Plastic Wood, premixed. Rutland Vinyl Wood Putty, powder, accepts stain well.

Sand paper. Two or three sheets each of medium, fine, and extra fine.

Wood Stain. Most paint manufacturers produce a penetrating stain. Minwax brand is very popular.

Paint brush (2). Nylon. 1 to 2 inches depending on size of piece. Keep one for varnish only.

Cloths. Cheesecloth, old T-shirt or diaper.

Tack cloth. A sticky square of cheesecloth, sold in paint stores.

Varnish. Polyurethane is easiest to use. A pint should be enough.

APPLY YOURSELF 4. In APPLY YOURSELF 1 you made a list of possible topics for a how to. Now choose one of those, decide on audience and context, and write a plan like the one just shown. Include a list of materials, if appropriate.

WRITING THE DRAFT

The plan completed, two alternatives are open to you. To further clarify your thinking about an audience and a context for the essay, it might help if you wrote one or more *trial* titles and leads before starting a draft. On the other hand, you might wish to begin writing without concerning yourself with these preliminaries. Then you would add these elements later. For my furniture-finishing article, the context is the general homeowner magazine such as *Better Homes and Gardens.* I have in mind as an audience people with little experience but much interest in home crafts projects. And I know that these readers like to do it themselves not only to save money but to gain personal satisfaction in creating something beautiful with their hands. With the audience and context clear in my mind, I'll draft first and incorporate the title and lead after.

Here is my first draft of how to finish unfinished furniture (I think that I have unconsciously chosen a working title and that's it). You'll notice that I've made some changes during the drafting, proving that writing and rewriting are not completely separate activities. Additions are indicated +like this+ and deletions /this way/. Generally, though, I prefer to keep writing while it's flowing well. I'll go back and polish more carefully after I've finished the first draft.

FIRST DRAFT: "HOW TO FINISH UNFINISHED FURNITURE"

Begin by filling all nail holes and cracks with wood putty. +Following directions on the package.+ Use your finger /to/ or a flexible-bladed putty knife to work the putty into the holes. Smooth, leaving /the/ +some+ putty +projecting+ slightly above the surface of the wood. This allows for /some/ shrinkage /of material/. You can sand away any excess /when the putty has dried/ later.

When the putty has dried /for the time recommended by the manufacturer/, sand all exposed wood surfaces. Begin with the medium-grade sandpaper, rubbing with the grain (that is, always in the direction of the lines of the wood.) Then sand again with the fine paper, and finally with the extra fine. If you would like a top-quality finish, continue to sand with the extra fine paper until a +wadded+ cloth pushed over the surface slides easily. Dust with a clean cloth, then with a tack cloth.

Applying the stain is fun because it changes the appearance of the piece quickly, giving you a great feeling of accomplishment. I recommend what is called a "penetrating" stain, which sinks into the wood giving some depth +to the finish.+ A light scratch will be less conspicuous with this kind of stain. Although manufacturer's directions vary somewhat, the application procedure is fairly standardized. You can apply the stain with a brush or with a folded rag dipped in stain. The brush keeps your hands cleaner but the cloth allows you to "feel" the wood better. Put on a generous amount of stain and let it soak +into the wood+ for 2 to 10 minutes, depending on the depth of color you want. +Then wipe off the excess.+ It's better to go for a shorter time and apply two or three coats than to let the stain penetrate too long, +making the wood darker than you desire,+ and have to remove it with paint thinner. Wipe off the excess stain, being sure to clean all surfaces. If the depth of color satisfies you, go on to the next step. If it is too light, repeat.

The next paragraph was added later in the drafting.

Most unfinished furniture is made of softwood. /and/ Stain will soak in quickly, but sometimes unevenly. If that happens and you don't like the effect, you can apply additional coats of stain to lighter areas to make them match. Higher-priced pieces are often made of birch, a very dense wood not easily penetrated by stain. You'll have to let the stain sink in longer and apply extra coats for a dark finish. With birch though, many furniture finishers skip the stain step entirely in favor of a light look, reminiscent of American Shaker furniture or contemporary Scandinavian finishes. To accomplish this, omit the staining and proceed to varnishing.

+ Assuming that you have decided to stain, after you have achieved the shade you want. + let the piece dry for 24 hours, then sand again lightly with extra fine paper. Dust thoroughly with a tack cloth. Any particle of dust left on the surface will mar the finish.

The final series of steps involves varnishing, a process where /care/ extra care pays off in a fine finish. If at all possible, do the varnishing /in a room/ where the piece can be left undisturbed for 4 or 5 days. Dust is the worst enemy of the wood finisher. If you varnish in a room with lots of traffic, dust will be stirred up and will settle on the wet varnish. If, like most of us, you don't have a spare bedroom or spotless workshop, do your varnishing the last thing at night, put out the cat, and go to bed. That way the varnish will have at least 6 or 7 hours of peace, usually enough to reach a tack-free state.

To apply the first coat of varnish, *stir* the contents of the can gently, scraping the bottom of the can frequently to mix up the solids. Do not shake the can; this will cause bubbles which will ruin your finish. Then /with/ dip a clean (preferably new) nylon brush into the varnish and tap gently against the lip of the can + to remove excess. + Do not scrape against the lip—this will remove too much. /The key to successful application of varnish is to *flow* it on./ If you're used to painting with a forceful back-and-forth, up-and-down motion, /forget it/ don't. With varnish, the secret is to *flow* it on. With a very light touch apply the wet brush to the wood and draw it along the surface in one direction only. The idea is to use the brush as little as possible in getting the varnish from the can to the wood surface. You should be able to see the varnish filling in the brush strokes behind the brush (called leveling). When this happens, you'll have a finish that you won't be able to see—and that's what you're after. Do be sure that you don't put the varnish on so thick that it begins to "run" or drip on vertical surfaces.

When you've applied the first coat, go away. Leave it alone for at least 24 or even better 48 hours. If you touch the varnish after 8 hours or so, it will seem dry. But for best results, let it cure thoroughly.

When the first coat is dry, sand *very* lightly with extra fine sandpaper, dust with your tack cloth, and you're ready to apply the second and final coat of varnish. Unless you're doing the top of a bar, two coats is all you need. /Apply/ Put on the second coat just as you did the first, then go away again. Once more, let the piece dry thoroughly. You're finished.

/You may want to protect your new piece of furniture with a coat of wax or lemon oil. Then/ Put your new piece of furniture in the living room or wherever and prepare yourself to respond modestly to all the compliments you'll /be getting/ get from family and friends.

THE NEXT STEP

Although I've written a draft, I'm not finished yet. The essay still needs a title, an opening, and some revision. When I've settled on an opening, I can write a title that relates to that, so let's put that aside for now. The purpose of the opening in this case is to attract the reader and to tell him what the essay is about. The first paragraph should make him want to read on.

Several ideas occur to me: the recession, inflation, how much you can save by finishing your own furniture, how widely available unfinished pieces are. But as I sit in my living room writing this, the table next to my chair, the one holding my coffee cup, catches my eye—and my mind. Here's a table that I finished myself last winter. Why not use that? Then I recall the circumstances of the table and I've got a lead.

> My mother-in-law did it again. Last Christmas she gave my wife and me a nice little butterfly table for our living room. You know the kind—drop leaves with swivel supports. But when I opened the box, I discovered that it was unfinished, /Oh, it was assembled, all right, but/ the wood /was/ raw and colorless. In giving us a nice Christmas present, she had also provided me with a way to spend several long, long Vermont winter evenings. I'd have to finish it myself.
>
> Truthfully, I was neither surprised nor dismayed. Long ago I had discovered that I couldn't live like a GM vice president on a teacher's salary, and over the years I had bought and finished a number of pieces of unfinished furniture for our home. And I have learned three things in the process. First, you can save lots of money by finishing it yourself. The butterfly table cost about 65 dollars; a comparable piece in a retail store about 150 dollars. Second, you can do a much better job than most manufacturers, who hastily machine sand and spray. And third, finishing furniture is a very enjoyable hobby that gives you a lot of satisfaction.
>
> If you've never tried to finish a piece of furniture for your own home, you can profit by my mistakes and successes. Just follow these simple step-by-step instructions to produce a warm, hand-rubbed finish.
>
> Wood stains come in a variety of hues, most representing the tones of furniture woods: mahogany, maple, oak, birch, cherry, walnut, even pine. Choose a stain that pleases you and enhances the style of the piece of furniture. While you're shopping for the stain, pick up the rest of the materials listed in the box below and you'll be ready to begin as soon as you get home.

I might try some other openings, but I like that one well enough, so I'll stick with it for now anyway. Notice the way this opening works. The first paragraph is the grabber; it tells a little story related to the topic. The second paragraph brings up the problem we all share—never having quite enough money to do what we want. It also gives other benefits of doing it yourself. The third paragraph tells what the essay is about and encourages the reader to try the process. The fourth paragraph wraps up the preliminaries and leads into the actual how to. It's not a bad lead, but it is too long. I'll get back to it as I polish.

Next, a title. "Create a Hand-Rubbed Finish on Your Furniture"? No. "Finish Your Own Furniture and Save"? That is descriptive and refers to money, an interesting subject. Maybe. Or how about a two-part title: "Do It Yourself and Save: Put a Fine Finish on that Unfinished Furniture"? Ugh! I'll go with the second one—it's short and to the point. Maybe I can come up with something better later on.

Now I'd like to deal with something that has bothered me since I wrote it: the ending of the essay.

> Put your new piece of furniture in the living room or wherever and prepare yourself to respond modestly to all the compliments you'll get from family and friends.

Two things are wrong with this as a concluding sentence. It's predictable; you've seen hundreds of essays end this way. And it's "cute." I hate "cute." If I go back to the opening, perhaps I'll get an idea.

How about something that connects the reader to my mother-in-law or his mother-in-law?

> You've done a job that you can take pride in for years to come. And next Christmas if your mother-in-law shows up with a big box, unlock the door and give her a kiss—it may be that dry sink you've been dreaming of for the dining room.

That's better, I think. Maybe I'll use it.

REVISING

So far in this chapter, we've examined the first two stages of the writing process as they apply to composing a how-to essay: prewriting and writing or drafting. The next step is rewriting, or revising. Rather than take the time and space here to explain all that is involved in rewriting, I'll refer you to Stage III, The Writer Revises. While you're reading that, I'll revise "Finish Your Own Furniture and Save." Who knows? Maybe *Popular Mechanics* or *Better Homes and Gardens* would be interested in . . .

APPLY YOURSELF 5. Now it's your turn. Plan and write a how to, either the one you started in Apply Yourself 4 or another. After you've chosen a process that you know well, you should ask (and answer) some key questions: Is this for the general reader or for someone with some knowledge of the field? For instance, one of my students wrote a care plan for a patient recovering from hip surgery. She knew that it would be read by other nurses, so she could use medical terms without defining them as she would have had to for a general reader. She could also determine that clarity was the prime requisite and that she didn't have to entice her reader to read on. Another question: What is the best method of development for this subject—order of time or order of importance? As you move along in the planning and into the drafting, ask if a diagram or some other visual aid would help the reader. Perhaps a list of materials or tools. When you've completed your first or second draft, ask someone who doesn't know how to do whatever you are explaining to read your article. Is it clear? Have you left out any important steps? The real test, of course, is when the reader actually tries to follow your instructions and perform the task.

Chapter Six
Classification—what is the pattern?

*T*he library at my university has over 800,000 books, a modest collection by some standards. Put yourself, if you will, in the position of the keeper of these volumes. How do you organize and arrange them? According to the colors of their bindings, thus a blue room, a maroon alcove? Pretty perhaps, but not very useful. By date of composition? More helpful maybe, but still of limited value. Back in 1874 a 23-year-old man faced a similar problem when he became acting librarian of Amherst College in Massachusetts: how to classify the books in the collection. He wanted a system that would enable readers to find not only any given book but other books on the same subject. His solution was to make ten major categories covering the general fields of human knowledge. Each category he subdivided for more precise identification. Thus young Melvil Dewey of Adams Center, New York, developed the Dewey decimal system of classifying books. An outline of his system is shown on the following page, along with a different solution to the same problem: the Library of Congress classification system. Your college library utilizes one or the other of these.

Any plan or scheme of classification is someone's attempt to organize things, people, events, or ideas (let's call them items) in a meaningful or significant way. Items that are alike in some specified way are put into a group; items that differ from these are excluded from that group and put into another. Each class or group, then, consists of items with similar characteristics.

The simplest sort of classification has just two classes: One contains items *with* the specified characteristics and one contains those *without*. Let's say you are beginning to plan your program of courses for next semester. As you go through the course schedule, you make a list of courses you consider taking, eliminating all others. Although in doing this you are establishing

LIBRARY CLASSIFICATION SYSTEMS

DEWEY DECIMAL

000–099	General Works		600–699	Applied Sciences
100–199	Philosophy and Psychology		700–799	Fine Arts and Recreation
200–299	Religion		800–899	Literature
300–399	Social Sciences		F	Fiction in English
400–499	Languages		900–999	History, Travel, Collected Biography
500–599	Pure Sciences		B	Individual Biography

Each of these major classes is divided into subclasses: the 820s is English literature, for instance. Finer distinctions are made by adding decimals.

LIBRARY OF CONGRESS

A	General Works		L	Education
B	Philosophy, Psychology, Religion		M	Music
			N	Fine Arts
C–D	History and Topography (except America)		P	Language and Literature
E–F	America		Q	Science
G	Geography, Anthropology, Sports and Games		R	Medicine
			S	Agriculture, Forestry
H	Social Sciences		T	Engineering and Technology
J	Political Science		U	Military Science
K	Law		V	Naval Science
			Z	Bibliography

Each of these major classes is divided into subclasses: PR is English literature, for instance. Finer distinctions are indicated by adding numbers.

two classes of courses (those you might take and those you won't take), you probably write down only those in the first category:

Courses I Might Take Next Semester
English 2
Math 9
History 24
Psych 1
Art 2
Philosophy 1
French 2
Chem 12
Phys. Ed. 27

Your system of classification is simple, but the characteristics of the category "Courses I might take" are several: must not require prerequisites I don't have, must count toward my requirements, must not be too hard for me, or must be a required course, and who knows what else. These are the bases of your system of classification. Only if a course meets all the criteria you've established does it go onto your list; otherwise it is rejected. In this simple kind of classification there are only two classes: items with the specified characteristics and items without them.

A second type of classification, called "complex," sorts items into several groups. Identifying characteristics are established for each class. Ordinarily, there should be classes to which every item of the larger group (universe) can be assigned. A system of classifying voters in your town would be incomplete if the only classes were *Republicans* and *Democrats*. What about *Independent*, *Libertarian*, and *Others*?

Another example of a complex system of classification is found in the field of economics. The author of a basic textbook begins his explanation of types of markets by observing: "There is no such thing as an 'average' or 'typical' industry. Detailed examination of the business sector of American capitalism reveals an almost infinite number of different market situations; no two industries are alike." Yet, to make manageable a study of various industries, an attempt must be made to classify, even if the results are imperfect:

> Economists envision four relatively distinct market situations. These are (1) pure competition, (2) pure monopoly, (3) monopolistic competition, and (4) oligopoly. The immediate task is to decribe the major characteristics of

each of these four market models. In doing so, we shall use the seller's side of the product market as a point of reference. We shall see later that the same general models also are relevant for the buying side of the market.

Campbell R. McConnell, Economics

In this example we see both the names of the classes and the basis of classification ("the seller's side of the product market as a point of reference"). The author of the text takes the next several pages to describe the characteristics of each of the classes.

THE BASES OF CLASSIFICATION

When Campbell R. McConnell classifies industries in the preceding example, he does so on the basis of "the seller's side of the product market." It is important for the classifier to specify his basis and explain why he chose it. The basis for Dewey's classification of books is subject matter, not authors or sizes or colors of bindings. A classification of suntan lotions would most usefully be made on the basis of sun protection factors, a rating of how well the lotion protects against ultraviolet radiation.

The basis of a classification, then, is the special significance that you are looking for in the items, the way in which you perceive the universe of your subject. So you don't classify *students*, you classify *students as roommates* or *students as social creatures* or *students as studiers*. By selecting your basis with care, you will ensure that your final classification has significance. Otherwise, the reader's reaction will be a yawn and a "So what?"

APPLY YOURSELF 1. Classifying livestock I. Listed below are nine kinds of livestock. (You might have to look some of them up in a dictionary.) Decide on a basis for classification, establish your categories, then put each of the nine items into one of the categories. The product should be a chart or diagram showing your classes and the items.

Stallion   Heifer   Ewe   Cow   Lamb

Mare   Bull   Colt   Ram

Because your basis will probably be different from someone else's, your classification scheme might be different too. There's no "correct" answer.

APPLY YOURSELF 2. Classifying livestock II. In the following excerpt from his fascinating book *Word Play*, author Peter Farb explains the process of classifying from the point of view of the language used. Please read the passage and answer the following questions: What is the "universe" that Farb classifies? What bases of classification does he employ? How do his bases compare to yours in Apply Yourself 1?

Everyone, whether he realizes it or not, classifies the items he finds in his environment. Most speakers of English recognize a category that they call *livestock*, which is made up of other categories known as *cattle, horses, sheep*, and *swine* of different ages and sexes. An English speaker who is knowledgeable about farm life categorizes a barnyardful of these animals in a way that establishes relationships based on distinguishing features. For example, he feels that a *cow* and a *mare*, even though they belong to different species, are somehow in a relationship to each other. And of course they are, because they both belong to the category of Female Animal under the general category of Livestock. The speaker of English unconsciously groups certain animals into various sub-categories that exclude other animals:

	LIVESTOCK			
	CATTLE	HORSES	SHEEP	SWINE
FEMALE	Cow	Mare	Ewe	Sow
INTACT MALE	Bull	Stallion	Ram	Boar
CASTRATED MALE	Steer	Gelding	Wether	Barrow
IMMATURE	Heifer	Colt/filly	Lamb	Shoat/gilt
NEWBORN	Calf	Foal	Yearling	Piglet

A table such as this shows that speakers of English are intuitively aware of certain contrasts. They regard a *bull* and a *steer* as different—which they are, because one belongs to a category of Intact Males and the other to a category of Castrated Males. In addition to discriminations made on the basis of livestock's sex, speakers of English also contrast mature and immature animals. A *foal* is a newborn horse and a *stallion* is a mature male horse.

The conceptual labels by which English-speaking peoples talk about barnyard animals can now be understood. The animal is defined by the point at which two distinctive features intersect: sex (male, female, or castrated) and maturity (mature, immature, or newborn). A *stallion* belongs to a category of horse that is both intact male and mature; a *filly* belongs to a category of horse that is both female and immature. Nothing in external reality dictates that barnyard animals should be talked about in this way; it is strictly a convention of English and some other languages.

Word Play: What Happens When People Talk

SUBCLASSES

For many purposes, the establishment of classes is only the first step in the process of organizing the universe of the subject. Further subdividing may be necessary to clarify finer distinctions. When Melvil Dewey devised his classification system for books, he realized that, while the ten major classes would be of some value, the introduction of subclasses was both possible and desirable. So he divided the class of literature (800–899) into subclasses:

800	Literature—general
810	American
820	British
830	German
840	French
850	Italian
860	Spanish and Portuguese
870	Latin
880	Greek
890	All other languages

Each of these subclasses is further divided:

810	American literature—general
811	Poetry
812	Drama
813	Fiction . . . and so on

The reader who knows Dewey's classification system can find poems by American authors by looking in the 811s, for instance.

Probably the most massive organizing scheme ever undertaken is the classification of all life forms of the planet Earth. The largest, most inclusive classes are called kingdoms, such as the animal kingdom and the plant kingdom. Each of these has a hierarchy of subclasses: phylum, class, order, family, genus, and species. The following segment of that classification scheme shows where modern humans fit. Originally devised for purposes of nomenclature and discussion, biological classification has assumed the subsequent purpose of depicting evolutionary relationships between living organisms.

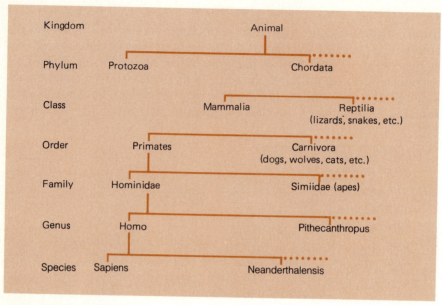

THE PURPOSES OF CLASSIFICATION

The first steps of classification are to identify the universe of your subject, to decide on a basis or bases, and to survey the items in order to establish the classes and their characteristics. Then you can set up a chart, or matrix, and fill it in with the items. Mr. Farb's matrix of livestock in Apply Yourself 2 is a good example. At that point, you have come to understand better the universe of your subject. But that understanding is only one of the purposes of classification. To communicate your understanding to someone else means to put it in writing.

Within an essay, classification can be a preliminary step in preparing the reader for the main topic. For instance, you might classify automobiles as a prelude to an explanation of how to select a true sports car. Another example: A pamphlet on heating with wood might begin with a classification of various species of trees by heat output.

A second purpose of classification is to provide the structure and true subject of an entire essay. Kinds of government, patterns of poverty, varieties of two-dimensional art, theories of knowledge are all subjects that lend themselves to exposition through classification.

APPLY YOURSELF 3. Preppies, Archies, and City Kids. As you read this tongue-in-cheek bit of classification, consider the following questions: What is Aldrich's purpose in classifying adolescents? What is his basis for making distinctions? What are the subclasses of Preppies? How accurate is his classification? What is his conclusion? If you perceive a different system of classification of the young, you might make that the subject of your writing for this chapter.

PREPPIES
The Last Upper Class?

WHERE DO PREPPIES RANK IN SOCIETY?

"Preppie" is a catch-all epithet to take the place of words too worn or elaborate for everyday use, words such as *privileged, ruling class, aristocrat, society woman, gentleman,* and *the rich.* Ideological struggle is too shaming to talk about these days. Life-style rivalry is the new engine of history. In this sort of society, Preppies pass for an upper class.

The middle class is made up of Archies. Many Preppies start out in life as Archies, attempt Preppieness for a time, then return to their original level. Archies, along with Jugheads and Bettys and Veronicas and the rest of the gang at Riverdale High, are distinguished by their sexual competitiveness, their fondness for automobiles and eating, and an amusing discomfort in the presence of all adults except their mothers.

The lower class is composed of City Kids. City Kids may be black or white, poor or rich, but mostly they're smart. Intellectually and physically, their motions are sharp, angular, and quick. In the company of City Kids, Archies tend to become angry and frustrated; Preppies, nervous and envious.

Some City Kids are sent away to prep school to become Preppies. So are many Archies. The Archies always become Preppies, for a few years anyway. The City Kids rarely do, and then only with the embarrassing enthusiasm of converts. This is because City Kids and Preppies represent rival ideals. The ideals lead them to compete for the distinction of living the best sort of life. Archies, on the other hand, have no ideals and do not live—they merely behave. City Kids and Preppies use their ideals to rank things, all things, in hierarchies of best to worst. Ranking things is their strongest passion. However, the only point of similarity between the Preppies' hierarchy of social life and the City Kids' is the rank they give to Archies. Archies are the worst.

WHETHER A PREPPIE IS BORN OR MADE

There are two sorts of Preppies, the self-made and the hereditary. Hereditary Preppies will have a Preppie parent or two—a parent, that is, who went to a prep school. But the purest of the type will go to the *same* prep school as his parent.

Contrary to widespread belief, most students at prep schools are not hereditary Preppies. At Groton and St. Paul's, prep schools that are famously and proudly "family oriented," only about 26 percent of the boys and girls are hereditary Preppies of the purest sort. Some of them are very pure indeed. At

St. Paul's last year there were thirteen great-grandchildren of alumni, one great-great-grandchild, and one great-great-great-grandchild; in this group were two descendants of the man who founded the school in 1855. At Exeter, on the other hand—an ancient prep school that would be offended if anyone thought to call it "family oriented"—only 13 percent of the students were children of alumni. This was closer to the prep school average.

But most Preppies are self-made in a more persuasive sense than the statistical. Few children today will go to a boarding school, any boarding school, just because their parents tell them to, or because of a funny family tradition. They go because they want to, more or less, and they stay for the same reason. By the same token, few prep schools spend much time enticing reluctant students or soothing the restless ones. With three to seven applicants for each place, they don't have to.

WHETHER A PREPPIE MUST BE A WASP

Historically, of course, most Preppies have been privileged WASPs. The Preppie ideal is therefore indelibly stamped with a certain privileged WASPishness.

WASPishness may be defined as a particular squeamishness. WASPs are readily revolted by the following facts of life: physical flabbiness, homosexuality, enthusiasm, Archies, cynicism, fearfulness, salesmanship, flamboyance, money, self-assertion.

More positively, WASPishness may be defined as a certain bravery in the face of other facts of life: disease, demonstrative women, impotent men, accident, disgrace, angry City Kids, and physical hardship (especially when suffered, or inflicted, in the name of a civic virtue such as patriotism).

Squeamishness and bravery are qualities found in City Kids and Archies as well as in Preppies. The differences are of degree and object, and these may be taught. The most efficient teaching of this sort—certainly the least expensive—goes on between parents and children. Thus, WASP children will be less resistant to some aspects of Preppie instruction than, say, the children of Hasidic Jews or Anglophobic Irishmen. Such, however, is the soft plasticity of adolescents, and so mordant is the stamp of prep school, that no sort of family upbringing may be said to foreclose the attainment of Preppie status by a boy or girl who is eager and willing to reach for it.

Nelson W. Aldrich, Jr., Atlantic

APPLY YOURSELF 4. No holds barred. For this exercise, your task is to write a classification of members of the opposite sex. Remember: Identify the universe of your subject (males, females), establish a basis for classification, determine the classes and characteristics, choose a purpose.

Chapter Seven
Comparison and contrast—what is it like?

Comparing and contrasting are among the most basic human intellectual acts. Even the youngest children recognize similarities and differences in colors and shapes. Tens of thousands of years ago primitive humans who followed migrating game into new territories must have noted the likenesses and differences of various subspecies of a favorite food plant. Today when we encounter a new experience, we're often reminded of a similar experience in the past. By comparing the two, we learn how to respond to the new challenge.

Comparison and contrast are types of analysis in which the writer explains similarities or differences between two or more objects, people, phenomena, or ideas. When similarities are stressed, the technique is called *comparison*. When the emphasis is on the differences, it is called *contrast*. Sometimes the distinction is ignored and the term *comparison* is used to refer to both types of analysis. This is especially true when they are combined and similarities and differences noted.

THE MANY USES OF COMPARISON

A versatile pattern of thought, comparison has many uses, which frequently suggest the means of development of an essay. Notice how each of the following functions also provides a built-in element of tension or opposition:

1. *To show the differences between similar items.* Ronald Reagan and Richard Nixon both served as American presidents in our lifetimes. Both are Republicans, both come from California. Both have been labeled "conservative" in their politics. Despite, indeed because of, their similarities, an

IT CAN RUN A MILE CHEAPER THAN YOU CAN.

The Rabbit Diesel runs a mile, and burns about 1.4 cents' worth of fuel.

Compared to that, you're a guzzler.

If you weigh 150 pounds, you'd burn around 90 calories per mile. Figure that as a mere fourth of a fast-food cheeseburger, and it comes to about 18 cents.

Fact is, if you were a car, you couldn't afford you.

So, don't walk. Run for a Volkswagen Rabbit Diesel. According to the 1979 EPA figures, it gets the highest mileage in America: an incredible 40 estimated MPG, and an even more incredible 50 estimated highway MPG. (Use the "estimated MPG" for comparison to other cars. Your mileage may vary with speed, weather and trip length. And your highway mileage will probably be less.)

In addition to giving you the best run for your money, the Rabbit Diesel doesn't require conventional tune-ups. There's nothing much to tune. No spark plugs, points or condensers. Not even a carburetor.

Like all diesels, the Rabbit Diesel has a great reputation for reliability. But unlike many diesels, the Rabbit Diesel responds like a shot from a gun (0 to 50 MPH in a mere 11.5 seconds). From its rack-and-pinion steering to its front-wheel drive, there's not a sluggish bolt in its body.

Obviously, all cars run on some kind of fuel. So do you. But what you save with a Rabbit Diesel, can fuel you with steak.

VOLKSWAGEN DOES IT AGAIN

©VOLKSWAGEN OF AMERICA, INC.

examination of their differences (contrast) could provide the reader with fresh insights. Additionally the unexpected contrast would add interest.

2. *To show similarities between different items.* This is a favorite technique of poets like Robert Burns, who wrote: "O my love's like a red, red rose that's newly sprung in June." The common ground shared by the otherwise dissimilar items is sometimes metaphoric, existing primarily in the mind of the perceiver. At other times it is literal and concrete, just not immediately apparent.

3. *To explain the unknown in terms of the known.* Imagine trying to describe a cactus to someone who's never even seen a picture of one. Or explaining a religious experience to a friend who is an atheist. One of the most successful ways of understanding and communicating the unknown is by comparing it to the known, fastening on specific elements that might be somewhat familiar. Your topic for a political science paper might be newspapers in the Soviet Union, for instance. Few of your readers have seen a Soviet newspaper (the unknown), but all are probably familiar with American papers. By contrasting characteristics of American papers (their parts and features, profit motive, ownership, local or regional distribution, etc.) to parallel characteristics of Soviet papers, you can explain the latter in an understandable way.

4. *To make a choice, express a preference, resolve an issue.* These uses or functions allow you to weigh alternatives, a common mental process. Which car to buy? Who to vote for? Which literature course to take? By comparing and contrasting several alternates according to their qualities, merits, weaknesses, outcomes, etc., you are able to make an informed decision and to persuade your readers of the wisdom of that choice. See Chapter 9, "Argumentation," for more information.

APPLY YOURSELF 1. Uses of comparison. For each of the uses of comparison just explained, choose a pair of subjects that would lend themselves to that use and explain briefly how you would make the comparison.

COMPARISON AND THE COMMON TOPICS

Now let's go back for a moment to something in Chapter 2 of this book, the common topics. Here are topics 2 and 3 from that list:

2. What is it like? Comparison
    In what ways?

3.   What is it different from?   Contrast
     How does it differ from things it may otherwise resemble?
     Is this a difference of degree or of kind?

In that chapter, I told you that the common topics are a means of discovering something to say about your subject. That's true, but they also can indicate the logical method of development. To use an example cited earlier: Your general subject for a course paper is newspapers in the Soviet Union. As you apply the common topics by asking the questions, it occurs to you that the best way to explain Soviet newspapers is by comparing them to American papers. You found both a topic and a way of treating that topic, of developing and structuring it: comparison and contrast.

WRITING THE COMPARISON ESSAY

Whether you need to show similarities, differences, or both, the process of planning and writing the comparison essay is the same. Understand and follow these steps and you'll master an essential pattern of written expression.

Step 1: Discover your true subject and purpose. By *true subject* I mean the sharpened topic that you found by narrowing the general subject. See the example in the preceding section. Several kinds of *purpose* are also explained.

Step 2: Make a list. Actually, brainstorm two lists, side by side. Enumerate all the similarities and differences you can think of. Put comparable items in pairs. In searching for an apartment off campus for next semester, for instance, you've narrowed your choices to two. Making up your mind will be easier if you compare and contrast their features.

Apartment A	Apartment B
Unfurnished	Semifurnished
Heat included	Heat not included
Two bedrooms (one small)	Two bedrooms
Living room 10 by 12 feet	Living room 11 by 14 feet
Close to downtown	Close to campus
$475 per month	$395 per month
Pets allowed	No pets allowed
Parking	Parking
First floor	Second floor
Fair condition	Fair condition

Not much natural light	Lots of windows
Air-conditioned	No air conditioning
Utilities not included	Utilities not included
In old house	In large brick building
Shower	No shower
Medium kitchen	Small kitchen
One-year lease	One-year lease

Step 3: Edit your list. When you've finished your list, you haven't really finished your list. You'll need to eliminate irrelevant items and, if your list is a long one, organize it by grouping similar items together. Let your purpose be the standard by which you decide when organizing your list. Returning to the example of the two apartments, one plan would be to classify all the features for each unit under "pluses," "minuses," and "neither." A second pattern is shown as follows, where the classifications are "size," "cost," and "other considerations."

Apartment A   **Apartment B**

Size

Two bedrooms (one small)	Two bedrooms
Living room 10 by 12 feet	Living room 11 by 14 feet
Medium kitchen	Small kitchen

Costs

$475 per month	$395 per month
One year lease	One-year lease
Unfurnished	Semifurnished
Heat included	Heat not included
Utilities not included	Utilities not included

Other

Close to downtown	Close to campus
Pets allowed	No pets
Parking	Parking
First floor	Second floor
Fair condition	Fair condition
No much natural light	Lots of windows
Air-conditioned	No air conditioning
In old house	In large brick building
Shower	No shower

With a list like this one, you could make a sensible decision about which apartment to rent or continue on to the next step on your way to writing an essay of comparison.

APPLY YOURSELF 2. Make a list. Choose two items to compare. They might be alternative majors or careers, summer jobs, or makes of cars. Or the items can come from courses you are taking: personality theories of Freud and Adler, the responsibilities of the executive and legislative branches of the federal government, the uses of color in early and late Picasso, or any other comparison that is relevant in your studies. Make a list like the one shown in step 2 above. Then edit that list as described in step 3.

Step 4: Make a plan. Your list complete, you can make a plan for the essay. Basically, there are two patterns of organization for comparisons, organization by wholes and by parts, although a third, mixed pattern is derived from these two.

Organization by Wholes

First you explain the whole (all the points) of subject A, then the whole of subject B. The plan looks like this:

Introduction

I. Subject A
    A. Point (or characteristic) 1
    B. Point 2
    C. Point 3, etc.
II. Subject B
    A. Point (or characteristic) 1
    B. Point 2
    C. Point 3

Conclusion

In other words, when you present your comparison "by wholes," you explain all the important characteristics of the first subject before treating parallel points of the second subject. This pattern of organization works best when the comparison is fairly brief: The reader can remember subject A while reading about subject B. You can help by listing the points of both subjects in the same order (e.g., size, color, weight, cost of subject A; then size, color, weight, cost of subject B).

Here's an example of a contrast organized by wholes:

> There are two types of exercises, power and rhythmic. Power exercises like weight lifting and isometrics require short, rapid, forceful movements. They put stress on the heart for short periods, and the stress on your muscle bundles during contractions tends to impede circulation rather than aid it.
>
> Rhythmic exercises like jogging, bicycling, swimming, brisk walking, stationary cycling—even vigorous dancing—use the major muscles repeatedly. I prefer jogging or running, which are cheap (total cost: shoes and shorts), aerobic, and produce physiological changes leading toward fitness. Jogging or running involve vigorous contraction and relaxation of the large muscles of the legs and trunk. Sustained for a period of time, this exercise will raise your body temperature, increase your heart rate and induce sweating. The rewards will be a greater ability to consume oxygen during a strenuous exertion, a lower resting heart rate, less lactic acid produced by your skeletal muscles (therefore less fatigue), reduced blood pressure and more efficient heart and lung action.

Bob Glover and Jack Shepherd,
The Runner's Handbook

Paragraph 1 introduces the contrasts and explains subject A (power exercises). Paragraph 2 explains subject B (rhythmic exercises). Notice that this brief contrast, in addition to showing the differences between power and rhythmic exercises, expresses the author's preference for rhythmic exercises and bases this choice on the differences between the two types.

Organization by Parts or Points

Here you present a point or characteristic of subject A, followed immediately by a parallel point or characteristic of subject B.

Introduction

A. Point 1
   1. Subject A
   2. Subject B
B. Point 2
   1. Subject A
   2. Subject B
C. Point 3
   1. Subject A
   2. Subject B

Conclusion

One advantage of organization by parts is the ease with which the reader can follow your comparison. One disadvantage is the tendency for the reader to develop "Forest Hills (or Wimbledon) neck." Like the spectator at a tennis match who has to turn right, left, then right again to follow the ball, the reader of a passage organized by points can quickly tire of the constant shifting of focus. This disadvantage can be overcome by the skillful writer, though, as the passage below illustrates:

> Early in the 1960's a male professor of anthropology at Vassar College startled his class by listing the parallels between the disabilities blacks suffer by virtue of their skin color and the disabilities women suffer by virtue of their sex. To begin with, neither women nor blacks could hide the respective facts of sex or race. Generalizations about blacks and women as workers relegated both groups to inferior status on the job. Both groups were regarded as a labor reserve, denied equal hiring, training, pay, promotion, responsibility, and seniority at work. Neither group was supposed to boss white men, and both were limited to jobs white men didn't want to do.
>
> Blacks were supposed to be better able to stand uncomfortable physical labor; women, boring details. Both had emerged from a "previous condition of servitude" that had denied them the vote, schooling, jobs, apprenticeships, and equal access to unions, clubs, professional associations, professional schools, restaurants, and public places. Strikingly similar rationalizations and defense mechanisms accommodated both denials of the central American ideal of equal opportunity.
>
> Both women and blacks were held to be inferior in intelligence, incapable of genius, emotional, childlike, irresponsible, and sexually threatening. They were supposed to be all right in their places, and were presumed to prefer staying there. (If they didn't, they were shamed, ridiculed, or slandered.) Both were viewed as treacherous, wily, "intuitive," voluble, and proud of outwitting their menfolk or white folk.
>
> *Caroline Bird with Sara Welles Brillers,*
> *Born Female*

The opening sentence of this passage establishes the comparison: the striking similarity of discrimination practiced against two minorities, women and blacks. The focus of the rest of paragraph 1 and of paragraph 2 is on treatment of these minorities in the workplace and elsewhere. In paragraph 3, both groups are shown to be victims of typical stereotypes. The authors have made organization by points work by careful paragraphing, choice of examples, and varied sentence structure.

The Mixed Pattern
The writer of a more sustained comparison develops a pattern of organization that retains the advantages and eliminates the disadvantages of both

"pure" patterns. Combining organization by wholes and by parts, the mixed pattern allows the writer to compare even the most complex of subjects. Here's the first paragraph of an extended contrast:

> The American and the English educational systems are different in purpose, structure, and method. Let us start with purpose. The two systems grew up in response to very different pressures and needs. In America, you have always been very conscious of the need to build up a new society. You have wanted to construct something bigger, richer, better than you have. This is said to arise from something in the American national character, but that seems to me to turn the logic upside down; it is the American national character that has arisen from the circumstances in which the American people have found themselves. From the start it was necessary to create a supply of ministers of religion, of lawyers, and of skilled artisans—I place them in the order of importance in which they were regarded at the time. Later on there came the obvious necessity of incorporating the great waves of immigrants into your society. Still later came the great task, in which you are still engaged, of knitting your varied economic, social, and racial groups into the harmonious and balanced society in which the principles of democratic government can work properly.
>
> *Geoffrey Crowther, "English and American Education"*

The first sentence establishes that the contrast is between the American educational system (subject A) and the British (subject B). It also informs the reader that three points will be contrasted—differences in purpose, structure, and method. Sentences 2 through 4 explain that the point of the contrast in this paragraph is *purpose* of education in America. The remainder of the paragraph explains the relationship of the purposes of American education to our needs over the centuries.

Now, if you've been following, you should see where this contrast of American and English educational systems is going. If you reread the first four sentences in the sample paragraph, you could even write an outline of the next five paragraphs of the essay. Try it. Cover the answer below with a sheet of paper and write the topics of paragraphs 2, 3, 4, 5, and 6. Then check your answer.

Based on the clues given in the first paragraph, the rest of the essay probably looks like this:

Paragraph 2 purpose—British
Paragraph 3 structure—American
Paragraph 4 structure—British

Paragraph 5 method—American
Paragraph 6 method—British

Of course the author of this essay might have chosen to develop some of these points more fully than others. Thus, British structure, for instance, might really be several paragraphs in length. That's fine. The point is that the reader is given a clear sense of the scope of the essay at the beginning. Although some readers and writers might find this particular pattern too mechanical, it does illustrate some advantages of a clear plan of development, especially important for the student writer whose essay is often just one of twenty-five or more read by a harried professor.

WRITING THE COMPARISON ESSAY—CONTINUED

To review: Step 1 was discovering your true subject and purpose. Step 2 was making a list, step 3 editing your list. Step 4 was making a plan.

The final steps are the same for writing a comparison as for any other kind of exposition:

Step 5: Write a draft.

Step 6: Revise the draft.

Step 7: Copy edit the final draft.

APPLY YOURSELF 3. Study the following examples of comparison and contrast. Then for each example answer the following questions: What is the writer's purpose? Is the piece organized by parts or by wholes? What is the central idea? Finally, working backward from the written passage, see if you can reconstruct the list that the writer might have used. Doing this is similar to outlining an important section of a textbook.

A.   "Boston: A City of Two Tales"
         Old Ironsides was there, the fabled U.S.S. Constitution. So was the 370-foot Spanish schooner Juan Sebastian de Elcano, the 253-foot sailing ship Denmark, from Copenhagen, and the 261-foot Guayas from Ecuador. With close to 2 million people watching, eight big square-riggers and dozens of other tall ships sailed into Boston Harbor last week to kick off a summer-long celebration of the city's 350th birthday. "We want to tell the world we are now a major world-class city again," proclaimed Deputy Mayor Katharine Kane. But behind the hoopla, one of the nation's oldest major cities is more than ever a study in contradiction. Cultured and prosperous, Boston is still plagued by ethnic tension and political conflict whose roots are as old as the city itself.
         "Contrast is everything," the city's official birthday greetings proclaim,

but in Boston the contrasts are so sharp that the city is really a jurisdiction of competing turfs. Founded by Puritans, its tone is now largely Irish Catholic. Known for its Brahmins and brainy academics, it is actually dominated by blue collars. Seen by many as the nation's most livable city—with newly restored mansions, markets and riverfront cafes that attract throngs of the well-to-do—Boston is also a collection of insular working-class neighborhoods, such as Charlestown, Roxbury and South Boston, where racial skirmishes can flare up in an instant. Few blacks dare go to baseball games at Fenway Park because they fear friction with antagonistic whites; many Irish-Americans rarely leave their communities to sample the culture and commerce downtown. "It's tribalism" complains Emory Jackson of the Boston Urban League. "People group around tribes, neighborhoods, turf"—instead of working for the city as a whole.

David M. Alpern with Phyllis Malamud and Ron Labrecque,
Newsweek

B. In person, Papandreou seems more the genial professor than the iconoclastic firebrand. He listens with gratifying attention to the opinions of his visitors, fumbling with his pipe, asking incisive questions and expressing his own views with reassuring temperance. He smiles easily, projecting a charm that never fails to impress those who meet him, regardless of their political beliefs.

But on the balcony, the primary soapbox of Greek politicians, his manner and his speech are transformed. He plants his feet in the stance of a prizefighter and slices the air with his hands, his heavy eyebrows drawing together, his voice mocking and indignant in turn. His rhetoric loses the careful moderation of his private conversations and crystallizes into slogans that touch Greek passions and are scrawled on walls all over the country: "Greece for Greeks!" "Out of NATO!" "Change!"

Nicholas Gage, New York Times Magazine

C. To make some sense out of a sprawling and ill-defined field, perhaps travel writing should be separated from *place* writing or *destination* writing. John McPhee's *Coming Into the Country* is a good example of the latter category. It is a high-spirited description of Alaska, boldly laid out with a clear eye for relevant detail, and stylishly written. It has almost nothing in common with the average travel book or travel article, loaded as they are with information on airline schedules, hotel accommodations, the comparative quality of discotheques, and details of the local landscape often described on an ascending scale of extravagance. There was a time in my life when, editing magazines dealing with travel, I waded through hundreds, perhaps thousands, of these articles. Now, I would unflinchingly choose the Iron Maiden rather than spend an evening with the Sunday travel section of the New York *Times.*

Caskie Stinnett, The Atlantic Monthly

D. In a stained-glass shop in town you can buy antique rose lampshades and geodesic terrariums and tear-drop mirrors in opalescent glass frames. The shop features two kinds of mirrors, silver and bronze. Most of us have seen the silver mirror. It's the common variety and we probably all have one in our bathrooms at home. The bronze mirrors are imported, and they have a slightly darker tone, as the name implies. The silver mirrors reflect things the way they are, but the bronze puts them in a better light. People look into one and see themselves tan and healthy, and tend to buy many more bronze mirrors than silver.

Paul Reese

E.   In Russia and Japan, as in most of the non-Western world, the urge to end economic backwardness was due to external humiliation. In Russia it came through defeat in the Crimean War and in Japan by the intrusion of American gunboats and the imposition of colonial type commercial treaties. In both cases, the first requirement for modernization was major institutional change, particularly in agriculture. In Japan, the process of reform was undertaken with breathtaking pragmatism and capitalist institutions became firmly en-trenched. In Russia the changes were half-hearted, agrarian reform was made in two stages in 1861 and 1906, and on the eve of the Bolshevik revolution half the peasantry still held their land in restrictive communal tenure. The Russian administration collapsed under the strain of war, and capitalism was abolished before it had fully emerged. The USSR then took on the more difficult and quite novel task of devising a workable institutional framework for production without the profit motive. It took the new communist regime ten years to consolidate its power and to define its economic strategy.

Angus Maddison, Economic Growth in Japan and the U.S.S.R.

THE "SO WHAT?" PRINCIPLE AND OTHER PARTING WORDS

Because comparing and contrasting is such a familiar process to most of us, we sometimes overlook principles that make this kind of essay interesting and informative. Often the student in a writing course, told to write an essay of comparison, shows mastery of the organizational patterns and of compe-tence in style, yet the essay lacks a purpose, a reason for being. After reading this comparison of high school and college or living on campus versus living off campus, the reader mutters "So what?"

If you don't want that ho-hum response from your readers, here's what to do (and what to avoid):

Don't make the expected comparison (Washington and Lincoln as presidents, dogs versus cats as pets) unless you have a fresh angle or a new insight.

Don't expect your essay to seethe with tension merely because you've written a contrast. Exciting intellectual tension may come, however, when the writer perceives similarities between dissimilar things or differences between similar ones.

Do explore the causes of similarities and differences or the consequences of them. The result then is a combination comparison and cause-effect analysis (see Chapter 8).

Do review your purpose as you draft. That and your subject determine the necessity for making your plan clear to the reader. If your subject is relatively simple and your purpose is primarily to entertain, see what you can do to make the plan disappear. It shouldn't intrude in this sort of essay. If, however, your purpose is to inform the reader about a relatively complex subject, you should make the plan apparent and use signals to indicate the movement. *On the one hand, first, second,* and *both* are examples of signals that keep the reader on track.

APPLY YOURSELF 4. "Mammoths and Men." Reproduced below is a passage from an essay on the prehistory of the human species. The author describes a conflict that occurred in the Pleistocene epoch, more than 12,000 years ago. Please read the passage and write responses to the following questions.

1. What is compared to what?
2. What seems to be the purpose of the comparison?
3. What are the *major* offsetting attributes of each side? What secondary characteristics does the author compare?
4. What signals of comparison does the author provide?
5. What are the implications or consequences of this comparison?

As compared with the contemporaneous mammoths, the Pleistocene men were probably scattered and certainly not very important; yet as they developed with the passing of time, they were destined to become increasingly disturbing to the animals around them—even to the mammoths, then the giants of the earth. For these early men were evolving a new thing under the sun, a giant intellect, which eventually was to overpower all of the beasts with which men had to contend.

With the gradual increase of the primate brain to a point where it became human, there developed a struggle for dominance between man and the animals around him, and not the least important of man's adversaries in this struggle were the elephants or mammoths. As has been pointed out, it was a contest between a giant physique and a giant intellect. Yet there were other factors involved, to make the struggle between man and the elephants of particular interest in retrospect. It was not only a struggle involving a maximum of body size against a maximum of brain development, but also one of intellect against intellect. The elephants are and always have been remarkably intelligent mammals, and even though their intelligence was no match for the cunning and the reasoning powers of primitive man, still it was sufficiently advanced to make the struggle between these two adversaries all the more intense.

Not only that, but there was a struggle in manipulation. Man had his two hands, which were not necessary for locomotion and therefore could be used for skillfully manipulating objects to his own uses. On the other side of the picture, the elephant had his trunk, an organ of almost unbelievable mobility, strength, and tactile delicacy, with which he could manipulate objects, likewise without regard for the necessities of locomotion. Yet the higher intelligence won, because it could fashion tools as an aid to the handling of objects, while the lesser intellect could use its power of manipulation only for direct contact with things—the tearing down of trees and bushes or the pulling up of roots.

Again, man, having fashioned tools or weapons with his hands, could use them to increase his effective strength. As compared with this, the elephants, particularly some of the extinct mammoths, had strong, efficient tusks that served not only as weapons but also as tools for digging and prying. Here again the higher intellect won out—tools in hands directed by a logically reasoning brain were more effective than powerful tusks, directed even in the most intelligent fashion by a brain of lesser abilities.

Edwin H. Colbert, "Mammoths and Men"

APPLY YOURSELF 5. Stereotypes. Through ignorance or lack of thought, most of us hold oversimplified views or uncritical judgments—stereotypes—of a race, an issue, a nation. When we finally confront the reality, we may discover how wrong the stereotype is. Write an essay in which you compare and contrast a stereotype with the reality that you have experienced or learned.

APPLY YOURSELF 6. Course challenges. College courses you are taking right now provide an ideal opportunity both to practice what you've learned about writing and to reinforce your mastery of the subject matter of a course. In political science, for instance, you learn that responsibilities are divided between the federal goverment and the states. In economics, you must know the differences between a perfectly competitive market structure and a monopoly. In literature, you may study both Greek and Shakespearean tragedy. All these topics lend themselves to comparison and contrast. Choose comparable topics, but not ones for which the professor or the text has already done the work of comparing for you. Write an essay, following the steps outlined earlier in this chapter. Your audience is another student in the course who is confused about the topics.

Chapter Eight
Analysis—parts and the whole

*T*o raise the question "What are its parts?" is to begin the process of analysis, for analysis is the exploration of the nature of a subject—the components or constituents that comprise it. The essential follow-up question, though, is "How do they work?" Here is an excellent definition of *analysis* given in Webster's *New World Dictionary*:

> a separating or breaking up of any whole into its parts, esp. with an examination of these parts to find out their nature, proportion, function, interrelationship, etc.

This definition points out the two essential qualities of a good analysis: an identification of the components of the whole and an examination of the relationship of those components to that whole. *Merely* to identify the components is just to name the parts, contributing little to your understanding of the subject and likely to prove of small value to the reader. Note, then, the second quality of analysis, an examination of the *relationship* of the parts to each other and to the whole. All kinds of analysis come down to that—parts and their relationships.

The subject or whole of analysis may be a physical object, a living organism, an event or a phenomenon, an organization, a work of art, or an idea or intellectual concept. Some examples:

Physical objects—cigarette lighter, book, pencil
Living organisms—leaf, human heart, jellyfish
Events—Battle of Cemetery Ridge, Stones Concert, election of 1948
Phenomena—wave, lunar eclipse, plant respiration
Organizations—New York Stock Exchange, ant colony, Congress
Works of art—poem, painting, movie
Ideas—theory of relativity, Buddhism, democracy

In other words, anything that has essential unity or wholeness is a suitable subject for analysis.

Just how you go about analyzing your subject depends on your interest in the subject and the purpose of the analysis. This chapter treats four kinds of analysis: structural, functional, process, and cause-effect. When you've mastered them separately and in combination, you should be able to treat virtually any subject for a large variety of purposes.

Purpose is as important in analysis as in any other type of exposition. Elsewhere I warned about the "So what?" problem, the reader's frustration at not getting any notion of why the piece was written. Often in a paper about a poem, for instance, the student identifies meter, figures of speech, rhyme scheme, and other elements correctly. So what? Tell me more than that. I want to know what the relationship is between, let's say, the iambic meter and the speaker's voice. Or between the images of light and dark and the theme of the poem. Whether it be a class exercise or a research paper, a sense of purpose must inhere in your writing. In analysis, as you move from a naming of the parts to an explanation of their "nature, proportion, function, interrelationship," you must discover and impose a purpose on your thought and your writing.

STRUCTURE

Perhaps the most familiar kind of analysis is structural. The listing of the parts of a Big Mac which begins this chapter is an example, as is this simple diagram of the parts of a bird.

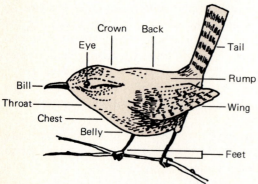

Just how you go about separating the parts of your subject depends on your purpose. Munching away on a bag of Doritos® Nacho Cheese Flavored Tortilla Chips, I found these three analytic lists (current as of November 1983):

NUTRITION INFORMATION
(Per Serving)

Serving size $1\frac{1}{2}$ ounces
Number of servings 1

Calories	220
Protein	3 grams
Carbohydrate	27 grams
Fat	10 grams
Cholesterol+ (0 mg/100 g)	0 milligrams
Sodium (610 mg/100 g)	265 milligrams
Potassium (240 mg/100 g)	105 milligrams

Percentage of U.S. Recommended
Daily allowances (U.S. RDA)

Protein	4
Vitamin A	2
Vitamin C	*
Thiamine	2
Riboflavin	2
Niacin	2
Calcium	4
Iron	2
Vitamin B_6	6
Phosphorus	8
Magnesium	6
Copper	8

+ Information on cholesterol content is provided for individuals who, on the advice of a physician, are modifying their total dietary intake of cholesterol.

* Contains less than 2% U.S. RDA for this nutrient.

Ingredients: Corn; soybean oil, partially hydrogenated; Cheese flavor, salt, Romano cheese from cow's milk, whey, flour, cheddar cheese, tomato solids, monosodium glutamate, buttermilk, onion, Parmesan cheese, garlic, artificial colors, dextrose, citric acid, sugar, spice, disodium inosinate, disodium guanylate, and lactic acid.

The nutrition information and the percentage of U.S. RDA represent somewhat differing ways of assessing the same thing—food value. The ingredients listing tells what went into the triangular concoction. Each of these
lists is a kind of structural analysis of a bag of Doritos® Tortilla Chips, each
performed for a different purpose and on a different basis. The reader needs
to know what the purpose and the basis are.

Analysis by structure is an identification of the parts or components of
a whole coupled with an explanation of the nature of those parts as they
relate to the whole. Depending on the subject, the analysis may be relatively
simple, such as the parts of a bird, or more complex like this analysis of lake
zones:

> Most lakes are divided into zones, as based on physical dimensions and
> biological characteristics. Each zone has a distinct identity and figures impor-
> tantly in the dynamics of lake life. Nearest the shore is the littoral zone,
> where shallowness and light penetration allow plants to root and grow making
> it the most biologically productive area. A marsh is really a highly developed
> littoral zone of a wide, slow-moving river that is, for all intents and purposes,
> a long lake. . . . Though often called the shore zone, the littoral zone is not
> just shoreline; some shallow ponds have nothing but littoral zone, since
> vegetation grows out to the deepest middle parts, covering the entire surface
> of the water.
>
> *Charles W. Johnson, The Nature of Vermont*

Notice how the author gives the basis of his analysis: "physical dimensions
and biological characteristics." When you've read the explanation of three
additional zones (the limnetic, the benthic, and the profundal), you have a
pretty good understanding of what makes up a lake.

Thus far the examples presented of structural analysis have all dealt
with physical objects—a corn chip, a bird, a lake. And so far the structures
have been evident. But some subjects are not physical and their structures
may well not be so apparent. An example of this kind of subject is the
concept of the human personality, a whole with no clearly observable parts.
For centuries students of the subject have explained the personality in a
variety of ways. Best known is Sigmund Freud's analysis, summarized in an
excellent little book, *A Primer of Freudian Psychology*:

> The total personality as conceived by Freud consists of three major
> systems. These are called the *id*, the *ego*, and the *superego*. In the mentally
> healthy person these three systems form a unified and harmonious organiza-
> tion.
>
> *Calvin S. Hall*

Freud took a concept—the human personality—and imposed his perceptions of order on it, something you too will have to do when the structure of your subject is not evident.

GUIDELINES FOR ANALYSIS OF STRUCTURE

1. Introduce your subject.
2. Explain the basis of analysis (e.g., food value, biological characteristics).
3. Explain the components.
4. Relate the components to the whole.

APPLY YOURSELF 1. Analysis of structure. Choose a simple subject suitable for a brief structural analysis, perhaps one page in length, make a plan, and write a draft. The purpose of this is to get some practice with the form, not to produce a major essay.

FUNCTION

When your interest in a subject leads you beyond the structure itself, beyond the parts to the *working* of the parts, you are ready for analysis of function. No longer is the question "What are the parts of this whole?" but "What do the parts do?" In functional analysis you explain how each part contributes to the operation of the whole.

To exemplify functional analysis and compare it to structural analysis, let's take a simple example—a pencil.

STRUCTURE

The heart of a pencil is the "lead" (actually a graphite-clay compound). Surrounding this is a soft wood cylinder, usually two or more strips glued together. The nonwriting end of the pencil is capped by a latex or gum rubber eraser in a metal ferrule.

FUNCTION

The heart of a pencil is the "lead," actually a powdered graphite-clay compound. It's the graphite that makes the mark, but alone it is too soft so clay is mixed in for strength. A wooden sleeve covers the brittle lead to give it support. Named for its function, the eraser was once a separate tool. Then an inventor who could never find his eraser when he needed it hit on the idea of attaching it permanently to the pencil. The metal ferrule does that job today.

The functional analysis of the pencil actually includes an analysis of structure as well, a very common combination. First explain the components and then relate their function.

Functional analysis is not limited to concrete subjects. Most of the examples listed at the beginning of this chapter are suited to functional analysis. Like analysis of structure, this method is often employed to explore the nature of intellectual concepts and ideas. Earlier, we saw a brief explanation of Freud's theory of the personality. The author moves quickly from that passage into analysis of the function of the three components or systems as he terms them—the id, the ego, and the superego.

The sole function of the id is to provide for the immediate discharge of quantities of excitation (energy or tension) that are released in the organism by internal or external stimulation. This function of the id fulfills the primordial or initial principle of life which Freud called the *pleasure principle*. The aim of the pleasure principle is to rid the person of tension, or, if this is impossible— as it usually is—to reduce the amount of tension to a low level and to keep it as constant as possible. Tension is experienced as pain or discomfort, while relief from tension is experienced as pleasure or satisfaction. The aim of the pleasure principle may be said, then, to consist of avoiding pain and finding pleasure.

Calvin S. Hall

GUIDELINES FOR ANALYSIS OF FUNCTION

1. Introduce your subject.
2. Explain the basis of analysis.
3. Explain the components.
4. Explain the function of each as part of the whole.

APPLY YOURSELF 2. Analysis of function. Choose a subject that lends itself to functional analysis. Then, following the guidelines in this section, plan and write an explanation of the way the parts contribute to the whole.

PROCESS

Practically every jar, can, and bottle that you have around the house or dorm contains a short process analysis. The can of shaving gel I use every morning gives explicit directions, as if I could read at that hour:

1. Wash face with soap and hottest water possible.
2. Leave face moist.
3. Put a small amount on finger tips and spread gel thinly over beard.
4. Gently rub into a lather and shave.

One kind of process analysis explains how to do something—repair a leaky toilet, get the ultimate tan, write an essay. Called the how to, this technqiue is treated fully in a separate chapter.

Here, we'll concern ourselves with two other varieties of process analysis. The first explains how something is done: how oil is refined, how asexual reproduction works, how a legislative bill becomes a law. The difference between this type of analysis and the how to is a matter of emphasis. The reader of the how to is given directions that he or she may follow to achieve the results. The reader of this second kind of analysis learns how the process operates without any expectation or likelihood of actually doing it.

The following passage is a good example of analysis of process, in this case the onset of a thunderstorm.

The barn doors were closed just as the first gusts of wind struck. The curtain lit up with flashes of lightning, and the thunder was sharp, crisp, ten seconds later, two miles away. Big silver raindrops exploded in the barnyard dust, and the cows, which had not taken notice until now, ran for the shelter of some trees. Now another stroke of lightning, searing across the sky to a hilltop. It was blindingly bright, and there was no time to gather one's wits before the thunder shook the ground. The sheet of rain obscured the hills as it drew closer. The tall elms at the far fence line bent, then disappeared behind gray torrents. Gusts of wind rippled across the unmown fields, blowing the grass one way, then another, and the rain struck. Another flash, a quick tearing sound, and bone-jarring explosion. The thunder seemed to jolt ten times more water loose from the clouds. There was no respite. Each [storm] cell was fully recharged twenty seconds after a lightning stroke, and ready to do it again. Up on a knoll, a pine tree began to tingle. Overhead, fingers of ionized air were reaching down, a little farther each time, toward the tree. A little ionized finger reached up from the tree, and the circuit was complete. A charge of millions of volts shot up the tree and into the cloud. The core of ionized air reached temperatures several times greater than the surface of the sun. The moisture in the unfortunate tree vaporized, and its heart exploded.

For five hundred feet, the shock wave traveled faster than sound. Then it slowed down and became a sound wave, sounding and resounding off the different air masses, and finally fading away.

Nathaniel Tripp, "Summer Storm"

Although this account of a summer storm is dramatized, it is not all that different in construction from an explanation that you might find in an encyclopedia. It shares with every other process analysis three basic qualities. First, it is composed of a series of steps. Second, these steps are presented in a logical time sequence. And third, it is narrative in nature, as if it were a story. When you come to write your own process analysis, be sure it contains these qualities.

Another variety of process analysis takes as its subject a single event and explains how it happened. Much history is written this way: how John F. Kennedy was assassinated, how American schools came to be desegregated, how Alaska became the fiftieth state.

In researching and planning any kind of process analysis, you need to be certain that you include all of the relevant information and none of the nonessential. This sort of analysis is often combined with analysis of cause and effect, the topic of the next section of this chapter.

GUIDELINES FOR ANALYSIS OF PROCESS

1. Introduce your subject.
2. Present the steps in sequence.
3. Show how the steps contribute to the whole.

APPLY YOURSELF 3. Analysis of process. Write an essay based on one of the following choices.

A. Analyze the process of the coming of spring or fall.
B. Analyze an event you witnessed during your years in high school— something like a teachers' strike, the big food fight of 1983, graduation. Write about it from the viewpoint of an outside observer, not a participant.

CAUSE AND EFFECT

Rooted deep in the Western mind is the idea of *causality*—the relationship between a cause and its effect. We believe vigorously that every change has a cause; one thing leads to another. We search for the cause whenever something good happens so as to repeat it. We are just as anxious to find the cause when something bad occurs so as to eliminate it.

"Why did that happen?" is an expression of interest in causes. Often we can understand a condition or an event better if we know what brought it about. Why is the divorce rate higher today than it has ever been? Why did Japan attack Pearl Harbor? Why did I get a cold?

Anything that produces a result or effect is a cause. In attempting to assign causality, we usually look to events that precede the effect in time. But merely because one event or condition occurs before another does not necessarily make it a cause. A black cat crosses the street in front of your car. A block later you have a flat tire. The cat did not cause the flat tire. Although this example is trivial, the danger of false reasoning from assigning a cause just because it precedes an effect is a serious one. Roman rhetoricians had a name for this kind of spurious logic: *post hoc ergo propter hoc*, meaning "after this, therefore because of this." Coincidence does not establish causality.

Multiple Causes

In any study of causality that you undertake, be certain to explore the subject thoroughly. An effect may well have more than one cause, as the following analysis of economic recovery points out. As you read, identify the multiple causes.

> Despite such worries, most economists believe that the recovery not only is gaining strength but should continue to register solid, if unspectacular, gains throughout 1983 and beyond. The analysts attribute the apparent vigor to various forces, ranging from an accommodative monetary policy at the Federal Reserve Board to smartly climbing productivity. But a paramount factor, it's generally agreed, is that the very severity of the recent slump has created strongly expansionary conditions—plentiful supplies of labor, ample productive capacity and sharply diminished inflation.
>
> *Alfred L. Malabre, Jr.,*
> *The Wall Street Journal*

Effects Become Causes

Effects themselves may become causes as the chain of causality extends. As an example, look at what happens when a ski area has a season of little or no snow (cause). Fewer skiers travel to the slopes (effect). Fewer skiers (cause) mean less income for resorts, gas stations, clothing shops, and restaurants (effect). Severely reduced income (cause) means layoffs for some workers (effect), and so on.

Multiple Effects

Multiple effects deriving from a single cause are not uncommon. Sometimes one or more of these effects is unanticipated and even undesirable. In the 1940s and 1950s, for instance, farmers used a wide variety of chemical pesticides and herbicides (causes) to control unwanted insect and plant life (effects). Only years later did it become widely known that these same pesticides and herbicides (causes) were harming desirable wildlife (effect) and producing cancer in humans (effect). The following passage points out the mixed effects of a lowering of world oil prices:

> Treasury Secretary Donald Regan told reporters Monday that a further major softening of world oil prices could put poorer oil-producing countries, such as Nigeria and Venezuela, in a bind. He added, though, that a decline in oil prices generally would be good for the world economy because it would ease inflation and provide more income for consumers. Treasury officials have estimated that prices would have to fall to between $22 and $26 a barrel before oil-producing countries would be seriously hurt.
>
> *Youssef M. Ibrahim, The Wall Street Journal*

Confusion of Cause and Effect

Strange as it may seem, cause is sometimes confused with effect in our thinking. This is especially common when the cause and the effect are circumstances of long duration or when they seem to occur simultaneously. The analyst needs to be insightful to untangle the relationship, as shown in the situation known as hyperventilation.

> Hyperventilation is another form of abnormal breathing which may occur during an acute anxiety attack, and results in a sense of overwhelming terror and impending death. This syndrome triggers overbreathing and creates frightening symptoms which generates even more anxiety. Numbness and tingling may develop in the hands and feet and around the mouth. Hyperventilation attacks are often mistaken for heart attacks, seizures or acute asthmatic attacks. The victim feels that the physical symptoms are the cause of his panic, but actually the opposite is true.
>
> *Emergency Handbook/Directory*

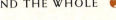

Your analysis will be easier to follow if you identify the causes with marker words like "because," "due to," "reasons," "produces." Effects can be marked by "results," "outcomes," "consequence." Aside from clarifying, words like these also signal transitions.

GUIDELINES FOR ANALYSIS OF CAUSE AND EFFECT

1. Introduce your subject.

2. Distinguish between causes and effects.

3. Include multiple causes and multiple effects when relevant.

4. Use marker words to show connections.

APPLY YOURSELF 4. Effects of the Tennessee Valley Authority. In his article noting the fiftieth anniversary of the Tennessee Valley Authority (TVA), the author explores the effects of the agency established in 1933. As you read the following excerpt from that article, make a list of positive and negative effects of the TVA. Also note which of the changes cited in paragraphs 4 and 5 might have had causes other than the efforts of this government corporation.

It was in that year [1933], on May 18, that President Roosevelt signed a bill establishing the Tennessee Valley Authority, a Government corporation charged with taming the Tennessee River, improving navigation, reforesting and restoring land and providing for the agricultural and industrial development of the valley.

From its birth the T.V.A. was swaddled in controversy as one of the foundation blocks in Roosevelt's New Deal. It has been criticized as an experiment in socialism and praised as one of the few Government experiments that worked.

It became the largest utility in the country, though it is now second, and probably the most effective regional development agency. It has struggled with politicians and snail darters and opponents of nuclear power. It has improved the overall quality of life in the region, but it has also flooded generations-old farmland and the birthplace of the Cherokee Indian nation; it has attracted industry but has polluted the skies.

Since 1933, the number of manufacturing plants in the region has increased by 400 percent. Per capita income has climbed to 77 percent of the national average. The river is tame and navigable for the entire 650 miles from Knoxville, Tenn., to Paducah, Ky. And in the fiscal year 1982, in a deeply recessionary economy, there were 273 announcements from industries planning to build new facilities or expand existing ones in the region.

In an area once speckled with the log cabins of ragged sharecroppers, the highways are lined with brick homes with late-model pickup trucks and outboard motorboats parked outside.

Wendall Rawls, Jr., The New York Times

APPLY YOURSELF 5. Cause and effect. Choose an event in your own life or in the life of your community or your friends about which you know a great deal. Sort out the facts as you understand them, identifying causes and effects, then write an essay of analysis.

APPLY YOURSELF 6. "Blue Haze." This short essay includes several kinds of analysis. What is the general subject (the whole)? What are its parts? What kinds of analysis are performed in paragraphs 1 and 2? In paragraph 3?

June, with its long days and rising temperatures, always entices me to visit the seashore and enjoy the special pleasures offered at this meeting point between land and sea. Shorelines are rich in natural phenomena just waiting to be observed and investigated. Some members of my family become amateur conchologists and disappear down the beach for hours in search of calcareous treasures. That is not for me. Between dips in the waves I like to sit and take in the local atmospheric and hydrospheric characteristics. First, I note whether the breeze is offshore or onshore, because of the important temperature consequences that follow. Next, I note the stage of the tide and whether it is coming in or going out, so that my nap will not be interrupted by any waves. And then I consider the character of the waves, whether they are long rollers caused by a distant disturbance or short, choppy breakers that I must respect.

Finally, I note the visibility. One phenomenon that has always interested me is the haziness of the atmosphere just above the breakers. That haziness is caused by particles of sea salt that have been carried into the atmosphere with the evaporating spray of breaking waves. It forms a dark curtain above the shoreline, which from a distance often appears bluish. The tinge results when the sunlight is scattered by the tiny salt particles. The blue light waves in direct sunlight are scattered more than are other colors and hence predominate in the haze, making it appear blue.

These tiny salt particles also fill an important role in the atmosphere's hydrologic process by forming the nucleus around which moisture condenses to form raindrops, and these, of course, eventually return to the seas in a never-ending cycle.

David Ludlum, Country Journal

APPLY YOURSELF 7. We all do it. Look for examples of the four kinds of analysis in your reading and bring them to class. Likely places to look: textbooks, college catalog, magazines, campus newspaper, even novels.

APPLY YOURSELF 8. The Edge of Nausea (courtesy of Tony Magistrale).

She: *Look, this is important to me, can I trust you?*
He: *You tell me—. . . am I worth your trust?*
She: *I hope so, but if I tell you about it, will you still respect me?*
He: *Is it really that important for you that I do?*

The above is a verbatim account of one of the more articulate conversations between two main characters on "The Edge of Night," a semiliterate phenomenon offered every weekday afternoon for the stimulation of tired homemakers, retired senior citizens, bored college students, stay-home-sick career folk, and perverted teachers of composition. As an exercise in comprehending American culture, watch one of these serials (remember that there are evening shows such as "Dallas" that also belong to the genre) for several days—three at least, more if you can stand it. Then choose three of the following five sets of questions and write a one-paragraph response to each set.

1. Who are the main characters? What is their social position in the world (i.e., banker, doctor, candlestick maker)? Do the actors in your program conform to certain stereotypes in the roles they play? To what extent, if any, were you able to identify with the characters?

2. In terms of the occupations portrayed, are they a fair or unfair representation? How are the sex roles managed? Do the men and women play "traditional" roles? Why or why not?

3. What are the major themes of your program? (Don't summarize the plot!) Why are these themes stressed at the exclusion of others?

4. Did your soap opera have any *intended* elements of humor in it? If so, how did it come off? Laughter is usually avoided in traditional soap operas. Why?

5. Consider the enormous popularity of the soap opera: Why do Americans take this sudsy world so seriously?

APPLY YOURSELF 9. Your professors in other courses are always assigning papers of analysis, although they may not call them that. For this assignment, you have two options:

A.   If you have to write an analytical paper for another course, work on it for this assignment too, but add a brief explanation for your English instructor, identifying examples and kinds of analysis used.

B.   A variation of the first option is to choose a subject from another course and write an essay of analysis. This would be a good way of understanding a difficult concept. You might try to anticipate an essay question for an exam. Append a brief explanation as in option A.

Chapter Nine
Argumentation—Prove It!

WHERE THERE IS MUCH DESIRE TO
LEARN, THERE OF NECESSITY WILL
BE MUCH ARGUING, MUCH WRITING,
MANY OPINIONS; FOR OPINION IN
GOOD MEN IS BUT KNOWLEDGE IN
THE MAKING.

John Milton

More than two thousand years ago, the Greek philosopher Aristotle made a study of rhetoric, the art of persuasive discourse. Mastery of the skills of persuasion was highly regarded in Athens, for public debate was the lifeblood of citizenship in the republic. Virtually every young man of the upper classes studied under a rhetorician like Aristotle, who taught the three appeals of argumentation and persuasion.

1. *Ethos.* Sometimes called the "ethical appeal," this method relies on the character and personal traits of the speaker or writer. The audience is moved in part, then, not by *what* is said but by *who* said it. Today celebrities are often used in advertising campaigns because of the recognition factor, but they do not have the kind of credibility that Aristotle had in mind. As a writer, you can acquire some measure of ethical strength by demonstrating during the course of your argument that you are an earnest seeker after the truth, unmotivated by selfish ends.

2. *Pathos.* Appealing to the emotions of the audience, pathos is the method of persuasion. Perhaps because it has been so often abused, perhaps because it has so often served ignoble ends, this approach has acquired a bad name. Yet rhetoricians from the time of Aristotle have known that men and women are emotional beings as well as rational. A responsible appeal to the

feelings of the audience, far from being reprehensible, is often necessary to create a frame of mind receptive to your logical arguments.

3. *Logos.* The logical method is directed to the rational faculty of the audience through the reasonableness of the piece. It employs facts, data, and evidence that the mind can weigh in assessing the truth or validity of the assertion. This is the classical mode of argumentation.

An argument is the process of reasoning for or against something. Its purpose is to convince the reader to agree with you or to do something you want done. Unlike *persuasion*, which is directed to the emotions of the audience, *argumentation* makes its appeal to the reason. Argumentation may employ singly or in combination the modes of definition, comparison and contrast, and classification, as well as the various kinds of analysis. In its simplest form, it consists of two parts: *thesis* and *proof.*

THE THESIS

The thesis of an argument is the claim, the assertion—in other words, the point the argument makes. It is not a subject but a statement about that subject. Not "suburban sprawl," but "Suburbs in America are gardens of alienation." For that reason, the thesis must be presented as a declarative sentence. In fact, the very structure of the declarative sentence is what makes the point.

Subject	Predicate
Suburbs in America	are gardens of alienation.

The word "predicate," when used as a verb, means to "affirm" or "assert." The grammatical predicate asserts something about the grammatical subject. The verb indicates the relationship between the predicate and subject. Here the verb "are" signals equality.

Subject	Suburbs in America
Relationship	are
Assertion	gardens of alienation.

Here is another example of the composition of a thesis:

Subject	The Dallas Cowboys
Relationship	have
Assertion	the best defense in the NFL.

The thesis may be negative ("Outlawing handguns will not solve the problem of the rising crime rate"), thus denying rather than affirming. It should not, however, be interrogatory: "Should first-year English be a course in literature instead of writing?" You may well begin your thinking with a question. Then your thesis will be the *answer* you give to that question: "Instead of dealing with writing, first-year English should be a college-level introduction to literature."

For the sake of clarity and unity, the thesis should be stated in a single sentence. You may want to lead up to that sentence, qualify it, or define a term in it. Fine, but those ends can be served in introductory or explanatory sentences clustered about the thesis. Somewhere early in your argument, write one sentence that states the thesis explicitly. You might even underline your thesis if you are writing an essay exam or a paper for another course. That will help you to focus on your purpose as you write. An added benefit not to be taken lightly is that it will call the reader's (professor's) attention to your main point.

One more point about the thesis: It must be argumentative. That should go without saying, but I've seen enough student essays to know that this isn't always understood. "Shakespeare was a great dramatist" is not likely to engender much disagreement. Nor is "A college education is a worthwhile investment" or "The dog is man's best friend." The way to test your thesis is to look at the other side or the negative. Would anyone argue that Shakespeare was *not* a great dramatist? Not likely. Some of the best argumentative essays I've read reverse the common wisdom, going against the stream: "Given high tuition costs and the loss of four years' income, a college education is not a financially sound investment." Or "The cat is man's best friend." Your thesis doesn't have to be highly controversial; it just needs to admit of other points of view.

> **The thesis is**
> a single,
> declarative
> sentence,
> placed early in the essay,
> that makes an assertion
> argumentative in nature.

APPLY YOURSELF 1. What's wrong here? Not one of the following sentences is a good thesis. Tell what's wrong with each and try to write an effective thesis statement for each topic.

1. Could we find a better solution to the housing needs of the poor than those large, ugly, impersonal projects?

2. The Soviet Union is a communist state.

3. I think that something is wrong with the way varsity sports are handled at large universities.

4. Law-abiding citizens should take a stand about the way drunken drivers are treated by the courts.

5. Single parents have a difficult time raising their children and holding down a job at the same time.

APPLY YOURSELF 2. Find the thesis. The following passages are taken from student essays of argumentation. Find the thesis in each one and decide how well it meets the criteria of a good thesis statement.

1. "To prevent nuclear accidents as serious as Three Mile Island, fundamental changes will be necessary in the organization, procedures and practices—and above all—in the attitudes of The Nuclear Regulatory Commission and, to the extent that the institutions we investigated are typical, of the nuclear industry." This conclusion was reached by The Presidental Commission designed to investigate the Three Mile Island accident. Fundamental changes only provide a start towards what needs to be done before nuclear power can be safely used. It is essential that we stop any further nuclear power plant construction immediately.

Allison Hill

2. Should the United States reactivate the draft? Since the United States has a long history of distrusting mandatory conscription, the volatility of this question is capable of provoking reactions of anger, hate and fear. However, no person viewing today's world can deny the need for a strong military position. The problem confronting the United States is one of method. Which course will produce and maintain a powerful military organization able to protect this nation? At this point, the United States has two options. One is to reinstate the draft. The other is to continue the All-Volunteer Forces (AVF) which replaced the draft in the early 1970s. After reviewing the evidence, the answer to the question is most emphatically Yes! The draft must be reinstated if the United States expects to properly defend this country.

Ginny Piper

3. Vermont Governor Richard Snelling will decide by July 1 whether or not he will ask the Legislature to convene a special session. The session would concern itself with six proposals made by Snelling to strengthen the state's criminal code. One of these proposals would change the juvenile justice code so that youths who have committed serious crimes would be tried as adults, giving the state the power to detain such youths after they turn 18. Snelling has reversed an earlier decision in which he stated that a special summer session wasn't desirable because there would not be time to fully consider the

proposals. Several legislators agreed with the governor, saying that they would meet in a special session only if it dealt with the single issue of juvenile justice. Some feel that the legislature should wait and discuss the issue at length during its next regular session, which would begin in January. Whether they address the issue now or in seven months, Vermont lawmakers should revise the juvenile justice code so that juveniles who commit serious crimes against another person are prosecuted as adults for those crimes.

Paul Reese

WHERE DO YOU STAND?

For many people in a writing class, one of the most difficult tasks is finding something to write about. This problem seems to become especially acute when it comes to the argumentative essay. "I don't really know anything about nuclear power, I'm not interested in whether there's a draft or not, and the issue of women's rights leaves me cold." Oftentimes the standard topics suggested in writing texts are of more interest to the writer of the text than to the students taking the course. Furthermore, these "standard" topics tend to result in "standard" essays, filled with canned ideas and lacking conviction. One friend of mine who teaches writing even gives her classes a list of proscribed topics, subjects they are not allowed to write on, such as abortion, euthanasia, the death penalty.

In "real life" you would write an argument only when you felt the need and were moved to persuade someone. The topic would force itself on you; you wouldn't have to go out looking for it. You become concerned about the lack of a crossing guard at a busy street corner that your child has to get across each day on her way to school. You write a letter to the board of education, urging them to assign a guard to that corner. Or you have a plan to reorganize your department at the office where you work to make it function more efficiently, so you write a proposal to your supervisor explaining the plan and arguing for its adoption. Or you are incensed that the state department of corrections is considering building a juvenile detention center in your community. Determined to do something to stop the project, your first step is to write a letter to the editor of the newspaper presenting your reasons for believing it to be unwise.

But this isn't the "real world," you say, and I have nothing to argue about. Not true. You are always arguing with someone, either in conversation or in your mind. Your parents plan to replace their old car with another tan station wagon. You want them to buy something with a bit more style. Or maybe your roommate wants to get a Labrador retriever when there's hardly enough space for the two of you in your 9- by 12-foot cell. What do you find yourself disagreeing with others about? Would any of these subjects make a good argumentative essay?

APPLY YOURSELF 3. Where do you stand? To help you practice formulating a thesis statement, answer the following questions. Your first response may be just a fuzzy answer. Sharpen it until it meets the tests of a good thesis: It must be a declarative sentence that makes an assertion argumentative in nature. Perhaps the questions will suggest other topics or theses to you.

1. Should someone concerned about the environment own a car?
2. When George Washington was president, he told Congress, "To be prepared for war is one of the most effectual means of preserving peace." Do you think that is good advice today?
3. Do you believe that college should be free to all qualified students?
4. Should a husband and a wife stay in an unhappy marriage for the sake of the children?
5. What do you think the United States should do if foreign nations cut off our supply of oil as they threatened in 1973?
6. Is alcohol abuse a problem at your school? Drug abuse?
7. What do you and your parents disagree about?
8. Many colleges and universities have a Gay Student Union sponsored by student association funds. Do you believe that some of your fees ought to be used to support an organization like this?
9. Write five different endings to this sentence: "I believe that . . ." Are any of them argumentative?
10. What do you think about cigarette smoking?

THE PROOF

Now that you have gotten some practice discovering issues that matter to you and formulating positions (theses) on those issues, it's time to move on to the second part of the argument, the proof. By definition the thesis makes an assertion, argumentative in nature. It may be an old argument to which you are bringing new evidence or it may be a new (to the reader) point of view that you prove with evidence that is verifiable. The writer has two systems of reasoning and thus of proof from which to choose: deduction and induction.

DEDUCTION

Deduction is the process of reasoning that begins with general assumptions and proceeds to a conclusion. When the assumptions or premises are acceptable to the reader and they are correctly related to the conclusion, there is certainty to the argument. An example of a deductive argument is the syllogism:

A.   All primates are mammals.
B.   The chimpanzee is a primate.
C.   Therefore, the chimpanzee is a mammal.

Sentences A and B are the assumptions (premises) upon which the conclusion, sentence C, is based. If the argument is to be persuasive, the assumptions must be acceptable to the reader. A reader who disagrees with either of the premises will not accept the conclusion.

   Although we don't often talk or write in pure syllogistic form, we frequently make use of abbreviated syllogisms sometimes called "enthymemes." Your roommate tells you: "I've got a blind date with Charlie. He must be gorgeous, he's in a fraternity." Poor roomie. If she stopped to analyze her thinking, she might not be so happy. Put into syllogistic form, her reasoning looks like this:

A.   [All fraternity men are gorgeous.] (premise)
B.   Charlie is a fraternity man. (premise)
C.   Therefore, Charlie must be gorgeous. (conclusion)

   I've supplied the first premise, an unspoken assumption she must have had in the back of her head when she reached the conclusion about her date's physical attractiveness. Only if sentence A is accurate is your roommate's reasoning sound.

   Syllogistic reasoning can become quite complex. There are rules to cover the manner in which the assumptions are stated and rules about what kind of conclusions may be drawn from given assumptions. It seems that one whole semester of my sophomore year of college was spent learning those rules in Logic 111. But the writer who exercises some common sense and intellectual honesty can develop a deductive argument without an exhaustive study of the rules of syllogistic reasoning.

APPLY YOURSELF 4. Enthymemes. Popular in ordinary reasoning, the enthymeme is a syllogism with one of the parts, usually a premise, missing. There's nothing wrong with employing this reasoning as long as you realize the need to examine the missing part. Only then can you tell if the reasoning is sound. Here are some examples. Reconstruct each as a syllogism and decide if the conclusion is justified.

1. Of course she's a good cook. She's Italian, isn't she?
2. They must be rich—they drive a Mercedes.
3. I don't care what you say. My son is really smart. He goes to college.
4. Your yard must smell good in the spring. Those are lilacs, aren't they?
5. "If prisoners are to learn to bear the responsibilities of citizens, they must have all the rights of other citizens except . . . that of liberty of person." *Attica: The Official Report of the New York State Special Commission on Attica*

THE DEDUCTIVE CHAIN OF REASONING

Although the three-part syllogism is the model of deductive reasoning, most of our thinking and writing demands a longer series of related ideas to prove a point. Calling this series of related ideas a deductive *chain of reasoning* emphasizes that only by connecting each step to the ones before and after can we construct a convincing argument. Here is an example of the main points or steps of such an argument:

1. Dependable sources of economical electrical power are essential to the welfare of our community.
2. Reserves of fossil fuels are dwindling, and supply of these fuels is subject to interruption.
3. Nuclear power plants have proved expensive and unreliable.
4. Hydropower facilities are now operating at capacity, and solar power would be prohibitively expensive in our region.
5. Studies show that burning municipal wastes is an economically feasible way of providing dependable energy.
6. Further, the quantity of wastes currently going into landfill sites is more than adequate to fuel a trash-burning plant of moderate size.
7. Private utility companies have refused to take initiative in planning such a plant.
8. Therefore, our city should build a municipally operated, trash-burning, electricity-generating plant.

I think you can see from this example the way a deductive chain of reasoning works. The writer begins with a premise (1) that nearly everyone would agree with. Points 2, 3, and 4 show that traditional modes of power production are *not* dependable and economical. Point 5 offers an alternative to these traditional modes. Point 6 explains the availability of trash as fuel.

"We found the engineer we needed with his nose stuck in The Wall Street Journal's classified pages."

Sensibly so, we'd add.

The best people find the best jobs in The Mart – the classified pages of The Wall Street Journal.

Which is why, conversely, the best jobs inevitably find the best people when they're advertised in The Mart.

After all, the man or woman who reads The Journal is precisely the sort of person you'd like to find.

Only The Journal reaches more than six million executive, professional and technical readers every single business day.

Which means that your recruitment ad in The Mart reaches far more prospects than it would in any other single medium.

Logically, the better your choices, the better your ultimate selection.

And that may just explain why those companies which advertise their position in The Mart seem to be a step ahead of the rest.

Career-minded people shop The Mart. In The Journal.

The right place to find the people you need.

The Mart in The Wall Street Journal.

Point 7 rules out help from the private sector. Finally, point 8 states the conclusion: Our city should build a municipally operated, trash-burning generating plant. There's a certain force of logic as you move from point to point. If the reader has accepted each of the points or premises in turn, the conclusion has a kind of inevitability about it.

The text of the preceding advertisement from *The Wall Street Journal* is a chain of reasoning, too. The argument concludes that employees will find the best-qualified job seekers by buying space in that newspaper.

APPLY YOURSELF 5. Deductive chain of reasoning. For each of the following theses, develop a chain of reasoning like that in the preceding examples. Strive for the same kind of step-by-step logic that carries the reader along with it, ending with the conclusion, which is in fact the thesis.

1.   Fraternities should be banned from college campuses.
2.   The traditional kind of marriage is unworkable in our society.
3.   Every American should know one foreign language.

FALLACIES OF DEDUCTION

Of the many varieties of erroneous reasoning, three fallacies are especially common to deduction. Watch for them in your reading. Listen for them in oral arguments and persuasion. Root them out of your own writing.

Ad hominem
This Latin phrase means "to the man," referring to an attack on the person, not the position or argument. Examples: "His idea for the party can't possibly be any good. After all, he spends all his time in the library." "How could a guy who wears white socks and black shoes know anything about sociology?" A variation on the *ad hominem* fallacy is name calling.

Faulty generalizing
Judging an entire group, race, class, or sex by the evidence of a few examples is one kind of faulty generalizing—stereotyping. Another kind is the glittering generality: "It's the real thing," the good old days, President Kennedy's "New Frontier." Both types of faulty generalizing obscure critical thinking.

Begging the question
Assuming that some part or all of the thesis or question is proved or agreed upon is the fallacy of begging the question. Example: A college professor

complains, "We must do something to stop grade inflation. I propose we give no more than 10 percent A's in every course." The professor is begging the question—whether grade inflation actually exists. Example: E. F. Schumacher asserts in his book *Small Is Beautiful*, "That things are not going as well as they ought to be going must be due to human wickedness." Who says things are not going as well as they ought to be going? What "things"? How "ought" they to go?

APPLY YOURSELF 6. Examples of deduction. Study the following examples of deduction, all excerpted from longer pieces. In each, locate the thesis and list the main points of the argument.

A. Assuming that Corporate America has political power, what then are the costs of increasing concentration of economic power? As economic diversity decreases, the number of units contributing to the political process decreases accordingly. And as political pluralism weakens, so does democracy.

Mark Green, The Progressive

B. Neighborhoods deserve and are getting new attention for supremely important reasons—not simply because neighborhoods may be practical but because they may be necessary. It may be necessary to revive and live in neighborhoods or face the possibility of simply having no place else to go.

In big cities, the institutions of larger scale which have marked city growth are clearly falling apart. The quality of life in every big city of America—and perhaps of the entire world—is being seriously questioned and being seriously described as deteriorating. At the same time the relationship of working people to the work they do is also falling apart, leaving more frustrations, less sense of accomplishment and meaning, more trash and less craft, more quantity and less quality. And around it all, the sense of citizenship is falling into a cynical decline. Politicians are expected to be corrupt and people generally expect that there is nothing to be done about it. A civic weariness has set in. There seems no real use to voting. The rascals all turn out the same. There seems little use to fighting city hall. The occupants all turn out to be the same. And so, people's heads turn toward—what? Toward home. Toward where they live. How they live. Going home, in this sense, means rediscovering the neighborhood.

David Morris and Karl Hess, Neighborhood Power

C. When we are at work we ought to be at work. When we are at play we ought to be at play. There is no use trying to mix the two. The sole object ought to be to get the work done and to get paid for it. When the work is done, then the play can come, but not before. And so the Ford factories and enterprises have no organization, no specific duties attaching to any position, no line of succession or of authority, very few titles, and no conferences. We have only the clerical help that is absolutely required; we have no elaborate records of any kind, and consequently no red tape.

Henry Ford, My Life and Work

INDUCTION

Induction is the way we learn most of what we know. Based on limited experience and knowledge, we form a conclusion that expresses a general truth. For instance, even before you entered kindergarten, you probably saw a picture of a yellow school bus in one of your books. You also saw your older sister get onto a yellow school bus every morning. From these limited experiences, you concluded that all school buses are yellow, although you hadn't seen all the school buses in the world.

The movement in inductive reasoning is from specific to general, from facts to principle. Diagrammed, the inductive process appears this way:

Fact 1
Fact 2
Fact 3
. . . and so on
Therefore, conclusion

If you were to fill in the diagram with survey data collected from a sample of first-year students admitted to the state university last year, your outline might look like this:

Fact 1: At the end of her first year Sally Smith, who graduated from Middletown High School, had an average grade of C−.

Fact 2: John Jones, also from Middletown High, had an average of D+.

Fact 3: Bill Brown's average grade for the year was B+. He came from Central High.

Fact 4: Jessica Jefferson, also from Central, had a cumulative average for the year of A−.

Therefore, we conclude that Middletown High does not do a very good job of preparing its students for college, while Central High does a much better job.

One point to notice about the parts of this inductive argument: The facts are not related to each other in the same direct way that the premises are in a deductive argument. They do have a common subject (here, the students' average grades), but they don't follow from each other. A second point is that when the researcher has listed all the facts, he hasn't really listed *all* the facts. To do so would require evidence on all the 2000 or so students admitted to State University each year. Yet, he goes on to make an assertion about the whole universe of State University first-year students from these two schools: Middletown High is inferior to Central High in preparing students for college.

The natural scientist makes extensive use of induction. In the passage that follows, we learn of some conclusions drawn as a result of the banding and close observation over several seasons of selected individuals in a herring gull colony:

> Every banded gull was watched, its nest located, and the bird caught when possible. Thus we caught eleven gulls in our colony at Wassenaar, ten of which appeared to be Wassenaar-born. Another colony on the famous bird island of Texel, about 65 miles from Wassenaar, yielded us fifteen banded birds, fourteen of which were Texel-born. This proved that herring gulls as a rule return to the colony where they were born, select a territory, and keep that territory during the rest of their lives.
>
> Nikolaas Tinbergen, "In the Life of a Herring Gull"

RULES OF EVIDENCE

A variety of evidence may be used to support a conclusion in the inductive process: personal observation, statistics, survey results, and so on. Whatever evidence is used, however, must meet certain tests. It must be sufficient in quantity and both authentic and representative in character.

Sufficient in quantity
How much evidence do you need? That question is impossible to answer for all situations. For the example given previously about the preparation of high school students for college, the four cases cited are not enough to make a compelling argument. Sometimes, though, a single piece is sufficient to prove the point. If you drive your car without oil, the results will be impressive. You don't have to repeat the mistake several times in order to learn that operating a gas engine without oil is fatal to the engine. Physical and chemical reactions tend to be regular; often conclusions about them can be supported with only a few observations.

Authentic in nature

By authentic, I mean both accurate and complete. If your evidence comes from direct observation, it must be accurately gathered. If it comes from authority, let's say a book, you must assess the source. What are the qualifications of the writer on *this* subject? (Joe DiMaggio may know a lot about baseball, but what does he know about coffee?) When and under what circumstances was the statement made? (Is the evidence out of date? Does it apply to a different situation?) What might the writer's biases be? (Does he or she have an ax to grind?) As for the completeness of the evidence, the honest writer will include all relevant data and observations, not just those that support the conclusion. Negative evidence must be accounted for.

Representative in nature

The editor of the campus newspaper urges that the dining hall concessionaire be replaced. "A survey of students shows that 75 percent are dissatisfied with the meals," she writes. If the editor had asked only four people, all of them vegetarians, she has gathered neither sufficient nor representative data. She should survey a cross section of students who eat in various dining halls on campus. Students polled should include vegetarians and non-vegetarians, as well as those with other special dietary needs. The number of students sampled in each category should be proportional to the number present in the student population. Then her data would be truly representative and a logical conclusion drawn from it credible.

THE INDUCTIVE LEAP

You've gathered your data and now you mull it over. Suddenly, with a flash of insight, you see the connection, the general principle that explains not only that data but the entire class to which it belongs. This is the inductive leap—the jump from considering your five or fifty observations to a conclusion about all cases of the same kind. No matter how carefully you have gathered data, regardless of how cautious you were in formulating your conclusion (or thesis or hypothesis), that conclusion is only a probability. The conclusion of an inductive process never comes with absolute certainty. On the basis of some data, a conclusion or prediction of all such data is made. The only way you could achieve certainty would be to survey all data, all instances.

We've all found ourselves in situations in which the evidence is small but the need to form a conclusion is pressing. For instance, for the last two or three days the neighbors' 12-year-old son has been shooting a BB gun behind our houses. Squirrels, birds, other kids are his targets. This morning when I got into my car, which was parked in front of the house, I discovered a small, circular chip in the windshield. It's hard not to jump to the conclusion that one of his BBs did the damage. Yet the evidence is insufficient to provide any degree of certainty. I hadn't seen him shooting at my car or any others. His can't be the only BB gun in the neighborhood. The limited evidence at hand suggests a working hypothesis or theory only. More proof is needed before I'll feel confident in confronting his parents with a bill for a new windshield.

Complex evidence may often admit of a number of possible conclusions. How do you know which one is "right"? My best advice is twofold. First, the more likely conclusion is the one that takes into account the majority of significant evidence and disregards none of the major negative evidence. Secondly, follow the principle that, other things being equal, the simplest explanation is the best.

APPLY YOURSELF 7. Examples of induction. Study the following examples of induction, all excerpted from longer pieces. In each locate the thesis or conclusion. How well justified is the conclusion, based on evidence presented in the passage? Would you need additional information before you would accept the thesis? Is it possible to draw a different conclusion from the same evidence?

A.   One of the problems with federal bailouts is that they can become habit-forming. One thinks of Lockheed, New York City and Chrysler. Now there's Whoops, more properly known as Washington Public Power Supply System or WPPSS.

"Another Bailout?" The Wall Street Journal

B.   For centuries, except for poor women who always had to work like horses, women were discouraged from building their bodies. We wanted women who were weak, fragile, clinging, round and soft. Since we have changed our attitudes about what constitutes female beauty and attractiveness, we've seen something interesting: Women now are breaking world records that were set by men ten years ago. Men, with additional training, are going beyond those records. But the amazing thing is how fast women have come close to even some current world records for men. What does that tell you? It tells you that the muscle strength of women can be improved enormously.

Estelle Ramey, interviewed by Stephen Barlas, Working Woman

C.   "Boys are simply more vulnerable to stress of any kind than girls," says Dr. Jerome Kagan, professor of psychology at Harvard University and a specialist in early childhood development. "Boys are more likely to have 90 percent of all human frailties, including aggression problems, neurotic symp-toms, phobias, difficulty with toilet training, even learning. Reading dis-abilities are seven times more common in boys than in girls. A boy born prematurely is less apt to survive than a girl," says Dr. Kagan. "A five-pound boy dies. The probability of a girl surviving is greater. That can't be learned. And no one knows why."

Cited by Linda Bird Francke, "The Sons
of Divorce," The New York Times Magazine

D.   But as opportunities for women have multiplied, so have their worries. An entire generation of female newscasters now is poised on the brink of middle age, and many are jittery about their career prospects.

Audience Research & Development, a Dallas media-consulting firm, surveyed 1,200 news anchors at local stations around the country and found that 48% of the men—but only 3% of the women—were over the age of 40. None of the female anchors—compared with 16% of the males—were over 50. Whether this reflects the belated entry of women into the profession or a concerted effort to ease them off the air as they mature isn't clear. Still, to many TV newswomen, the statistics are ominous. "After 40, the career lines just seem to end for most women," says a young woman recently hired as a correspondent for ABC's "World News Tonight." "It's a little eerie."

Jane Mayer, "TV Anchorwomen Never Die,
They Get Replaced by the Young,"
The Wall Street Journal

APPLY YOURSELF 8. Induction: Formulating a conclusion I. What conclusion could you draw from the following facts?

In recent years, scores made by high school students on standardized tests such as the Scholastic Aptitude Tests have shown a steady decline. College entrance requirements have eased, demanding fewer courses in math, the sciences, and foreign languages. College graduation requirements have shown a similar loosening. Young people in the age groups 16–18 and 19–25 have the largest disposable income ever. Bookstore sales have dropped off, while record sales and concert attendance continue to grow. Illicit drugs are now readily available in every city and town to anyone with the money.

What alternative hypotheses would you have to consider? What addi-tional evidence would you need before settling for certain on an explanation or in order to defend your conclusion against attacks by others? What additional facts will your hypothesis explain?

APPLY YOURSELF 9. Induction: Formulating a conclusion II. Often the facts available are presented to us in the form of tables or charts summarizing observations or data collection of others. Consider, for example, the following presentation of summary data from the U.S. Department of Agriculture:

VITAL STATISTICS ON U.S. FARMS

	1960	1970	1981
TOTAL U.S. POPULATION	181 million	205 million	228 million
POPULATION ON FARMS	16 million	10 million	6 million
NUMBER OF FARMS	3,956,000	2,954,000	2,419,000
FARM OUTPUT (1967 = 100%)	91%	101%	106%
CROP PRODUCTION PER ACRE (1967 = 100%)	89%	102%	132%
FARM OUTPUT PER HOUR OF LABOR (1967 = 100%)	65%	115%	209%
WHEAT SURPLUS (at start of harvest)	1.4 billion bushels	0.8 billion bushels	0.9 billion bushels
CORN SURPLUS (at start of harvest)	2.0 billion bushels	1.0 billion bushels	1.6 billion bushels

What conclusions can you derive from the preceding data? What additional facts would you like to have so as to be more confident about the validity of your conclusions? What recommendations might you make about agricultural policy?

WHY DO PEOPLE WRITE ARGUMENTS?

People write arguments to change the opinions, beliefs, and behaviors of others. More specifically, they argue to influence voters and government officials, to persuade consumers to buy things, to convince their professors or bosses that their point of view is correct or their performance laudable. They write to move their readers to action.

THE AUDIENCES OF ARGUMENTATION

Arguments are written to three kinds of audiences. Sometimes a single piece will address all three, sometimes just one kind of audience is selected and strategies chosen accordingly.

Those on Your Side

If your audience is already with you, why bother? You might preach to the converted to urge greater effort on behalf of your shared cause, or perhaps to maintain group solidarity, especially in the face of persuaders from the opposition. Your argument can provide the less well informed with reasons for doing what they do as well as with information they can use to influence others. Strategies: Although this would seem to be the easiest audience, it has needs the writer should recognize and meet. Provide your reader with reasons for the position and faults in the opposing view. Use specifics and examples.

The Uncommitted

This audience is more difficult to address than those already on your side. Some readers may be undecided about an issue or course of action because they are confused, others because they are uninformed. Some are indifferent—they just don't care. Others care a great deal, so much that they want to weigh all evidence and arguments before reaching a decision. Strategies: These depend greatly on which specific part or parts of the uncommitted audience you are addressing. You'll certainly need to begin by attracting the interest of these readers. After that, establish your credentials as an openminded researcher and writer. Rely on facts, rather than opinions. Present your case without slurring the other side.

Those on the Other Side

If their minds are made up, why take the trouble? Perhaps you write for them in the belief that they don't fully understand; if only you could make a clear enough presentation of the facts and the reasons, they would see it your way. Perhaps you are writing not to try to change their minds but to persuade them to be tolerant of your position. Strategies: With this audience, as with the uncommitted, you need to convey a sense of responsibility and fairness. An organizational pattern that I find effective begins with the presentation of evidence that is unassailable factually and emotionally. Evidence that gains the assent of readers before they are aware of where it is taking them. Then show where that evidence leads—to the conclusion, which is your thesis. The danger with this approach is that it might gain resentment at having been tricked rather than grudging agreement that maybe you have a point. If you come across as credible and fair, you stand a good chance of avoiding this reaction. And never patronize your audience, at least not if you hope to gain their goodwill and respect for you and for your position.

THE ORGANIZATION
OF AN ARGUMENT

"There is no new thing under the sun," Ecclesiastes reminds us. Indeed, the basic structures of argumentation have been tested and proven for more than twenty centuries. Although each writer may make modifications according to circumstance and need, these structures remain as useful as ever. The primary arrangement may be called "rhetorical" and, a variation on that, "dialectic."

Rhetorical Arrangement

Based on the work of Aristotle and other Greeks concerned with public speaking, rhetorical arrangement is a description of the sequence and functions of the parts of an argument. Each part has a clearly defined job to perform, so the arrangement of an argument is more than a mere outline of your notes. Applied intelligently, rhetorical arrangement provides flexible guidelines, not a rigid blueprint, for the writer.

The rhetorical arrangement of an argument has five major divisions:

1. Introduction
2. Context
3. Presentation
4. Refutation
5. Conclusion

1. INTRODUCTION

The function of the *introduction* is to prepare the reader psychologically and intellectually for the discourse. The process of introducing your argument begins with the title of the essay and may continue through the next several paragraphs. This is where you seek to gain the interest of the audience and make the reader receptive to the arguments which will follow. The introduction announces the subject and purpose of the essay. It is also the place to establish your credentials in the field and your fair-minded and reasoned approach (ethical appeal). Not every argument you write will require that the introduction accomplish all of these ends. You will need to judge which are essential according to your purpose and audience.

2. CONTEXT

The function of the *context* section of the argument is to inform your readers of the history or background of the subject, to explain what has led to the present state of affairs. Context is not a necessary part of every argument. Where it is used, it should be presented in a clear, forthright, noncontroversial way. Continue to build ethical appeal in the treatment of this phase of the argument.

3. PRESENTATION

The function of the *presentation* is to assert your position and to prove it. This is the heart of the argument, the place to use what you have learned about deduction and induction. The presentation consists of two parts: thesis and proof. Ordinarily, the thesis comes first, followed by the proof. You tell the reader what you're going to prove and then you prove it. Very logical. There can be advantages, though, to reversing the order. If your audience is likely to be resistant to your point of view, you might set forth the cases or evidence first, hoping that your reader will perceive their value and begin to agree with your thesis even before you present it.

As for the sequence in which you present evidence, the general principle is ascending order. Put the strongest, most persuasive last. That way everything in the essay leads up to it. It has the spotlight and remains in the reader's mind. If you begin with your strongest point, the reader is conscious of a weakening of the argument as the proof tapers off. If you have two or more strong cases or facts, lead with the second strongest, follow with the weaker ones, and end with the most compelling.

4. REFUTATION

The function of the *refutation* is to acknowledge the opposing view and to show its weaknesses. You could avoid the opposition entirely, but then the knowledgeable reader is led to question the true strength of your argument. Better to face up to the arguments of the other side, even if you can't refute every one of them. No issue you are apt to argue has a clear-cut solution. It will always be a trade-off. If, however, you can refute most of the strongest points of the opposition and present a convincing case yourself, you will win the reader's respect. Although the traditional position of refutation is after presentation, you may find reasons to treat it before. Demolishing the position of the other side leaves you free to convince the reader of your alternative.

5. CONCLUSION

The function of the *conclusion* is to sum up and round off the argument. The word "conclusion" used in this sense is not the same as the endpoint of the logical process of induction. Here you make a restatement and amplification of your key points. The conclusion also affords you the opportunity to

5. Conservation alone is not an energy policy

As the administration prepares its energy policy against an April 20 deadline, official after official keeps stressing that conservation will be a cornerstone of the program. But in our view, conservation, laudable as it may be, is not the total answer—new domestic supplies will be needed.

The graph clearly shows why. In the past decade, oil consumption has risen at an annual rate of 3.7 percent. If it continues to rise at this rate, Americans will consume 25 million barrels of oil a day by 1986. If it doesn't rise at all, they will still use over 17 million barrels a day.

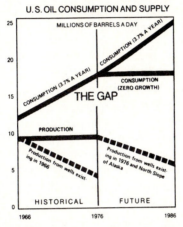

U.S. OIL CONSUMPTION AND SUPPLY

Furthermore, counting too heavily on conservation would impose on this country a regulatory superstructure that could deprive Americans of their freedom of choice. It could force them to give up many of the conveniences and even some necessities of their accustomed life-styles—force them to restrict their personal mobility and turn from private houses to energy-efficient apartments.

Worse still, those who would be hardest hit are the very Americans who are still struggling to extricate themselves from substandard housing, unemployment, and poverty, and the young who will require jobs in the next two decades. Their path to a better life would be blocked because energy is needed for economic growth.

Meanwhile, domestic oil production in the past 10 years has failed to keep pace with increasing consumption. Ten years ago, American oil fields produced 9.6 million barrels a day; last year, they yielded 9.7 million. Only because there was an infusion of some $75 billion of capital, to find and open up new oil fields and improve output from existing ones, was it possible to keep production on an even keel and hold the gap between U.S. production and U.S. consumption to less than 8 million barrels a day.

The graph also shows what would have happened if America had relied solely on the oil wells existing in 1966. The gap would have been more than 13 million barrels a day. It also projects what is likely to happen if the nation coasts along on presently existing wells plus production now anticipated from Alaska's North Slope.

Obviously, even with extreme austerity, the gap would widen. Conservation can help. But if conservation were pushed to the extreme of allowing zero energy growth, it would still fail to bridge the gap that oil imports now fill.

A parallel situation exists with natural gas. Together, oil and gas now supply 75 percent of the nation's energy, and they must continue to bear the burden of supply through the rest of this century. Increased use of coal and nuclear power can improve the situation. But the more exotic energy options—solar, geothermal, synthetic fuels—are too far in the future to affect the gap significantly in the next decade or so.

It should be noted that further improvement of air and water quality will require large amounts of energy. It also takes energy to *conserve* energy. True, in the long run, some conservation measures will result in a net saving; but their short-term impact will be to consume more energy than they save. Moreover, some conservation ideas now being considered are fallacious—they will never reduce consumption. Take one example: The energy required to build, equip, and operate some rail mass transit systems could exceed the energy used by transportation systems based on buses and private automobiles.

It should be clear that a national energy policy must place equal emphasis on eliminating energy waste and on substantially improving domestic energy supply. The fastest, most direct way to stimulate supply is to create an economic climate in which exploration and development of oil and natural gas are encouraged, along with the construction of refinery capacity and necessary pipelines, and the development of coal and nuclear energy potential. This means that energy prices must reflect the replacement cost of energy resources in order to foster adequate supplies. Such a climate would, of itself, encourage a degree of conservation.

Conservation should be used only to eliminate waste; like many remedies, it can be harmful if the proper dosage is exceeded.

Mobil

suggest the complications and consequences of your position or solution to the problem. If appropriate, urge the reader to action. Throughout the essay, your audience has assessed your character and intentions as well as your reasoning. Don't let up now. End on a calm, rational note. Make no claims here for which you haven't already laid the foundations. If you've done your research and followed these guidelines, you've swept away the opposition and won a convert—your reader.

An Example of Rhetorical Arrangement

In recent years a number of major corporations have been running series of newspaper and magazine advertisements designed not to sell their products but to influence public opinion on important national issues. Mobil corporation ran the preceding advertisement in the *New York Times* in 1977 when Jimmy Carter was president. It's an excellent example not only of rhetorical arrangement but also of the use of a graph to dramatize the argument. Use the following outline to help you study the techniques of the author, including the sequence of proof:

> Introduction—title and paragraph 1
> Context—paragraph 1
> Presentation
>> Thesis—paragraph 1
>> Proof—paragraphs 2–8
> Refutation—paragraph 9
> Conclusion—paragraphs 10 and 11

Dialectical Arrangement

The dialectic arrangement of an argument is so called because it resembles people talking. An argument framed as dialectic is somewhat like the give and take between friends who disagree on an issue. You state your position, then your friend asks a question or gives a reason against it. You counter that and give another bit of evidence or support for your position.

> "I'm going to drop German."
>> "That's dumb. Why?"
> "Because I'm doing really lousy. It'll pull down my average."
>> "You could study more."
> "You know that I do work at it, more than any other course. And if I drop it, I can put that time into history and zoo."

"Maybe, but the drop period is over, so you'll need the dean's permission to 'withdraw pass.' You won't get that without a pretty good reason."
"I didn't know that. . . ."

The dialectic is a favorite form of persuasion of writers of television commercials. You've seen the two homemakers who meet in the grocery store: "Are you really going to buy that brand of peanut butter (or dish detergent)? Don't you love your family? . . ." Put to more serious uses, the dialectic is just as effective. The International Institute for Economic Reseach has sponsored a series of radio broadcasts to present its positions in this fashion. Adam Mouse speaks for capitalism and free enterprise, Karl for the controlled economy of socialism.

MOUSE WISDOM: THE TERRIBLE COSTS OF CHOICES

The two philosopher mice who live in my office—Adam and Karl—were again comparing meditations about the nature of the economic world. As usual, Karl was complaining and criticizing.

"I have long known it, and I have tried to tell you, but you wouldn't listen," he exploded in righteous triumph.

"What truth have you latched onto this time?" Adam responded calmly.

"This newspaper story proves that consumers have too many options," Karl announced.

"That *is* fascinating knowledge," Adam agreed. "I have supposed that it is a happy situation for consumers to have lots of options among which they can choose. Not only is it nice to have alternatives at any given moment, but the existence of alternatives reflects a situation of competition. I love to have many producers and suppliers working very hard to please me."

"Well," grumbled Karl, "you may believe that a marketplace with many competing sellers is attractive, but you neglect the costs involved. Competition is very costly to consumers."

"My, you fairly exude fascination today," said Adam with a touch of sarcasm. "Please tell me how I am worse off when I can pick and select among many sellers when I spend my money."

"In the first place," replied Karl in a professorial manner, "it is confusing to the customer when confronted by dozens of brands of cigarettes, breakfast cereals, beer, and soap. It would save time and strain on the brain if there were just one kind of any sort of good. Second, producing many brands of a good has to be wasteful. Both silly psychological and trivial physical differentiating of products is too costly, and should be forbidden."

"I don't deny that life would be *simpler* if most choicemaking were eliminated," agreed Adam. "But would it be *better*? I *like* to have some variety in my consumption of cereal."

"You surely don't need thirty or forty brands to choose from," snapped Karl impatiently.

"No," said Adam. "Probably no consumer uses *all* of the brands available of any kind of product. But if only a very few brands are to be produced, who is to choose the ones to survive, and on what basis is the designation to be made? Are you willing to let me decree which brands can henceforth be made?"

"Of course not," grumped Karl. "You might not select the kinds I prefer."

"Precisely," Adam replied. "People have different preferences. And those preferences can change over time. So each of us votes for his favorites with his money expenditures in the market. If we make it worth the while of a producer to provide Crunchie cereal, he will provide it. We indicate our preference; the producer gains by responding to that indication. Both parties gain from free expression which guides production. It is not wasteful when preferences are profitably satisfied."

"OK, OK," said Karl in exasperation. "Since the rest of you have so many strange tastes, I guess it makes sense to let those tastes be registered and catered to in a free market."

William R. Allen, Midnight Economist

This farfetched dialogue between two mice contains all of the parts of a conventional argument: introduction, context, presentation, refutation, and conclusion. See if you can identify them.

When dialectic is used in a formal written argument, three of the elements are usually carried over from rhetorical arrangement and continue to perform the same functions: introduction, context, and conclusion. The dialectic does the job of both presentation and refutation.

Rhetorical Arrangement	Dialectic Arrangement
Introduction	Introduction
Context	Context
Presentation ⎫ Refutation ⎭	Dialectic
Conclusion	Conclusion

When dialectic is the arrangement of an argument, the thesis is stated and followed by a point from the opposition, then a counterpoint from the pro side and so on. Not all dialectic arguments take the form of dialogue, however. In fact, most formal dialectics do not. What matters is the pro-con arrangement, combining the functions of both presentation and refutation.

Let's consider the following simplified plan for a dialectic argument:

Pro	Con
Thesis: Dogs on campus should be leashed.	
	It's true that some of them are well behaved. . . .
But even those often frighten passersby.	
	Some owners argue that dogs are natural creatures and need their freedom.
These owners overlook the dangers of injury or even death to the animal from cars and trucks on our congested streets.	
Further, free-roaming dogs are destroying many of our trees and shrubs and littering the campus green.	
Inconsiderate dog owners are depriving the rest of us our own rights and not serving the best interests of their pets by letting them roam freely.	
Therefore, a leash regulation would protect both people and dogs.	

Notice the combination of presentation and refutation in the preceding plan. For each point of the opposition (con), the pro has a rebuttal. Then, in the last three sentences, the writer shows that the dialectic is not merely a defensive arrangement. Additional arguments are presented followed by the conclusion. Although not indicated in this example, any point of the dialectic may be developed at greater length than other points. Ordinarily, the pro side would show this additional development, thus strengthening the argument.

Now, examine the following passage to see how the plan of the dialectic looks fleshed out. The author of this piece on control of public schools includes the four elements of dialectic arrangement.

LOCAL BOARDS SHOULD HOLD REINS OF EDUCATION

As one who has sat through (1) many local school board meetings, (2) many state school board meetings, and (3) many congressional education committee meetings, I have to agree (for a change) with President Reagan: The federal government has no business trying to run the schools.

Just look at the constituencies. Local school board members, small-minded and prickly as they often are, nonetheless are primarily interested in their own kids, who just happen to be the schools' clientele.

State boards, while they do recognize that the attractiveness of their state to new families and big-buck industries hinges on the quality of schools, nonetheless are mainly interested in keeping state legislators off their backs.

House and Senate committees have as their constituencies teachers' unions and states whose main interest is money. There are always a few U.S. lawmakers really interested in the school kids, but their concerns get lost in the money stampede.

So, in principle and often in practice, the local folks should be in charge, just as Reagan said in his Tuesday press conference.

Carol Richards, Gannett News Service

The effect of the dialectic is dramatic. The objections and questions of the opposition are put forth as part of a lively conflict. This confrontation is also persuasive, often more persuasive than the extended rhetorical argument. The skeptical reader has a voice, a spokesman for his point of view. Thoughtful use of the dialectic assures that you will develop your argument with your audience in mind.

APPLY YOURSELF 10. Dialectic arrangement. Study the arrangement of "Local Boards Should Hold Reins of Education" and identify introduction, context, dialectic, and conclusion. Then make a two-column diagram of the dialectic and conclusion like the preceding one about leash laws.

APPLY YOURSELF 11. Dialectic plan. As preparation for writing an argument in the dialectic:

A.   Select a thesis, perhaps one you worked out in Apply Yourself 3.
B.   Make a list of all the significant objections that could be made to your thesis.
C.   Make a second list of your responses to those objections and additional points you would want to raise.
D.   Write a plan combining these lists. Set it up like the plan for leash laws.

APPLY YOURSELF 12. Your written argument. You've studied deduction and induction, rhetorical and dialectic arrangement. Now choose an argumentative subject that matters to you. Formulate a thesis and plan an argument in the rhetorical or dialectic arrangement.

Chapter Ten
Search and research

*I*t's the class after the midsemester exam in art history. Your instructor, having finished reviewing the exam, puts down his papers and perches on a desk near the windows. "If you'll check the syllabus I gave you at the first class, you'll find that a term paper is required in this course. Now is the time to get started on that, if you haven't already done so. Acceptable topics? Anything related to the subject matter of this course. Library research required. Length is ten typed pages. Your paper is due at the last class before the final. Any questions?" Silence. Unless "Huh?" is a question, you don't have anything to say.

This scene is repeated every year all over the campus, all across the country. In courses in history, education, business, English, and virtually every other academic subject, students are asked to "write a paper." Although the details of subject, length, and special requirements certainly vary, a common core of skills and procedures apply to all these situations. It is the common core that this chapter treats.

In many ways, writing the research paper is like writing the other papers you've done in this course. You still use the process approach—prewriting, writing, revising. Your research paper will take as its form one or a combination of the modes already studied—comparison and contrast, perhaps, or analysis or argumentation.

What's different about the research paper then? What's different is that, in preparing and writing this kind of essay, you rely heavily on the ideas, opinions, and facts of other writers. Although many activities come under the heading "research"—experimentation, observation, polling, interviews—the kind of research that is required of most college students most of the time is done in the library. By reading in books and periodicals, you gather information about your subject. By thinking about the ways in which this information from a number of sources relates to your subject, you derive a new way of looking at the problem or a new approach that reflects your interest in the topic. The magic that happens in research is that you begin with the ideas and facts of other writers and recast them in a fresh way that is meaningful to you. A good research paper is more than a summary of what others have said about the subject, then.

WHERE DO YOU BEGIN?

Commonly, writers start a research project in one of two ways: with a question or with a general subject about which they need to write. Questions: Why have some animals become extinct? How do wages affect prices? What causes a volcano to erupt? What happened to all the Okies who went to California in the 1930s? What is literary Marxism? Subjects: European Jews during the Holocaust, timber management in the national forests, irrigation in modern Egypt, Hemingway's *The Sun Also Rises*, genetic engineering, Gandhi's revolution. Each of these questions or topics is a good beginning if it is relevant to the assignment and interesting to you.

WHERE DO YOU GO FROM THERE?

From this starting point, work on a research paper divides into three subprocesses: thinking, reading, and writing. As you proceed, you'll continually shift back and forth between them. Because of this shifting and frequent overlapping, it is difficult to present a simple sequence of steps that every student should follow from the start of the research project to the stapling of the typed final draft. What I can give you, though, is a rough guide that may be of some help to you as you write your first research papers in college. Although this guide is presented in two columns to suggest the different kinds of work the researcher does, you should notice the dependencies of the steps.

Thinking/Writing

1. Establish research subject or question. Write it down.

Thinking/Reading

2. Survey reading. The purpose is to get a sense of the scope and complexity of the subject and the availability of resources. Consult card catalog, general encyclopedias, periodical indexes, bibliographies. No extensive notes yet.

Thinking/Writing

3. Narrowing the subject. As survey reading nears its end, begin to sharpen the focus of the general subject or question and thus of the search.

5. Clarification of subject. As you build your working bibliography, continue to refine your subject. Establish subtopics as needed. Define your purpose.

7. As you read and take notes, your sense of topic will sharpen. Consider organization: order of development, subtopics, use of charts or graphs. Write a preliminary plan of the paper.

9. Make final plan, including subtopics.
10. Draft, then revise your research paper.

Thinking/Reading

4. Develop working bibliography of important sources. Skim tables of contents and introductions to establish their potential value. Make bibliography cards.

6. Note taking. With a clear sense of your true subject, begin to read intensively and take notes. Be sure to indicate sources.

8. Your plan complete, you'll probably need to fill gaps in your knowledge of the topic with additional reading and note taking. This prevents a thin or poorly balanced presentation.

FINDING THE TRUE SUBJECT

The research subject or question that you start with in step 1 is seldom the true subject of the final paper. As you work through the processes of reading, thinking, and writing, you narrow, sharpen, and perhaps even change your subject completely. Your survey reading (step 2) may suggest important aspects of the general subject that you hadn't considered: recurring themes or subdivisions in the treatment by other authors, for instance. Also, as your interest in the general subject grows with your increasing knowledge, one or two aspects of the general subject may become more appealing than others. As you work through steps 3–7, continue to ask

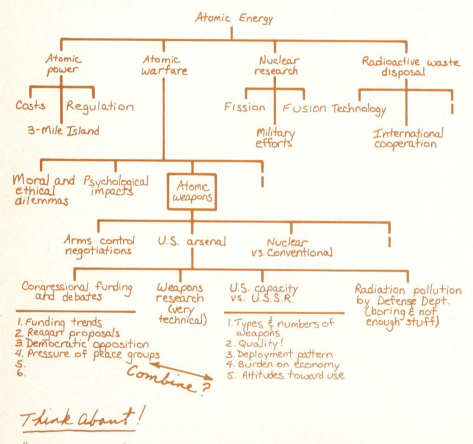

yourself these questions: Is my subject as I perceive it interesting enough to me to write ten (or whatever number) of pages? Is it appropriate for the course in which it was assigned? Is it narrow enough to treat in depth?

As an example of the kind of discoveries you may make about your subject, study the diagram of the general subject "atomic energy" one researcher made after survey reading in the library card catalog and the *New York Times Index*. This is not an outline of a paper; it is one student's attempt to understand the complexities of a broad subject in order to find the true subject to write about. After preliminary exploration of the major divisions of the subject (atomic power, atomic warfare, nuclear research, radioactive waste disposal), this writer decided to narrow the subject to "atomic warfare." "Atomic warfare" was still too big, so it was narrowed to "atomic weapons." Just how far you should proceed in this limiting of the subject depends on the purpose of the paper and the resources at your disposal. The writer of the outline chose to stop with subdivisions of "U.S. arsenal." At this point, three possible topics suggested themselves. They appear at the foot of the diagram.

APPLY YOURSELF 1. Finding the true subject. Using the library card catalog and either the *Readers' Guide to Periodical Literature* or the *New York Times Index*, develop a subject diagram on "recreation in the United States." Your diagram should resemble the preceding one, although you may not need as many levels. Then write three possible topics appropriate for an eight- to ten-page paper.

THE LIBRARY

Facilities of college and university libraries range tremendously from the small collections of new community colleges to the awesome holdings of the major state universities and the centuries-old private colleges. Moreover, new technology has revolutionized information storage and retrieval procedures through innovations like informational data banks and machine-readable catalog copy. Any reasonably complete introduction to the use of the library would take dozens of pages and would still fail to familiarize you with your own school's collection and practices. For these reasons, I won't even attempt such an introduction. Many college libraries offer individual and group tours. Perhaps your instructor can arrange a class visit. Other libraries provide printed guides. Make use of whatever assistance is available.

Your library is staffed with knowledgeable people who are anxious to help you with your research. The librarians at my university express the attitude of thousands of their colleagues around the country:

> The single most important thing to remember when using the library is this: *if you have a question, ask someone.* The most valuable resource of any library is people. And the people to ask are reference librarians. Every time you use the library you will be engaged in a dialogue, asking questions and finding answers. Reference librarians can help you to find and to learn to use sources such as encyclopedias, from the general encyclopedias like the *Americana* and the *Britannica* to very specialized and scholarly works like the *International Encyclopedia of the Social Sciences*. Manuals, handbooks, dictionaries, yearbooks, and statistical compendia also collect information from diverse sources. Abstracts and indexes—the *Reader's Guide to Periodical Literature* is but one among hundreds—and bibliographies are tools that lead you to information in many different types of publications. A reference librarian can help you match your needs to the sources of information available in the library. The librarian helps establish a dialogue through which you can communicate with the persons whose ideas and experiences are represented in the books and other materials housed in the library. As you engage in this dialogue and use the communications system that makes it possible, you will learn about yourself and the rich variety of experience that arises from the world in which you live.
>
> Welcome to the library!
>
> Milton H. Crouch,
> *Assistant Director for Reader Services,*
> *Bailey/Howe Memorial Library*

Once you've become at home in the library, it's time to get to work.

THE USE OF SOURCES

An essential mark of the good research paper is careful, responsible use of sources. Imprecise quotations and paraphrasing and missing, incomplete or inaccurate references signal more than mere carelessness in documentation. They suggest very strongly that the writer has little respect for the original sources used and little understanding of the intellectual process of research. Read this section carefully. Learn what it has to teach. Then, when you are engaged in your research and writing, double-check everything.

The researcher who uses the ideas, facts, or line of reasoning of other writers has three means of employing them: *quotation, paraphrase,* and *summary.* Each of these means has its own values and techniques. Each requires that you give credit to your sources.

The following paragraph, taken from a *Newsweek* article on working mothers, represents the original material that a researcher might encounter and want to use.

> No one toils harder at living two lives than the 5.5 million working mothers of pre-school children, the fastest-growing segment of the work force. Over-all, 43 percent of married mothers with children under 6 now work outside their homes. These mothers have 7 million small children to worry about while they earn needed paychecks—and there are precious few places to put them. Counting public, private and commercial facilities, the United States now has fewer licensed day-care slots available than in 1945: 1.6 million openings. That leaves another 5.4 million kids to be parceled out among babysitters and nursery schools—or left alone. "We are one of the few developed nations in the world that does not have serious child-care programs," says feminist Betty Friedan. "We force women to make agonizing choices" (Langway, 72).

QUOTATION

Quotation is using the exact words of the source. It's appropriate when the language in which the information is contained is so apt or unusual that you wish to share it. Or when the author is a well-known authority. Use quotation sparingly: It is uneconomical of space, and too frequent use implies that you haven't digested the information. Quotations must be precise in wording, spelling, and punctuation. The sample quotation that follows is taken from the *Newsweek* source.

> "Counting public, private and commercial facilities, the United States now has fewer licensed day-care slots available than in 1945: 1.6 million openings" (Langway, 72).

The next example uses single quotation marks within double quotation marks to indicate that part of this quotation has been quoted from another source.

> " 'We are one of the few developed nations in the world that does not have serious child-care programs,' says feminist Betty Friedan. 'We force women to make agonizing choices' " (Langway, 72).

When you use a short quotation, blend it in with your own writing so that it seems a natural, inevitable element. Example: Franklin Delano Roosevelt's powerful words, "The only thing we have to fear is fear itself," were spoken in the depths of national depression. Example: These issues are complex. College president Hiram Foss claims that "not all of our problems stem from lack of money. Lack of commitment is right up there."

Different rules apply to the use of longer quotations. Two or more sentences in prose which are four or more typewritten lines should be set off from the body of your paragraph by indenting four spaces from the left margin and single spacing:

> Counting public, private and commercial facilities, the United States now has fewer licensed day-care slots available than in 1945: 1.6 million openings. That leaves another 5.4 million kids to be parceled out among babysitters and nursery schools—or left alone (Langway, 72).

No quotation marks are used because the indentation and spacing signal quotation. A quotation within the longer quotation would have double quotation marks. Set off two or more lines of poetry similarly, but center them instead of indenting four spaces.

> Season of mists and mellow fruitfulness,
> Close bosom-friend of the maturing sun;
> *John Keats, "To Autumn"*

Deleting Material from a Quotation

Skillful, accurate editing is often called for if you are to use quoted material effectively. To emphasize a point, you may omit part of a quoted passage by using ellipsis periods (. . .) to signal the deletion: "Whoever thinks that art is a luxury . . . would do well to study the Parthenon." When ellipses mark the end of a sentence, use four periods: "No one toils harder at living two lives than the 5.5 million working mothers of pre-school children. . . ." The researcher must guard against distorting the meaning of the original passage by the use of ellipses.

Adding Material to a Quotation

Excerpting a quotation from its context sometimes requires you to clarify its meaning by adding a comment or correction. To do this, use brackets [ ] to enclose the added material. This practice tells the reader that the added words are yours, not the original author's. Example: The senator claimed that "they [the Russians] have never kept their word."

PARAPHRASE

Paraphrase is the use of ideas or examples or line of reasoning of another writer but converted into your own words. A paraphrase is usually about the same length as the original passage. Here is an acceptable paraphrase.

> Feminist Betty Friedan complains that while most of the world's industrialized nations have extensive day-care establishments, the American mother may have to choose between career or children (Langway, 72).

Compare it to the original quotation.

Like quotation, paraphrase must be credited. You'll learn how later in this chapter. Indicate by your wording where the paraphrase begins, as well.

> In a recent article on women and careers, *Newsweek* asked: When mom goes to work, where do the kids go? Working mothers in this country have 7 million children under the age of six. Licensed day-care centers can hold only 1.6 million of these pre-schoolers. The rest—5.4 million—are handled in a variety of ways ranging from spending the day in Grandma's kitchen to roaming the streets (Langway, 72).

A paraphrase is *not acceptable* when it follows the source too closely, reproducing the sentence structure and repeating many of the words of the original. This so-called close paraphrase is actually plagiarism—even if it is footnoted.

ORIGINAL

No one toils harder at living two lives than the 5.5 million working mothers of pre-school children, the fastest-growing segment of the work force (Langway, 72).

UNACCEPTABLE PARAPHRASE

No one works harder with their dual lives than the 5.5 million working women who have children under the age of six (Langway, 72).

Here a few words have been changed and one phrase dropped from the original, but the sentence structure and the order of ideas are the same. Even though the passage is footnoted, this is plagiarism. One more example of unacceptably close paraphrase (plagiarism):

ORIGINAL

Counting public, private and commercial facilities, the United States now has fewer licensed day-care slots available than in 1945: 1.6 million openings (Langway, 72).

UNACCEPTABLE PARAPHRASE

Counting all public and private centers, America now has fewer licensed day-care openings than in 1945—only 1.6 million (Langway, 72).

SUMMARY

Like paraphrase, summary employs the words of the student-researcher. The major difference is that summary is apt to be a brief statement of the central idea rather than an attempt to follow fairly closely the pattern of another's argument or explanation. Because it is economical, use summary instead of paraphrase when you have a choice. The following summary presents the central idea of the original paragraph on working mothers. Even summary requires a credit.

> Nearly half of all mothers of pre-school children hold down other jobs, but as observed in a recent issue of *Newsweek*, finding adequate child care is usually their most difficult assignment. Licensed day-care is available for only 1.6 of the 7 million children of these mothers; the rest have to settle for other, usually less satisfactory, alternatives (Langway, 72).

APPLY YOURSELF 2. Use of sources. Please read this passage, then follow the directions that appear after it.

> To be a Red Brigader is to cut every tie with home and family. The mother of Mario Moretti, wanted by police as a key figure in Moro's kidnapping, had thought her son was long dead until she saw his name in the papers. Elaborate rules govern everyday conduct in the underground. A printed handbook found in one of their safe-houses instructs "regular" Brigaders to keep their rented or purchased safehouses modest, clean, orderly, and decorous (curtains, lamps, doormats, potted plants on the balcony, etc.); to shave, cut their hair, and dress well; to pay gas and light bills promptly; to turn radios down at night, avoid neighborhood newsstands and bars, stay out of the landlord's sight; to stock the flat with plenty of food and a first-aid kit; to have incriminating documents always ready-packed for a fast getaway; and to practice strict economies, especially for their vast fleet of cars.
> Even with scrimping, the care and maintenance of a Red Brigades "regular"—food, clothes, flat, guns, travel, forged documents, electronic

equipment, general overhead—runs to around a thousand dollars a month. It is thought that there are 400 full members for project design and execution, thus adding up to a $5 million annual budget. True to the teachings of Lenin, who financed the Bolshevik Revolution that way, they "expropriate" the necessary funds by kidnapping or robbing banks. Once they get the hang of that, it is pretty easy: "When you realize the enormous advantage of having that gun in your hand, there's nothing to it," an anonymous terrorist told the Italian weekly *Panorama*. A single haul from the kidnapping of a wealthy Genoese in 1977 netted more than enough to cover the Brigades' expenses in the Moro operation. They are in fact "immensely rich," says an Italian official, and their German counterparts are also awash in money (Sterling, 39).

A. Copy, in the correct form, a quotation from the passage.
B. Write an acceptable paraphrase of some part of the passage.
C. Write a summary of one aspect of the passage.

BIBLIOGRAPHY CARDS

The bibliography card is your record of a source consulted or to be examined. At a minimum it contains the following information:

For a book

> Library call number
> Author's full name
> Complete title of work (underlined)
> Name of editor or translator, if there is one
> Facts of publication
>> Place of publication
>> Publisher
>> Date of publication

For an article in a periodical

> Author's full name
> Title of article (in quotation marks)
> Name of periodical (underlined)
> Volume number, if there is one
> Date
> Page numbers

You'll find the necessary information for a book on the title page, for an article on the cover or contents page and the article itself. Here are examples of bibliography cards:

For a book

303.4973
K 122 c

Herman Kahn
The Coming Boom: Economic, Political, and Social
New York

Simon and Schuster
1982

For a periodical

Sharon A. Mayes
"Women in Positions of Authority:
  a Case Study of Changing Sex Roles"

Signs
4
Spring 1979
pp. 556-568

Although these cards show the information that you should collect for each source, the form commonly used for recording that information differs from that given here. To save space on the card and to arrange the bibliographic information in the correct order, you should follow the pattern shown in the next section of this chapter. The sample card at the end of this section illustrates the correct form.

You should make a bibliography card for each source you uncover in your initial survey reading and subsequently. This enables you to keep track of your working list of sources. Some researchers will keep the card even if the source proves useless. That way they have a record that they did consult the source.

A second function of the bibliography cards is to note possible uses or a brief summary of sources. Such a note will rescue you from a faltering memory days or even weeks later, sending you back to just the source you need.

B

Mayes, Sharon A, "Women in Positions of Authority: A Case Study of Changing Sex Roles." Signs 4 (Spring 1979): 556-568

Survey of University Staff. Sex roles in small groups under stress. Concludes:

1) women evoke different reactions from men

2) males fear work changes mean new norms of behavior in everyday life.

no statistics --- easy to read

NOTE TAKING

When you read, you take notes—notes that summarize relevant passages, quote important wording, copy figures and statistics. Although some writers use large pads, one page to each source, most students will find the organization and writing stages much easier if they use file cards or uniform slips of paper. Each major idea or quotation gets a separate card, even if it is taken from the same source as other cards. The value of this practice will become apparent to you as your research notes pile up and you begin to organize. You will be able to sort through your cards, arranging them into smaller piles by subtopics. This aids you in integrating your ideas with those from several other sources.

Here is a sample card written on the subject of women as executives:

> *male attitudes about female bosses*
>
> Men simultaneously wanted "strong, nurturant, supportive females "and wanted" to retain control over the traditional male roles which require weak, passive, obedient, and sexually available females."   566-567
>
> Sharon A. Mayes, "Women in Positions of Authority"

The parts of the note card

1. *Key phrase or subtopic.* A word or two to identify the contents of this note. Useful in organization.
2. *The note.* This one combines both summary and quotation. Page numbers are essential.
3. *Source.* Author's name and title of source. Complete bibliographic information is written on a separate bibliography card.

There's not much more that needs to be said here about taking notes. Make clear whether you are summarizing, paraphrasing, or quoting. Copy bibliographic information and quotations accurately and double-check them.

DOCUMENTATION: CREDIT WHERE CREDIT IS DUE

Earlier in this chapter, I explained when and how to quote, paraphrase, and summarize. After you've used these skills in taking notes on the books and articles that are your sources, after you've put it all together into a research paper, you must attribute these words and ideas to their authors. Many academic disciplines have their own ways of writing notes and listing works cited. A professor who asks you to write a paper should tell you what the requirements are or direct you to the guide for that field. In English courses the standards established by the Modern Language Association (MLA) are usually followed. Recently MLA published new, simplified guidelines. In the absence of directions to the contrary, I suggest you use the MLA style.

Most striking about the new MLA style is the lack of notes.[1] Instead you include the author's name and the page number in the text for the first entry. Subsequent entries list only the page number.

> "No one toils harder at living two lives than the 5.5 million working mothers of pre-school children, the fastest-growing segment of the work force" (Langway, 72).

If you cite more than one work by an author, your references would be author, shortened title, and page number.

> "The code word for criticism of science and scientists these days is 'hubris'" (Thomas, *Medusa*, 58).

Instead of a bibliography, your essay should end with a list of "Works Cited." Include here every source that you quoted, paraphrased, or summarized in your paper. Arrange items alphabetically by author's last name. If you include more than one work by an author, do not repeat the name; substitute an eight-space line followed by a period (_____.). If the author's name is not given, alphabetize by the first key word of the title. Use hanging indention as shown in the following samples.

The examples that follow should explain how to credit any source you are likely to use. If you can't find the answer to a problem here, consult with your instructor or the reference librarian. To see how documentation is handled in an actual paper, look at the last chapter of this book.

"WORKS CITED"
SAMPLE ENTRIES FOR BOOKS

One Author

Brinton, Crane. *A History of Western Morals*. New York: Harcourt Brace and Company, 1959.

---

[1] Except for content or informational notes like this one which become "Endnotes" just before the list of "Works Cited."

Two Authors

Wellek, René and Austin Warren. *Theory of Literature*. 3rd ed. New York: Harcourt, Brace & World, 1956.

More than Two Authors

Spiller, Robert E., *et al. Literary History of the United States*. Rev. ed. New York: Macmillan Company, 1960.

No Author Given

The Hammond World Atlas. Maplewood, N.J.: Hammond Inc., 1973.

Article, Chapter, or Component in a Collection

Hawthorne, Nathaniel, "Young Goodman Brown." In *Anthology of American Literature I*. Ed. George McMichael. 2nd ed. New York: Macmillan Publishing Company, 1980, 1135–44.

SAMPLE ENTRIES FOR PERIODICALS

Newspapers

Franklin, Ben A. "Congressional Panels to Review Mine Safety." *New York Times*, 15 Feb. 1982, A.11.
"Accord Fails on Treating Disabled Infants." *New York Times*, 29 April 1984, E.9.

Popular Magazines

Rubinstein, Carin. "Regional States of Mind." *Psychology Today*, Feb. 1982:22–30.

Journals

Sweterlitsch, Richard. "Ballads and a Mississippi Badman." *Mississippi Folklore Register*, 12 (Spring 1978):47–57.

SAMPLE ENTRY FOR INTERVIEW

Taylor, M.D., John A. Burlington, VT, 22 October 1984.

APPLY YOURSELF 3. "Works Cited." The following is a list of five items you might have used in preparing a research paper. Compile a list of "Works Cited."

A. You have copied a drawing from page 196 of a 1969 work called the teddy bear book. The book was written by Peter Bull and published by Random House in New York City.

B.   You have used a direct quotation from page H1 of an article appearing in the Sunday New York Times on May 22, 1983, written by Sally Bedell Smith. The article was entitled as MTM goes, so goes quality in TV programming.

C.   You have summarized significant parts of an essay by Raúl Prebisch which runs from page 29 through page 52 of a book called Latin American Radicalism, published by Random House in New York in 1969. The essay is called the system and the social structure of Latin America, and the editors of the volume are Irving Louis Horowitz, Josue de Castro, and John Gerassi.

D.   The Economics of Crime: Punishment or Income Redistribution was written by Sheldon Danziger and David Wheeler. It was published in the October 1975 issue of Review of Social Economy. The October issue is in volume 33 of the journal, and the article ran from page 113 through page 131.

E.   You have paraphrased from page 101 of this book.

THE IDEA OF SYNTHESIS

Synthesis means "putting together." In the case of research, it refers to your creation of an essay that weighs your research sources and melds them with your own ideas and perspective on the subject. As you read and take notes, you come to a clearer understanding of your subject and of the various sources. Shuffling note cards and thinking about your topic, you begin to see the structure of the subject and the relationship of its parts. Only when you've digested what you've read and thought about the subject can synthesis occur.

Sometimes a student turns in a research paper that looks like this:

Introduction
Summary of source A
Summary of source B
Summary of source C
Conclusion

The outline demonstrates that there is no synthesis. This research suffers from indigestion, a failure of the writer to chew the information thoroughly. To avoid producing this kind of paper, give yourself the time to read and time to reflect on what you've read. And accept the challenge to create a unique view of your subject.

APPLY YOURSELF 4. One-paragraph research essay. This assignment is intended to give you practice in many of the skills needed to write a full-scale research paper, but at a more modest level. Reading, note taking, formulating a thesis, organizing, synthesizing, and documenting are all called for. The product will be a one-paragraph research essay, not more than one and one-half pages long, on the subject of the disposal of nuclear waste. The idea for this project comes from Susan Peck MacDonald of Eastern Connecticut State College. I've had several classes write this assignment with excellent results. And students report that it enables them to master important skills they never really understood before.

Several articles dealing with the problem of disposing of radioactive wastes are listed after the following paragraph. These are the only sources you'll need. They should be available in most college libraries. To minimize conflicts between students using the materials, your instructor may have already put copies of these articles on reserve at the library.

The assignment: Using at least three of these articles, write a one-paragraph essay of no more than one and one-half pages, typed, double-spaced, on some aspect of the disposal issue. Start by reading all of the articles to get a feel for the many different ways this subject can be approached. In one page you cannot possibly say everything about waste disposal or summarize each article. Instead, you must settle on a clearly expressed central idea or thesis—a topic sentence probably should start off your essay—and you will have to synthesize those aspects of the articles that relate to your topic. Take care to integrate the source material into logical subtopics with good transitions between them. You will want to use a variety of direct quotations and paraphrasing intermixed with your own reasoning to support each of your subtopics. Credit sources as appropriate. Attach a list of works cited including only the articles you used.

The sources:

A. "Radwaste: Out of Sight" in *Science News.* Written by Ivars Peterson, this article appears in volume 121 on January 2, 1982, beginning on page 9.

B. An article in *Congressional Quarterly Report* with no author given. Entitled "Nuclear Waste Legislation Begins to Move in Congress," it appears on pages 1967–1970 in volume 39, published on October 10, 1981.

C. Barnaby Feder's piece in the *New York Times* entitled "Nuclear Waste: Disposal Issue." It appeared on page D4 on February 4, 1982.

D. On January 10, 1983, *Time* ran an article called "Too Hot for the Usual Burial" on page 19.

E. "Atomic Headache: What to Do with Deadly Waste?" by Kenneth B. Sheets was published in the August 31, 1981, issue of *U.S. News and World Report*, on pages 58–60.

F. *Science* ran "U.S. Considers Ocean Dumping of Radwastes" on pages 1217–1219 on March 5, 1982, volume 215.

APPLY YOURSELF 5. The research paper. If you've studied this chapter and written the exercises, you've mastered the skills needed to write a research paper. Although at first the job may *seem* monumental, you understand that taken a step at a time it is manageable, even satisfying, especially if you choose a subject interesting to you.

The assignment is to research a subject and to write an essay incorporating that research. Your instructor will establish guidelines for appropriate subjects and length. I suggest the following stages be used as checkpoints. Your instructor might ask you to turn in a written product at each stage. Alternatives are a conference with the instructor or a consultation with your workshop group.

The stages listed below are keyed to the steps of the process outline on pages 156–157. Review that outline before you begin, and refer to it and the explanations that follow it as your work progresses.

Stage 1. Establish the research subject or question, do survey reading, narrow the subject (steps 1–3). Product: a subject chart like the one on page 158.

Stage 2. Develop working bibliography and clarify subject (steps 4 and 5). Product: bibliography cards with summaries like the sample on page 167.

Stage 3. Take notes (step 6). Product: note cards.

Stage 4. Decide on your true subject and make a preliminary plan (step 7). Product: written statement of true subject and plan or outline.

Stage 5. Do supplementary reading and write final plan (steps 8 and 9). Product: written plan with subtopics.

Stage 6. Write draft and revise. Product: your paper with list of works cited, ready for comments and further revision (step 10). Congratulations!

WORKS CITED IN CHAPTER 10

Langway, Lynn, *et al.* "The Superwoman Squeeze." *Newsweek*, 19 May 1980, 72.

MacDonald, Susan Peck. "A Proposal for a One-Paragraph Research Paper." *The Leaflet* 79 (Fall 1980):32–38.

Sterling, Claire. "The Terrorist Network." *Atlantic*, Nov. 1978, 39.

Thomas, Lewis. *The Medusa and the Snail: More Notes of a Biology Watcher.* New York: Viking, 1979.

Stage III
The
Writer
Revises

This section of *Writer to Writer* will guide you through the difficult steps of rewriting and revising. Chapter 11 shows techniques for rewriting the entire essay as well as ways of revising paragraphs and sentences. This is a chapter that you'll want to refer to throughout the course for hints on paragraph development and sentence clarity. Also discussed are style, sentence structure, and basic rules of punctuation.

Chapters 12 and 13 treat the openings and the endings of essays, parts that have their own special needs. Of course, you may already have your starter parts from the thinking you did about audience in the early stages of the paper. And your ending may be the logical conclusion you drew from the development of your argument. I've placed these chapters here in the revision section because most writers review the overall rhetorical effect of their work at the last, and it is at that point you might well want some help with beginnings and endings.

Chapter 14, written mostly by a student, is the story of writing an essay. Sarah Buntenbah explains how she used the principles of this book—prewriting, drafting, revising—to write a research paper on the promise and danger of genetic research.

Placing revising at the end of this book has its dangers. The reader might infer that revising comes only after the last draft has been completed. That inference is untrue, as the following chapters illustrate.

Chapter Eleven
Revision

*T*o the inexperienced writer, *revision* often means taking the first draft and checking for errors in spelling and punctuation, replacing repetitive words and, perhaps, substituting action verbs for verbs of being. Then to the typewriter. More experienced writers know that this is not what revision is all about.

Revising is rewriting, not proofreading. We're talking about major surgery, not a haircut. Now I'd be lying to you if I claimed that experienced writers always tear apart their first drafts. Some, knowing exactly what they want a piece to do, agonize over each word and sentence as they go along. One writer of fiction spends up to 6 months per story composing this way. But, by and large, most accomplished writers expect to make extensive revisions. It's no accident that they have large wastebaskets.

What does this mean for you? In their book about the teaching of writing, Karen Burke LeFevre and Mary Jane Dickerson tell about one student writer's experience.

> A student enrolled in a writing course—call her Jennifer—wrote three drafts of an autobiographical essay over a week's time. Jennifer's first draft told about a turkey hunt—getting up early, dressing, riding in the truck, watching for turkeys, shooting her first turkey. But her final draft, called "The Killing Never Bothered Me," mentioned the word "turkey" only once. The essay had changed drastically into a piece that dramatized several different hunting scenes, showing how the writer had always felt compelled to impress her father, to be the perfect daughter, to try to succeed in one hunt after another and to fall short of that goal. The central point of Jennifer's experience came not from her first draft, in which she recited activities that had to do with hunting, but from her revisions, with their detailed descriptions of particular episodes that showed why she felt compelled to hunt. "In my first draft I had been writing *around* the actual point that I wanted to be writing about," she

commented later. "Without revising I never would have reached the final draft and discovered what I really wanted to say."

Until I See What I Say

Jennifer learned what the word "revision" truly means: to see again. To see again most clearly, you need some distance from the draft. Here, time is a great ally. The old advice to put the draft away for a while and then come back to it still makes sense. Of course, midnight drafting for 8:00 a.m. class doesn't permit that. Usually, you have at least a week between receiving the assignment and the due date. Make use of that time. Write a first draft within 48 hours, then put it away for another 48. When you reread it then, you have a chance to "see it again" in a fresh light. Another way to gain distance from a draft is to read it aloud, preferably to a friend. Reading aloud has a strange effect. When you *hear* the writing, it seems different, almost as if someone else wrote it. You can be more critical. And if you have the benefit of a listener, your friend can ask questions and point out weak sections.

To begin revising your paper, think big. Look first at the largest elements: overall organization, central idea, focus, purpose. Does the essay say what you really want it to say, or is it, like Jennifer's first draft, a circling of the true subject? Where is the heart of your ideas? Amazingly, many student papers get started only in the last page or so. They remind me of a dog getting ready to lie down in a grassy field. The dog walks in a circle a few times, treading down the grass and looking for just the right place to settle. Writers sometimes do that for a few pages. The remedy is to eliminate those early pages and develop the true subject in the space saved. After that you can write a new introduction, including a sharpened thesis.

Test overall organization by outlining the draft *after* you've completed it. Strange as it may sound, this procedure enables you to reassess the sequence and relationship of your ideas. You may find that a different order makes your presentation easier to follow or more persuasive. Look at the section "Rewriting the Outline" in Chapter 2 for an illustration. And if you contemplate moving large sections of your essay, use a common shortcut: scissors and adhesive tape. Cut up your draft (or a photocopy) to make rearranging easier. Tape paragraphs onto blank sheets.

When you are pleased with the overall form of your essay, try this: Type a new draft, triple-spaced. Don't let strikeovers bother you. This draft is for your eyes only. The rationale for this typed version is that it allows you to see your essay differently. The triple-spacing gives you plenty of room to work out revisions. And don't forget transitions, those connections between ideas. You'll need new ones now that you have moved things around. Only when you are satisfied with these larger elements are you ready to move downward in scale in revising—to paragraphs, sentences, and words.

The value of revising is probably the hardest lesson for the writer to learn. It's certainly one of the most difficult to teach. Yet often, as in Jennifer's case, only through revising do you discover your true subject. Even when the outcome is not so dramatic, the finished product is truly that—finished, not merely done.

THE PARAGAPH

After you have revised for true subject, focus, and overall organization, you encounter the paragraph. Usually the essay's largest subdivision, the paragraph is difficult to define. Descriptive paragraphs differ from narrative paragraphs which differ from expository paragraphs. You'll find paragraphs as short as one sentence and as long as a dozen or more.

What *can* we say about the paragraph, then? The paragraph functions as a unit of thought, a sort of supersentence. It is to the essay what the sentence is to the paragraph. Just as putting words into sentences arranges and controls their meanings, putting sentences into paragraphs arranges and controls their meanings. And like the sentence, the paragraph usually has a single core of meaning, sometimes a single idea, sometimes several closely related ideas.

This core of meaning may be expressed or merely implied. When expressed in a single sentence, that is called the *topic sentence*. In stating the core of meaning, the topic sentence determines what is relevant to the paragraph. To see what I mean, let's look at this somewhat flowery topic sentence: A bird feeding station in your yard can become a magnet for these colorful creatures with their melodious songs. The core of meaning or topic of the paragraph is *a feeding station will attract birds to your yard*. Any sentence that supports or furthers that idea may enter the paragraph. Any sentence that does not must stay out. This principle, called *unity*, assures that the paragraph has a singleness of meaning.

Occasionally, though, the core of meaning is only implied and not stated in any single sentence. That doesn't mean the paragraph isn't limited to a single topic, only that the topic is not directly expressed. Although I'm not unbending on the matter, I do advise my students to write topic sentences in their expository essays for two reasons: First, because constructing a topic sentence forces the writer to clarify the core of meaning and the purpose of each paragraph, and second, because the topic sentence increases readability.

Topic in hand, the writer's next concern is *coherence* in the paragraph. Coherence means "sticking together" and "systematic connection." It refers to the smooth, logical flow from sentence to sentence. Each sentence relates to the one before, the one after, and to the main idea of the entire paragraph. The writer ensures coherence by arranging thoughts in a logical order and by using several specific techniques. These are transitions, pronouns, parallel structure, and repetition.

Transitions:	words like *also, certainly, for instance, because, at the same time, if, first, although,* usually leading off the sentence.
Pronouns:	words like *it, these, this, who, they, many,* used alone when their reference is clear, otherwise attached to nouns: *these causes, many models.*
Parallel structure:	use of similar sentence structure to show related ideas: *When you type your paper, use white unruled paper and double space. When you write your paper longhand, use white lined paper and skip alternate lines.*
Repetition:	repeating key words creates links between sentences: *Topic in hand, the writer's next concern is coherence in the paragraph. Coherence means "sticking together" and "systematic connection."*

Study the following paragraph, noting the author's use of these techniques for achieving coherence.

Many teachers of photography start their students off making photograms. They are very easy to do, and they help you understand how photographic film and paper work. I will mainly discuss paper, although film is very much like it—except that it is transparent rather than opaque. Both materials are coated with a very thin emulsion consisting of hardened gelatin in which are suspended thousands of minute crystals of a silver compound which can be chemically changed by light. Both must be exposed to light to form images. And both are run through a short series of chemical solutions to bring out images; many times you can even use the same chemicals for film and paper, although it's usually better to use different developers.

Ralph M. Hattersley, "Photograms Teach
You How," *Popular Photography*

APPLY YOURSELF 1. Coherence. Most well-written expository paragraphs have an inner logic and unmistakable marks of sequence: coherence. You can prove this to yourself in this exercise. Each of the following items contains all the sentences of a paragraph, but the order has been scrambled.

See if you can rearrange the sentences to make a coherent paragraph of each. Then explain what clues you used to arrive at this order.

A.   1.   When they have found themselves faced with three parties, they have killed one at the polls.

       2.   The American people plainly want a two-party system.

       3.   During the past two hundred years, whenever they have found themselves with only one party, they have split it in two or started a new one.

*David Cushman Coyle, The United States
Political System and How It Works*

B.   1.   But the life of the core is limited.

       2.   The capacity of such a reactor is roughly 1,000 megawatts (one million kilowatts) of electricity, enough for a city of 600,000 people.

       3.   A large reactor operating today holds tens of thousands of fuel rods in which are sealed some eight million uranium pellets weighing about a hundred tons.

       4.   A third of the fuel must be replaced annually during the expected 30–40 year life of the reactor.

*Kenneth F. Weaver, "The Promise and
Peril of Nuclear Energy," National Geographic*

C.   1.   The causes of skin disorders are varied.

       2.   Whatever the underlying cause, emotional problems may increase the frequency and severity of attacks.

       3.   Bacteria, viruses, and physical and chemical irritants are important in others.

       4.   They may even be the fundamental cause of some disorders.

       5.   Heredity plays a role in some.

*Ted A. Grossbart, "Bringing Peace to
Embattled Skin," Psychology Today*

THE FOUR-PART PARAGRAPH

A colleague of mine, John Clarke, has studied paragraph logic and come up with an interesting and usable explanation of how paragraphs work. He sees the sequence of sentences in a paragraph as a model of a learning cycle. The writer answers questions asked by an imaginary reader. These answers become the sentences of the paragraph. Because of the nature and order of the questions, the paragraph moves from the general to the specific.

     Here are Clarke's questions, along with the names he gives to the answers:

1.	What is true? What does what to what? (under what circumstances?)	Leader	(L)
2.	Why is the leader true? How does it happen? What do you mean?	Clarifier	(C)
3.	When can we see (feel, touch, taste, measure, etc.) the leader happening?	Example	(E)
4.	So what? What does the example show?	Interpretation	(I)

Although not every paragraph need follow this plan, Clarke explains that "this set of formulaic questions will always generate a paragraph that meets some basic needs of readers."

A test run with these questions might produce a paragraph like this one:

Leader (L)	These days the most popular books among kids are about
Clarifier (C)	the supernatural. By supernatural I mean stories about
Example (E)	vampires, werewolves, ghosts, and the like. *The Amityville Horror* was passed from hand to hand until its covers were stained and torn and the pages began to fall out. I wonder
Interpretation (I)	if the Greeks enjoyed their myths of Perseus and Hercules as much as we like our chilling tales of the other world.

While this may not be a very sophisticated example, it does have an inner unity and a logic in its development.

(L) Inner unity and logical development must inform any paragraph. (C) The value of this approach to paragraph development is that it enables you to see and understand the relationship of the parts: (E) how the clarifier, by its specificity, explains the leader, how the example offers concrete evidence of the truth of the leader. (I) Each sentence has a definite function to perform.

Variations on this pattern, while adhering to the principle, allow writers to generate paragraphs that fit their needs. One type of variation results by doubling (or tripling) any part. For instance, you may have two clarifiers or three examples. A second variation is dropping one of the parts that isn't necessary, often done when other parts are doubled. The possibilities for variation are too numerous to list. Perhaps a few illustrations will give you the idea, though.

DOUBLED EXAMPLES

L	A good electric drill can do more than merely make holes.
C	With the right accessories, you can use it to sand, grind, polish, stir
E	paint, and drive screws. Some models can be sped up or slowed

E down to fit the job you're doing. Some can even reverse themselves
I to back out of tight spots or to remove a batch of screws. In short,
an electric drill is a virtual must for the do-it-yourselfer working on
anything but the simplest tasks.

Consumer Reports

TRIPLED LEADERS

L   The big oil companies adjust their prices to the prevailing
L market price, rather than to their costs in obtaining oil. The big
utilities adjust their prices to reflect higher fuel costs, with an
L additional profit percentage on those costs. The big manufacturers
adjust their prices to account for higher fuel costs and higher utility
costs, with a profit percentage on both. The consumer, who has no
I price to adjust, falls victim to the explosion of costs in the economy.

John Clarke

TRIPLED EXAMPLES

E   That year, farmers in the valley had to plant corn three times
E to get one harvest. They were out all night pulling mired cows out
E of mud holes. They fenced in new pastures and refenced after
I washouts. Farmers couldn't farm at all if they didn't have faith in the
future and a strong sense of humor.

John Clarke

Except as an exercise, nobody writes paragraphs according to a for-
mula. Yet your study of this approach might help you understand a little
better the internal relationships of the paragraph. In the preceding samples,
notice that doubled or tripled elements in each paragraph share a similarity
of structure. For instance, "Some models can be . . ." and "Some can
even . . ." Similarity of structure signals the reader to expect similarity of
function. The exercise that follows gives you a chance to test your grasp of
the four-part paragraph.

APPLY YOURSELF 2. The four-part paragraph. For this assignment you'll write
three new paragraphs and revise one old one. Identify the function of each
sentence: L for leader, C for clarifier, E for example, and I for intepretation.

A. Write a "standard" four-part paragraph—leader, qualifier, example,
interpretation.
B. Write two variations of the pattern. Use doubles, triples, and drops.
C. Choose a paragraph from an earlier essay, one that dissatisfied you.
Rewrite the paragraph.

APPLY YOURSELF 3. From facts to paragraph. "Oh dear," thought Ellen, "why did he have to ask that one? I don't know where to begin." Professor Steele has just handed out a surprise quiz question in his music appreciation course, and Ellen must write a coherent paragraph or two about the sonata. She hasn't had time to order her thoughts on the subject because she didn't know the quiz was coming. She tries to regain her composure by scribbling everything she knows about sonatas on the first page of her exam book:

There are two kinds: classical sonatas and Baroque ones.

Bach, Handel, and Vivaldi fall into the Baroque period 1660–1760; from Haydn and Mozart on, it is classical—1760 (includes Beethoven).

Symphony follows same structure as sonata does; a symphony is a "sonata for orchestra" it says somewhere in our textbook.

Beethoven wrote a lot of sonatas, but many of them don't follow the same structure as typical sonatas.

Sonatas are written in four movements.

Sonatas are the most important form of instrumental music from the Baroque right through to the present.

Almost all classical sonatas have these "movements": (1) allegro (fast, exciting); (2) adagio (slow, emotional); (3) minuet (dancelike); (4) allegro (fast, energetic).

"Movements" in music are essentially independent sections of a piece.

Sonatas mostly are written for piano alone or for a solo instrument with piano accompaniment.

Baroque sonatas were mostly written for small groups of instruments.

Your assignment is to take Ellen's information and assemble it into a coherent essay of one or two paragraphs for Professor Steele's command: "Tell me about the sonata form." As you plan and write, you may decide to eliminate some of the notes. And don't forget what you've learned about topic sentences, unity, coherence, and paragraph structure.

A FEW WORDS ABOUT STYLE

The way something is done—that's style. When we describe the style of a tennis player, a painter, or a teacher, we mean not so much what they do but how they do it. Style, then, is the manner, not the matter, the form, not the content. Applied to a written composition, the word "style" refers to the sum of the choices the writer made. Just what are those choices, and how do you make them?

In the broadest sense, the seminal choices are made in the prewriting stages. Decisions about purpose, audience, and voice determine and limit later choices about paragraphing, sentence structure and variety, and vocabulary. These matters are treated in Chapter 3, but let me summarize and illustrate here. Let's say your subject is black holes in space. If your audience is the average 10- to 12-year-old, you will have to accept certain constraints: short paragraphs composed of fairly simple, brief sentences, analogies or comparisons within the reader's understanding, a basic vocabulary whenever possible with explanations of unfamiliar terms. Writing an essay on black holes in space for your astronomy professor, on the other hand, calls for a more mature, objective style: longer paragraphs composed of more complex sentences, numbers to express magnitudes, a scientific vocabulary, and citations of research sources.

Your purpose, too, will affect decisions about matters of style. The primary function of an essay may be argumentative or informative or even contemplative. Each function offers its own opportunities and imposes restrictions that you must consider in overall organization, paragraphing, sentence variety, and word choice.

Voice, the last of the prewriting decisions, demands a consistency of treatment. An argumentative essay written in a conciliatory tone can be ruined by the injection of sarcasm, for instance. An elegant two-dollar word can be just as jarring in a playful, familiar childhood reminiscence as a piece of current slang in a course paper about Plato's *Republic*.

The man who created Lilliput, the land of tiny people in *Gulliver's Travels*, Jonathan Swift, claimed that "proper words in proper places make the true definitions of style." By *proper* he didn't mean nice or polite; he meant suitable or appropriate. Appropriateness to the subject, the audience, the purpose, and the voice—this is the first concern in the development of your writing style.

As a writer, you have many more options than you suspect. Take the first step toward an adaptable style by understanding those options. Do you use common words (like *curving, crazy, strange, get used to, rotten*) or unusual ones (like *sinuous, maniacal, fey, habituate, putrescent*)? What difference does it make? Are you conscious of the sound values of words and able to put those values to use? Single words have their own effects, pleasant or otherwise: *topaz, cranky, stipple, sleazy*. When you put words together, the effect can be memorable or distracting: *a secret ministry, that faint, fleeting smile, liquid lapse of murmuring streams*. Words can be abstract or concrete, English in origin or Latinate. Study the effects of word choice in your own writing and in the work of writers you respect. Use a dictionary, a thesaurus, and a book on usage like Follet's *Modern American Usage*. And this above all: Strive for the right word, the word that has precisely the shade of meaning desired, that is appropriate for the voice of the piece.

ECONOMY

To some, the notion of economy runs against common sense. When the English assignment calls for a minimum of 500 words or the history paper at least eight pages, the student writer's purpose often is not to avoid waste but to produce it. How else to meet that minimum bulk? Practicing the kind of economy explained here won't hamper your efforts. It will in fact convey to your reader a sense of control without flabbiness and padding.

In a way economy is a negative virtue, like chastity. It means doing without—without words that contribute nothing to the sense of your work. Without redundancy. If you study the following examples, you should get the idea. Then practice the principle in the Apply Yourself at the end of this chapter and in your own writing.

1. Original: *There are the voices of children nagging mom for candy.* I don't like sentences beginning "there are" or "it is" for two reasons: *there* and *it* are not the true subjects of such sentences, only stand-ins, and forms of the verb *to be* lack the force of action verbs.
    Revision: Children's voices nag mom for candy.

2. Original: *Villi cover the lining of the intestine. They are like the tentacles of a sea anemone.*
    The simile comparing villi to tentacles is excellent, but the sentence should probably be combined by changing one of the main verbs to a participle. What is the difference between the versions below?
    Revision 1: Resembling the tentacles of a sea anemone, villi cover the lining of the stomach.
    Revision 2: Covering the lining of the stomach, villi resemble the tentacles of a sea anemone.

3. Original: *The boat was leaking from neglect. It finally sank.*
    By placing the participle next to the noun modified, we can delete *was* and *it* and improve the sound.
    Revision: The boat, leaking from neglect, finally sank.

4. Original: *She supposed she would probably take another year of French.*
    Supposed and *probably* both convey some uncertainty. Choose one, but note the difference.
    Revision 1: She supposed she would take another year of French.
    Revision 2: She would probably take another year of French.

5. Original: *The Interfraternity Council, which is composed of all the sororities and fraternities on campus, plans the Winter Carnival every year.*
    Nothing wrong with the sentence, but you can eliminate *which is*.
    Revision: The Interfraternity Council, composed of all the sororities and fraternities on campus, plans the Winter Carnival every year.

6.   Original: *Most small cars that are now on the market have front wheel drive.*
The words *that are* contribute nothing to the sentence.
Revision: Most small cars now on the market have front wheel drive.

7.   Original: *Italian, which has been an unpopular course for years, will be dropped from the curriculum.*
Dropping *which has been* yields an appositive.
Revision: Italian, an unpopular course for years, will be dropped from the curriculum.

SENTENCES: VARIETY AND STYLE

Malcolm X and Benjamin Franklin both did it. They are just two of many people who have taught themselves to write by emulating the work of established authors. By transcribing effective prose, you can begin to learn how it works. By imitating sentence patterns, you can increase your knowledge of their structure. The following three simple techniques show you how to control sentence elements and enrich your style.

Transcribing or Copying

The practice of transcribing calls for you to copy word for word passages from masters of English prose style as well as favorite authors. Really! Although this might seem pointless, many writers find that transcribing well-written pieces gives them a much truer sense of sentence structure and style than even the most careful reading. The purpose of this exercise is not to adopt someone else's style for your own writing. By copying several authors you'll get the feel of a variety of styles. Select a passage you can copy in 20 minutes or less and read it through first, then copy slowly and carefully. You might want to do this and the following writing exercises in your journal. The effects of this technique are not immediately apparent, but if you practice four or five times a week for several weeks, you'll probably notice a greater flexibility and variety in your own writing efforts.

Variations on a Sentence

Good experience in understanding the effects of word choice and sentence structure is to write as many variations as you can of a single sentence. The only rule is that you must keep the sense of the original.

Example: The north wind blew down the old shed.
Rewordings: The old shack did not withstand the north wind's fury. Stronger than the shed, the north wind achieved an upset.

Boreas's force toppled the small, ancient building.
Hit by the intensity of the air current from the north,
the shanty collapsed.

Imitation

Imitation will challenge your wits and give you a grasp of a variety of
sentence patterns. The idea is to follow a model sentence, reproducing its
structure but not its ideas. You should use the same number of adjectives, for
instance, and the same kind of verb. A prepositional phrase should be
replaced by another prepositional phrase. The point is not to learn the styles
of other writers but to experience numerous ways of fashioning sentences.

Original: Because of the moon's gravitational pull, the oceans expe-
             rience daily tides.

Imitation: Due to the dollar's growing strength, American tourists
             encounter lower prices.

Original: I went to the woods because I wished to live deliberately,
             to front only the essential facts of life, and see if I could
             learn what it had to teach, and not, when I came to die,
             discover that I had not lived. —Henry David Thoreau,
             Walden

Imitation: He sought out an analyst because he wanted to perceive
             clearly, to understand the deep springs of his nature, and
             discover if he could cherish what he found there, and not,
             when he reached old age, realize that he had never been
             himself.

APPLY YOURSELF 4. Transcribing. Carefully and slowly copy the following
passages. You might also jot down any observations you make in the
process.

A.   Vanity of vanities, saith the Preacher, vanity of vanities; all is vanity.
What profit hath a man of all his labour which he taketh under the sun? One
generation passeth away, and another generation cometh: but the earth
abideth for ever. The sun also ariseth, and the sun goeth down, and hasteth to
his place where he arose. The wind goeth toward the south, and turneth about
unto the north; it whirleth about continually, and the wind returneth again
according to his circuits. All the rivers run into the sea; yet the sea is not full;
unto the place from whence the rivers come, thither they return again. All
things are full of labour; man cannot utter it: the eye is not satisfied with
seeing, nor the ear filled with hearing. The thing that hath been, it is that

which shall be; and that which is done is that which shall be done: and there is no new thing under the sun.

Ecclesiastes

B.   The allurement that women hold out to men is precisely the allurement that Cape Hatteras holds out to sailors: they are enormously dangerous and hence enormously fascinating. To the average man, doomed to some banal drudgery all his life long, they offer the only grand hazard that he ever encounters. Take them away and his existence would be as flat and secure as that of a moo-cow. Even to the unusual man, the adventurous man, the imaginative and romantic man, they offer the adventure of adventures. Civilization tends to dilute and cheapen all other hazards. Even war has been largely reduced to caution and calculation; already, indeed, it employs almost as many press-agents, letter-openers and generals as soldiers. But the duel of sex continues to be fought in the Berserker manner. Whoso approaches women still faces the immemorial dangers. Civilization has not made them a bit more safe than they were in Solomon's time; they are still inordinately menacing, and hence inordinately provocative, and hence inordinately charming.

H. L. Mencken

C.   In this refulgent summer, it has been a luxury to draw the breath of life. The grass grows, the buds burst, the meadow is spotted with fire and gold in the tint of flowers. The air is full of birds, and sweet with the breath of the pine, the balm-of-Gilead, and the new hay. Night brings no gloom to the heart with its welcome shade. Through the transparent darkness the stars pour their almost spiritual rays. Man under them seems a young child, and his huge globe a toy. The cool night bathes the world as with a river, and prepares his eyes again for the crimson dawn. The mystery of nature was never displayed more happily. The corn and the wine have been freely dealt to all creatures, and the never-broken silence with which the old bounty goes forward has not yielded yet one word of explanation. One is constrained to respect the perfection of this world in which our senses converse. How wide; how rich; what invitation from every property it gives to every faculty of man! In its fruitful soils; in its navigable sea; in its mountains of metal and stone; in its forests of all woods; in its animals; in its chemical ingredients; in the powers and path of light, heat, attraction and life, it is well worth the pitch and heart of great men to subdue and enjoy it. The planters, the mechanics, the inventors, the astronomers, the builders of cities, and the captains, history delights to honor.

R. W. Emerson, "The Divinity School Address"

APPLY YOURSELF 5. Variations on a sentence. Choose one of the following sentences and write at least ten variations of it.

A.   Please stop making so much noise.

B. The weather last winter was terrible.

C. A liar should have a good memory. *Quintilian*

APPLY YOURSELF 6. Imitation. For each of the following sentences, write an imitation according to the instructions given earlier.

A. Riding a wave of popularity, the convertible has brought car buyers back into the showroom.

B. The rain stopped as Nick turned into the road that went up through the orchard. *Ernest Hemingway*

C. When the fit had spent itself, he walked weakly to the window and, lifting the sash, sat in a corner of the embrasure and leaned his elbow upon the sill. *James Joyce*

D. From birth to age eighteen, a girl needs good parents. From eighteen to thirty-five, she needs good looks. From thirty-five to fifty-five, she needs a good personality. From fifty-five on, she needs good cash. *Sophie Tucker*

E. I have too great a soul to die like a criminal. *John Wilkes Booth*

THIRTEEN COMMON EDITING SYMBOLS

agree	faulty agreement of subject and verb or of pronoun and antecedent	¶	begin new paragraph
cap	capital letter	*p*	error in punctuation
cs	comma splice	*run on*	run on sentence
frag.	sentence fragment	*sp.*	error in spelling
lc.	lower case	*trans*	transition needed
no ¶	no new paragraph	*ww*	wrong word
		mm	misplaced modifier

CORRECTNESS, MATTERS OF

When the last word has been written about unity, coherence, and style, your readers will expect your work to reflect those conventions of mechanics and usage that still apply in this changing world. Although no one pays much attention these days to the fine points like the distinction between "shall" and "will," many readers are distracted by spelling errors, incomplete sentences, and lack of agreement between subject and verb. Punctuation errors can cause misreadings. For these reasons this book includes a brief summary of those rules of usage and mechanics that cause student writers the greatest number of problems. If you need more help than this section delivers, your instructor can recommend a good handbook.

The Sentence

Permit me to be the fourth (eleventh? twentieth?) teacher to tell you what a sentence is: A sentence is a group of words that contains a subject and a verb and expresses a complete thought.

This is a sentence:

> My car got a flat tire.

This is not:

> After my car got a flat tire

What's the difference? It seems ironic that by *adding* a word to the first utterance (My car got a flat tire) we get something less than a sentence (After my car got a flat tire). Obviously the word "after" has changed the sentence somehow. Both groups of words have a subject, *car*; both have a verb, *got*. The reason that "after my car got a flat tire" is not a sentence is that it doesn't express a complete thought. To see what I mean, read it aloud. The listener (reader) is left hanging—after my car got a flat tire *what?*

This nonsentence is an example of one kind of *sentence fragment*. Because a fragment doesn't express a complete thought, it cannot stand alone—it must be attached to a complete sentence.

> After my car got a flat tire, I took it to the garage.

This kind of fragment is called a "dependent clause," *dependent* because it cannot stand alone, *clause* because it has a subject and verb. "I took it to the garage" is an *independent* clause: It has a subject and verb and can stand alone.

> I took it to the garage.

A sentence, then, *must* contain an independent clause. It may contain other elements as well.

TWO INDEPENDENT CLAUSES

I took it to the garage, and the mechanic told me to leave it.
      independent   independent

ONE DEPENDENT CLAUSE AND ONE INDEPENDENT CLAUSE
When I took it to the garage, the mechanic told me to leave it.
      dependent   independent
Beth took the camera that wasn't working.
     independent   dependent

Subordinators

Subordinators are words that have the power to change an independent to a dependent clause. One kind of subordinator is the *relative pronoun*, which stands for a noun and relates the dependent to the independent clause. The word *which* in the preceding sentence is a relative pronoun as are the following words: *that, who, whom, what,* and *whose.* To add one of these to a clause is to make it dependent. The subordinating conjunction is a second kind of subordinator. *After* and *when* in the preceding examples are *subordinating conjunctions* as are *although, as, because, before, if, unless, until, when, where.* This list is not complete, and some of these words may function as other parts of speech. Like the relative pronoun, the subordinating conjunction, added to a clause, makes it dependent.

So what? If you've followed this very brief, very simplistic explanation, you'll appreciate the consequences for your writing. First, about sentence fragments—don't write them. English teachers don't like sentence fragments. Editors don't like sentence fragments. Students are ingenious in devising a variety of sentence fragments, almost always without realizing what they're doing. Fragments *can* be used for effect—to add emphasis or to break rhythm, for instance—but because they do not express a complete thought and because they are viewed as incorrect, you're better off avoiding them. If you get a paper back with a clause marked "fragment" or "frag," look near that clause for the sentence to which it belongs.

The second consequence of what you've just learned is positive— subordinating conjunctions and relative pronouns can be used in your writing to indicate causal or temporal relationships and to link ideas.

Original	Her ankle was twisted. She won the race.
Relationship expressed	*Although* her ankle was twisted, she won the race. (subordinating conjunction)
Original	Daylight savings time started last night. I was late for practice.
Relationship expressed	*Because* daylight savings time started last night, I was late for practice. (subordinating conjunction)

Original	Terry is a skilled potter. She works in her Soho studio every afternoon.
Relationship expressed	Terry is a skilled potter *who* works in her Soho studio every afternoon. (relative pronoun)
Original	We saw poverty and disease in the South Bronx. It was appalling.
Relationship expressed	The poverty and disease *that* we saw in the South Bronx was appalling. (relative pronoun)
Relationship expressed	We saw poverty and disease *that* was appalling in the South Bronx. (relative pronoun)

Comma Splice and Run On

When independent clauses are joined in one sentence, you may use a comma plus *and, but, or, nor, for,* or *yet,* or a colon, or a semicolon. Common violations of this rule are the comma splice and the run-on sentence.

Wrong	In the spring of 1776, a miserable Colonial Army retreated from Montreal, they were survivors of Col. Benedict Arnold's unsuccessful campaign on British Canada. (comma splice)
Correct	In the spring of 1776, a miserable Colonial Army retreated from Montreal; they were survivors of Col. Benedict Arnold's unsuccessful campaign on British Canada.
Wrong	Isabel is an orphan with no fortune, she is willing to accept any invitation to experience more of life, she is not willing to accept restrictions. (comma splice)
Correct	Isabel is an orphan with no fortune; she is willing to accept any invitation to experience more of life; (or "but") she is not willing to accept restrictions.
Wrong	Laura is not like that she is outgoing, friendly, and capable. (run on)
Correct	Laura is not like that: she is outgoing, friendly, and capable.

Agreement

The subject and the verb must agree in number. If the subject is singular, the verb must be singular. A plural subject requires a plural verb.

Wrong	The *values* placed on human life by the two countries *differs* drastically.
Correct	The *values* placed on human life by the two countries *differ* drastically.
Wrong	Mass *media has* successfully brainwashed us.
Correct	Mass *media have* successfully brainwashed us. (*media* is plural; the singular is *medium.*)

A pronoun must agree in number with its antecedent, that is, the word it replaces.

Wrong	This *type* of person has a complete lack of initiative. *Their* life is full of indolence.
Correct	This type of person has a complete lack of initiative. *His* or *her* life is full of indolence.
Wrong	Of course the *hallways* are not crowded if there are no students in *it!*
Correct	Of course the *hallways* are not crowded if there are no students in *them!*

Modifiers

To avoid confusion, phrases or clauses should be placed as close as possible to the words they modify.

Confusing	When taking hurdles, the helmet must have a chinstrap.
Improved	When you take hurdles, you must use the chinstrap on your helmet.
Confusing	Bouncing off parked cars, I saw the driverless truck.
Improved	I saw the driverless truck bouncing off the parked cars.
Confusing	Jeff asked me before I left to call him.
Improved	Before I left, Jeff asked me to call him.
Confusing	Our agency rents cars to salespeople of all sizes.
Improved	Our agency rents cars of all sizes to salespeople.
Confusing	When risen, you punch down the bread dough, cover it with a weight to keep it down, and let it rest for 24 hours.
Improved	When the bread dough has risen, you punch it down, cover it with a weight to keep it down, and let it rest for 24 hours.

Don't shift verb tenses unnecessarily.

Wrong	I *entered* the large room, and facing me *are* two tall windows, dressed only in venetian blinds.
Correct	I *entered* the large room, and facing me *were* two tall windows, dressed only in venetian blinds.
Correct	I *enter* the large room, and facing me *are* two tall windows, dressed only in venetian blinds.

Punctuation

Over the years punctuation practices have been eccentric, excessive, and changeable. Even the last decade has seen a trend toward simplified, less formal application of rules. That doesn't mean that anything goes, however. The primary function of punctuation is clarity, and most rules have clarity as their purpose. No fashion or expression of the writer's personality should ever take precedence over that. Other rules derive from convention: the colon after the salutation in a business letter, for instance. Your readers won't fault you for using punctuation conventionally.

In the following sections, we'll look briefly at some of the rules for the most common or troublesome situations. No attempt is made to be exhaustive; one useful book on the subject, Harry Shaw's *Punctuate It Right!*, is 176 pages long!

COLON

The colon is generally used to introduce a word, phrase, or clause that fulfills or explains an idea in the first part of the sentence. It is also used to introduce lists.

If you plan to go to Europe next summer, be prepared: millions of other American tourists will have beat you to it.
(Introduction or fulfillment)

I'm looking for three qualities in my next car: good gas mileage, low maintenance, and a little style.
(List or enumeration)

Some students see the colon as a kind of grammatical equal sign (=).

Her answer was simple: no.
(Answer = no)

One other important use of the colon is to separate the title and the subtitle of a book:

Time of Need: Forms of Imagination in the Twentieth Century

SEMICOLON

The semicolon is a mark of separation, stronger than a comma, weaker than a period. It can be used only between independent clauses not joined by *and, but, or, nor, for, yet.* Its use is optional: When you wish to emphasize the close relationship between clauses, use the semicolon; otherwise use a period.

> Skiing isn't easy; it just looks that way.
> Vegetable gardening can help a family budget; in some cases food bills are reduced as much as 30 percent.
> Health care costs skyrocketed in the 1970s; no relief is in sight for this decade.

The semicolon is but one of three ways of relating independent clauses, all correct. The difference is in the shades of meaning gained.

> The city's task force on crime met for nearly 3 hours. No decision was made about extra police patrols.
> The city's task force on crime met for nearly 3 hours, but no decision was made about extra police patrols.
> The city's task force on crime met for nearly 3 hours; no decision was made about extra police patrols.
> The city's task force on crime met for nearly 3 hours; however, no decision was made about extra police patrols.

COMMA

The most versatile, most frequently used mark of punctuation, the comma is also the most difficult to master. It is a relatively weak mark of separation, much less emphatic than the colon, semicolon, or dash. The major uses of the comma follow:

Before *and, but, or, nor, for, yet* when they join independent clauses:

The turnout for the rally was light, but everyone agreed they had made their point.
Exception: very short clauses
He drove and I walked.

To separate items in a series:

Rightly or wrongly, the Swiss people are thought to be thrifty, hard-working, and a bit stolid.

To set off interrupters:

I heard that Gary Trudeau, the cartoonist, is going to speak on campus.
(Appositive)
He should remember, by the way, that I warned him about that lamp.
(Parenthetical expression)

After an introductory adverb clause:

When you called, I was getting ready to work on my French.

After a series of introductory prepositional phrases:

On the way to the store in the rain, I lost my wallet.

Do *not* use a single comma between subject and verb

Wrong: The senator's statement, obviously rehearsed blamed the blunder on the president.
Correct: The senator's statement, obviously rehearsed, blamed the blunder on the president.
Correct: Obviously rehearsed, the senator's statement blamed the blunder on the president.

OTHER MARKS OF PUNCTUATION

A few other marks of punctuation cause student writers enough problems to merit mention here. These rules do not exhaust the uses of these marks.

Apostrophe

Used to show omission of a letter or numeral:

> doesn't (does not)
> won't (will not)
> the '80's (the 1980's)
> summer of '42 (1942)

Used to show possession

> Singular or plural noun not ending in *s*: add apostrophe and *s*:
> > Jim's
> > men's
> > girl's
> Plural noun ending in *s*: add apostrophe:
> > trees'
> > girls'
> > boundaries'
> Singular nouns of one syllable ending in *s* or *s* sound: Add apostrophe and *s*:
> > Henry James's novels
> Singular nouns of more than one syllable ending in *s* or *s* sound: Add apostrophe:
> > Socrates' philosophy
> Indefinite pronoun: Add apostrophe and *s*:
> > somebody's idea
> > anyone's guess
> Do *not* use an apostrophe with possessive pronouns:
> > his, hers, yours, ours, theirs, whose, its (*it's* means "it is")

Dash

Used to show an abrupt break in thought:

> We were on the Mountain Road—but I told you about that.
> When you arrive—assuming you get there—you must visit the castle overlooking the river.

Used to separate or announce an idea in the conclusion of a sentence, much as a colon does, but less formally. Emphasizes what follows:

If you were planning to look for a job in Alaska next summer, my advice to you is—don't.

They began about 10 years ago—the complaints that Johnny can't write.

Used to set off for emphasis (instead of using commas or parentheses):

Of the two novels we read—*The Sun Also Rises* and *A Farewell to Arms*—Hemingway's tale of the lost generation is my favorite.

Do not use the dash unless you know why you are using it. It is still a controversial mark of punctuation.

Quotation marks

Used to set off direct quotations:

Professor Herbert asked, "Is your paper late again, Johnson?" (Direct quotation)

Professor Herbert asked me if my paper was late again. (indirect quotation)

Exception: long quotations are indented and single spaced and quotation marks are not used (see Chapter 10).

A quotation within a quotation uses single marks within double marks:

In his convocation address last month, Dean Spicer summed up: "Remember President Kennedy's words, 'Ask not what your country can do for you—ask what you can do for your country.' "

Used for titles of short stories, poems, essays, articles, and chapters of books:

"The Scaffold" chapter in *The Scarlet Letter*
Robert Frost's poem "Stopping by Woods"
Swift's essay "A Modest Proposal"

Note: titles of books, full-length plays, magazines, and newspapers are *italicized* or *underlined*, not placed in quotation marks.

APPLY YOURSELF 7. Revising sentences. Each of the following passages needs work. Some sport outright errors of punctuation or agreement. Others are wordy, repetitious, or awkward. Review "A Few Words about Style" earlier in the chapter" and "Correctness, Matters of." Then revise each sentence to make it clear, economical, and correct.

A. Both books became favorites with the public for their unique insights. *Black Elk Speaks* for its eloquent expressive English filled with metaphor and simile. *Bury My Heart at Wounded Knee* for its exposé of the half-truths of our history.

B. There are several types of problem drinkers in our society today. One type of problem drinker is one who drinks before being called upon to do something he dislikes. If he had to speak before an audience or go visit his mother-in-law are just a few examples.

C. The sun is the driving force in our hydrological system. Its solar radiation evaporates the water from the oceans turning it to water vapor. Evaporation occurs when there is enough heat energy to break apart water molecules. When this happens the water changes from a liquid to a vapor.

D. The undaring beginner can buy an "instant beer" kit at any hardware-garden center. For a small pittance (10 dollars) you can buy a complete kit, except for the bottles, to make a full case of beer.

E. The low pH level in the precipitation has many adverse effects. The formation of acid lakes is one of them. In the Adirondacks alone over three hundred are present. These lakes contain so much acid that all marine life is killed. A trademark of crystal clear water results from their lack of fish and vegetation. Acid lakes have caused problems in Norway also. Small fishing villages have literally been wiped out of economic existence.

Chapter Twelve
Starter parts—
capture your audience

$\mathcal{I}$t's important that your reader *want* to read your essay even if he has to. Much of the time we write under compulsion and read out of necessity. College students write term papers for their professors. Department heads write quarterly reports for their regional managers. The professor *has* to read that term paper, the regional manager *has* to read that quarterly report. Under these conditions, what an advantage you'd have if you could only make the reader forget that he or she *has* to read the piece. Make him or her *want* to read it instead. Ways exist to do this. That's what this chapter is all about.

What if you're not writing for a captive audience? Making the reader *want* to read your work then becomes a matter of survival. As far as I'm concerned, something I write doesn't even exist unless and until someone reads it. Whether it's a publicity release for your organization, a free-lance feature for your local paper, or an article you hope to sell to a national magazine, you have to persuade at least two people to *want* to read it—an editor and a reader. This chapter will show you how to accomplish this goal.

TITLES

Often overlooked entirely or hastily tacked on, the title not only announces the subject of the essay but also plays a large role in interesting or prejudicing the reader. Because the title must be brief yet effective, its composition is demanding. Look at each of the examples below to see how it works.

"Invasion from Mars" (David B. Parker)
  Little green men? UFOs? Danger?
"The Craft and Craftiness of Henry Kissinger" (Philip Geyelin)
  Play on the word "craft." Love him or hate him, Kissinger is still news.

"Hi! Sex Is Not Located Only in the Head" (Herbert Gold)
> *"Hi!"?—First time a title ever said that to me.*
> *"Sex"—now I've got your attention. I didn't know sex was located in the head.*

"A Very Easy Death" (Simone de Beauvoir)
> *Seems to be a contradiction, easy and death.*

"I Want a Wife" (Judy Syfers)
> *Why would somebody named Judy want a wife?*

"Eat Better, Spend Less" (Carol Brock)
> *Food is one of life's chief interests. It comes third after money and sex, or is it sex and money?*

"What Every Child Should Know About Grownups" (Eda LeShan)
> *Reverse of the expected, which is what every parent should know about children.*

"Q. How Much Are You Worth?
 A. More than You Think" (Barbara Gilder Quint)
> *The question and answer form is striking, although easily overdone. What do you mean, "how much am I worth?"*

LEADS

The opening paragraph arrests the reader's attention. It should also reach out to the reader in his world and connect that world with the world of the essay.

> The problem with tourists visiting New York City for the first time is that they will immediately spend over fifty dollars to see a Broadway show when they could get forty times the entertainment for only one-fortieth the price.
>
> *Adam Bodian*

> An 1875 then-and-now advertisement for the American Meat and Vegetable Chopper depicted a weary grandma huddled by the fireplace, bowl in lap, knife in hand, laboriously mincing the ingredients for her Christmas pies. A second picture showed a then modern mother, at ease, book in hand, watching her young daughter crank the mechanical chopper, accomplishing in four minutes what had once taken an hour. Today, the food processor performs the same operation with a flick of the wrist in a few seconds.
>
> *Meryle Evans, " 'A Good Egg Beater Is a Treasure,' " Antiques World*

The lead is *not* the introduction. It is a separate element the sole purpose of which is to favorably dispose the reader toward your essay. The functions of the traditional introduction are met by the billboard, described later in the chapter.

Just what makes for a good lead? The answer to that question depends in part of your purpose and your audience. If you are writing to convince department heads in your organization to change a company policy regarding marketing procedures, you probably wouldn't want a lead that was cute, but that doesn't mean it has to be dull.

Some kinds of leads seem to be perennially successful. The *anecdote* is at the top of my list. Let's say your topic is the deplorable state of nursing homes for the aged and you want to provoke your reader to action. Your lead might recite the case of *one* patient, giving concrete descriptions of her living conditions, appearance, and treatment. Your anecdotal lead makes a huge national problem more understandable by showing it at the human level. Here is an effective example of the anecdotal lead:

> Not long ago in Austin, Texas, a motorist—furious because the driver ahead of him had stopped to make a left turn—got out of his car, grabbed the other man's tie and pulled on it till the man nearly choked.
>
> Julie Candler, "Secrets of Defensive Driving," Woman's Day

Closely related to the anecdote is the *example*, a specific instance of a general situation. An analysis of U.S. foreign policy in the 1980s might begin by citing the example of the Iranian seizure of American hostages. The value of the example lies in its concreteness. The following opening contains several examples of the quest for sleep:

> In Baltimore, all-night walking tours have been arranged for insomniacs. In Lee, Massachusetts, where a man named John Boyne had the wit to name his small motel The Morpheus Arms, would-be sleepers have to be turned away by the hundreds all summer long. If we are not lying awake thinking about our own sleep, we are worrying that one of our children will wet the bed or walk in his sleep. The babble about sleep ailments is all but deafening; specialists terrify us with the news that many people stop breathing the minute they go to sleep, or their hearts stop, or both. Sleep clinics have become big business from coast to coast, and what it can cost to have your insomnia studied will really wake you up.
>
> Ruth Mehrtens Galvin, "Probing the Mysteries of Sleep,"
> The Atlantic Monthly

A third kind of lead that works well is the *conflict*. Embodying tension, opposition, controversy, it gets your essay off to a dynamic start. Osteopath versus physician, farmers versus the power company, the draft versus the volunteer army. Human nature is attracted to conflict as the schoolyard fight between two eleven-year-olds demonstrates. This kind of lead can effectively be combined with the anecdote for a certain winner.

When it's relevant, the lead I call the *striking fact* makes an irresistible opener. Here are a few examples:

> Oddly enough, the year 1979 marks not only the tenth anniversary of man's first landing on the moon, but also the *one hundred and tenth* anniversary of the first artificial satellite.
>
> Bartlett Gould, "New England's First (and only) Manned Satellite," Yankee

> There is an ancient Chinese legend, dating from 300 B.C., describing how the organs of two men, Lu and Chao, were interchanged by a surgeon named Pien Ch'iao. This story is almost certainly apocryphal but at least it suggests that the idea of transplanting organs from one person to another entered man's mind at an early date.
>
> William A. Nolen, M.D., "Organ Transplants: What We Know Now," McCall's

"You can earn 25, 50, even 200 dollars by selling your essays. And it's legal." Does that lead get your interest? Would you like to learn more about it? Would you read the rest of the article that begins that way? If you answered yes to those questions, you've proved my point—people are interested in money, making it and saving it. The *money* lead takes advantage of that fact of human nature. Here's one example:

> For more than 2,000 years, *le vendange* (the gathering in of grapes) has been one of France's most widely noted late summer and early autumn traditions. We all know that.
> But did you know that you can actually get paid ($15 to $25 a day, plus—in most cases—a daily bottle of wine) for taking part in this almost-mythical harvest. . . .
>
> Roger Mann, "You Can Work Your Way through Southern France!" The Mother Earth News

Mann hits the reader with a one-two punch that's unbeatable—you can indulge a fantasy *and* get paid for it.

Several other kinds of leads work well too: humor, quotation, arresting questions, powerful description. Do be careful that your lead isn't so gimmicky or cute that it repels readers instead of attracting them. Then whatever kind of essay you write, let the lead arrest the readers' attention and, meeting them where they are, bring them into your world.

BILLBOARDS

Closely related to the lead is what one writer-editor has called the billboard. Let him explain:

The lead paragraph in a magazine article must be seductive. The final paragraph must be arresting. But between the two, near the top, there should be a paragraph which—if written resourcefully—is practically invisible. If it is not written at all, the entire article will probably fall apart.

What is this paragraph that often makes or breaks articles? I call it the *billboard*, and I've never bought an article that didn't have one.

Billboards do what the name implies. They succinctly summarize the article. They tell the reader what he is about to read. In fact, you have just read *my* billboard.

Every magazine article must make its intentions known early because readers want to know what they are going to read about. . . .

Brian Vachon, "Be a Billboard Artist," Writer's Digest

Here Vachon not only explains the lead and the billboard, he exemplifies them. Paragraphs 1 and 2 are the lead—they create interest, introduce a little suspense (just what *is* this paragraph that's so important?), and imply a surefire device for selling articles. Paragraph 3 is the billboard. "Billboards," Vachon summarizes later on, "develop the tone, introduce the theme, state the article's reason for being, and then disappear." In paragraph 4 the writer has moved on to the body of the essay.

What if you never intend to write a magazine article? You still need a billboard. Every response to an essay exam, every course paper calls for a billboard. If you reread Vachon's piece substituting the word "essay" for "article," I think you'll see what I mean.

APPLY YOURSELF 1. Titles, leads, and billboards. Study the following examples. Analyze each title. Does it work for you as a reader? Try to write another and perhaps better one for this subject. Find the lead. How does it do its job? Does it work? Is there a billboard? Does it do what Vachon says a billboard should?

MICROSTEREOS: GREAT SOUND IN TINY PACKAGES

Remember when buying a car meant falling under the spell of horsepower and chrome? It's still much that way in the stereo trade. The ultimate in high-fidelity sound systems is a superpowered, room-dominating monster with the technological panache of a Star Wars rocket cruiser.

But now there is an alternative to the bigger-is-better ideal. A year or two ago a few pieces of sleekly understated and undersized equipment appeared in some stereo showrooms, and within the last few months there has been a further shrinking in size and weight. You can now buy stereo components, even speakers, that fit in a shoe box.

Changing Times

ZOOMING IN ON TV AUDIENCES

A sizeable group of young men who are blue-collar workers watches sports events on television less often than most groups of female viewers.

One large group of television viewers is rural Southerners, many of them black, who lack educational advantages and look to television, particularly public television, to expand their horizons.

Adolescent boys tend to favor situation comedies that poke fun at male authority figures, while adolescent girls from fairly affluent families like satires of family life in general.

One segment of the national TV audience is composed largely of elderly women who use television as a means of coping with loneliness.

Given the pervasiveness of television in our culture, it is sobering to realize how little we really know about what kinds of people watch various programs and why. The four observations above may not seem startling in themselves. But they are drawn from one of the few intensive surveys that seeks to look closely at the nation-wide television audience to determine whether it can be broken down into specific interest groups, and, if so, to pinpoint what uses each group makes of the medium.

Ronald E. Frank and Marshall G. Greenberg,
Psychology Today

APPLY YOURSELF 2. Write your own openers. Here are some ideas for essays. Try to write an effective title, lead, and billboard for each one. Since these starter parts will be influenced by your purpose and intended audience, you'll have to settle those questions first.

1. Some aspects of do-it-yourself car or home care (e.g., changing the oil and filter, painting your house)
2. The life history of some species of bird or animal
3. Careers in public health, law enforcement, medical care, or another field
4. The story of a community's plan or handling of its teenagers, growth, waste disposal, energy needs
5. An idea or ideal relevant to contemporary society such as privacy, equality, faith, education

APPLY YOURSELF 3. Revising one of your essays. Select an essay you have written this semester that needs to be revised; a piece done for this course would be ideal. Then, based on what you've learned from this chapter, rework the opening of that essay. Strengthen the title, lead, and billboard.

Chapter Thirteen
Endings—getting out gracefully

*I*n the last chapter we considered ways of making an initial appeal to readers—getting them interested in our writing and then leading them into our world. The problem that this chapter deals with is how to show them out the door graciously when the party's over.

Some people seem to have no trouble writing endings. I'm afraid I'm not one of them. In 60 seconds I can think up two or three leads for just about any subject under the sun. But it usually takes me as long to write the last paragraph of an essay as it does the preceding six. Yet knowing that the final effect is as important as the first impression, I'm willing to take the time. Understanding the various functions that an ending can perform for your essay does seem to help wrap things up more effectively—and with an emotion that can approach pleasure, or at least satisfaction.

You can end a piece effectively in any of two dozen ways. Five of these techniques follow. For the sake of clarity, each one is explained and exemplified separately. In practice, though, a writer often combines two or three methods in concluding an essay.

SUMMARY

A summary is a brief retelling of the major points of the essay, a recap. It is especially useful at the end of a long argument, a complex process, or a technical piece, where it is likely to be a point-by-point restatement to reinforce the material of the essay.

> The evidence appears clear. Teachers' incompetence rests at the base of the learning problem. How can we expect students to learn if their teachers lack sufficient knowledge of the subject? Why should they want to learn if teachers continue to prohibit outside classroom exploration or exhibit apathy

about the subject? Test scores must stop dropping. Teachers should be required to pass achievement tests prior to classroom exposure. Colleges must impose tougher curricula for education majors. With the surplus of teachers existing today, we can afford to weed out those who fail to reach adequate standards and replace them with competent educators.

Rachel E. Prentiss, "Educate the Educators"

Perhaps the worst ending is the unnecessary summary: a point-by-point recap of the two main points in a one and one-half page essay on a simple topic such as choosing the right breed of dog for you. Please don't ever write this kind of summary. If you can't find another way of ending, just stop.

EMPHASIS

This kind of ending drives home the central idea or thesis of the essay. "Drives home" may be too strong an expression, for it suggests forcing the "message." Subtlety usually works better.

> Animals in the wild are becoming increasingly scarce due to many "improvements" man makes for himself. Behind every new development lies a wake of destruction. The fate of endangered animals is somewhat of a paradox. It is through man's ignorance and greed that these animals live on the verge of extinction; however, it is only with man's help and protection that they can begin to survive.
>
> *Debra S. Merone, "This Time There'll Be No Ark"*

JUDGMENT OR LOGICAL CONCLUSION

Most commonly used to close an argument, the judgment or logical conclusion is the final step in a series. The sequence may be: proof$_1$, proof$_2$, proof$_3$, therefore conclusion. Or if A, then B; if B, then C; therefore conclusion. Here is the closing paragraph of an argument in favor of capital punishment.

> When, in 1976, the Supreme Court declared death to be a constitutional penalty, it decided that the United States was not that sort of country [in which the desire for vengeance prevails]; most of us, I think, can appreciate that judgment. We want to live among people who do not value their possessions more than their citizenship, who do not think exclusively or even primarily of their own rights, people whom we can depend on even as they exercise their rights, and whom we can trust, which is to say, people who,

even in the absence of a policeman, will not assault our bodies or steal our possessions, and might even come to our assistance when we need it, and who stand ready, when the occasion demands it, to risk their lives in defense of their country. If we are of the opinion that the United States may rightly ask of its citizens this awful sacrifice, then we are also of the opinion that it may rightly impose the most awful penalty; if it may rightly honor its heroes, it may rightly execute the worst of its criminals. By doing so, it will remind its citizens that it is a country worthy of heroes.

Walter Berns, "For Capital Punishment," Harper's

CALL FOR ACTION

You've made your case, pointed out the problems, accused the wrongdoers. Now you want your reader to take the next step—to do something. This is where the call for action comes in. Although this kind of ending might be a stirring cry, "to the battlements," more often it takes the form of a mild urging, as in this example.

> In the end, children and adults find themselves caught in a cycle of anger, fear and violence. But it is a part of our adult responsibilities to break that cycle, to find ways of communicating with our children and to give them the feeling that they are indeed the future. The first step we can take is to conclude that we can no longer afford to lose so many of them to violence.
>
> *Joel Dreyfuss, "Our Violent Children," Family Circle*

DRAWING THE CURTAIN

Has this ever happened to you: When reading an article in a magazine, you get to the bottom of the page, then turn to the next page only to find that the article has ended? And you didn't realize it? The problem is not with your poor reading; it's the author's poor writing. The end of an essay should contain quiet but unmistakable signals that the end is at hand. The writer "draws the curtain" the way the stagehand does at the end of a play. In addition to the four functional kinds of endings just described, several other types work primarily to draw the curtain and give a sense of completion to the essay.

1. Looking to the Future

Projecting the present situation as outlined in the essay into the future is a popular method of drawing the curtain.

> I looked at those two young islanders bending to the oars—one in his twenties, the other just at the edge of manhood. I knew that they, too, would

ɔ into exile, seeking a new life across the sea. Like generations of Celts
them, each would add a bright strand of individuality to life in other
nations. And bear an aching hunger for an ancestral land so poor in livelihood
yet so rich in beauty and legend and memory.

Merle Severy, "The Celts," National Geographic

2. Inverting the Funnel

Just as the funnel shape (moving from general to specific) often characterizes
the opening of an essay, the reverse, the inverted funnel, makes an effective
ending. Notice the movement from specific to general in the example below, written by a student.

> Despite the stand taken by the Carter administration, the Navy's uni-
> formed chief, Admiral Thomas Hayward, is urging the return of peacetime
> conscription. *The Burlington Free Press* reported on Friday, June 20th, that
> Admiral Hayward believes pay raises and improved benefits will not help the
> failing all volunteer force. Admiral Hayward points the way for the country to
> follow. The arguments in this very volatile issue make that fact clear. Consid-
> ering current world problems and the U.S. position as a guiding force and
> moral leader, Congress must support the draft. We can once again have a
> military that commands respect at home and abroad and the capability to
> protect the ideal of freedom for *all*.

Anne Smith, "The Draft"

3. Anecdote

An anecdote or terse, pointed story can crystallize an important idea of the
essay in a memorable fashion.

> The Corsicans have a reputation for being unfriendly. They certainly
> look gloomy, and their character is incontestably dour; but they are not smug
> or critical, they can be helpful, and they seem genuinely interested in
> strangers. "Simple in manner and thoroughly obliging," wrote Edward Lear,
> "anxious to please the traveler, yet free from compliment and servility." One
> old woman in the market at Ile Rousse told me in pidgin Italian that she
> thought Americans were "sweet." It is not a sentiment I have heard expressed
> anywhere else in Europe.

Paul Theroux, "A Circuit of Corsica," The Atlantic

4. Striking Quotation

Like the anecdote, a quotation can give lasting flavor to the theme of a piece
of writing, as this student's final paragraph demonstrates.

The lure of excitement and danger attracts a certain type of man to the profession. Those who can take the physical demands and risks are the ones that get rehired. A sort of 'survival of the fittest' has developed over the years. This has resulted in a particularly strong and rugged breed of men with an intense dedication. Darcy Marsh summed it up best when he said, "We provide people an eye into a world that most will never see. If I don't capture it with my camera, all that remains is my verbal account, and who's going to take the word of an Irishman?"

Keith Pierce, "The Dangerous Lives of Outdoor Cameramen"

5. Closing the Circle

An image or motif, first presented in the opening, is repeated in the ending. As the reader's memory is jogged, the point is made and the circle closed.

OPENING

The visitor to Vermont usually arrives with a preconceived picture of the typical Vermonter—big boned and sinewy, leaning on a fence post in faded bib overalls with a chaw of tobacco bulging his cheek—a man of few joys and even fewer words. Calvin Coolidge, "Silent Cal," was to many Americans the embodiment of this stereotype, hardworking and virtuous but without passion or mirth.

ENDING

In the early decades of the state's development, satires were usually of a political nature, like Thomas Rowley's "When Caesar Reigned King at Rome," Thomas Fessenden's "Eulogy on the Times," or, later, Leonard Marsh's delightful burlesque *A Bake-pan for Dough-Faces*, and the influence of foreign literary styles and techniques was strong. But as the Enlightenment and Neoclassical spirits waned, Vermont authors began to focus on the daily rounds of life, and the influence of Pope and Sheridan gradually gave way to the richness of native humor. What the tourist failed to notice about the overalled farmer was the twinkle in his eye.

A. W. Biddle and P. A. Eschholz, The Literature of Vermont

6. Changing the Rhythm

Probably the most common method of changing the rhythm is to follow several lengthy, perhaps complex, sentences with a short one. You know it's over. The principle is shown in the sentence below.

At a time when teachers are returning to basics, a fillip like values education may turn out to be an idea whose time came—and quickly went.

"Do Moral Values Belong in Schools?" Newsweek

A student altered the rhythm in the brief concluding paragraph that follows.

> The bicycle is a hybrid between the vulnerable pedestrian and the powerful automobile. When you realize that we provide all other forms of transport with their own "highways," you begin to wonder, "Why not have roads just for bicycles?" Indeed, why not?
>
> *George Eckert*

Changing the rhythm can be done very simply, as in the preceding two examples. Or it can be a very sophisticated business. The following paragraph is the ending of an essay on risk-benefit analysis, the planning tool that compares the costs of a course of action to the benefits to human life expected to follow. Its purpose is to help set priorities in matters of health and safety. The rhythmic effect of this paragraph is created very skillfully. The cumulative power of the four "mights" is undercut first by "perhaps," then by "but." The fifty-six syllables and three punctuation pauses of the next-to-last sentence are countered by the nonstop six syllables of the final sentence.

> But issues of equity and distribution and pie-cutting make up the backbone of our politics, and I see no reason to believe that we will cope any worse (or better) with these questions posed by risk-benefit than we have coped with other such issues in the past. One might even argue that we ought to face these inequities, to address honestly the realities of our distribution formulas. Perhaps. Risk-benefit might allow us to watch more closely than before what our government does, and therefore make us a more democratic society. It might allow us to discover and correct some serious inequities in our present programs, and make us more equal. It might, while doing this, make us safer and healthier. But the technique in its present state of development is too raw; the benefits it brings to the support of some values are not enough to compensate for the damage it does to other, equally important, values. Health isn't everything.
>
> *Fred Hapgood, "Risk-Benefit Analysis: Putting a Price on Life,"*
> *The Atlantic*

APPLY YOURSELF 1. See what you've learned. If you analyze each of the following examples, I believe that you will get a better sense of the ways an ending works. What technique(s) has each writer used?

1. All you can do is keep giving the dog chances to find grouse. When he handles the bird improperly, correct him. Then, once he's doing a good

job, start tempting him to break (stop pointing). When he breaks, show him he must never do that again. It takes time, patience and birds, birds, birds, but if a genuine grouse dog is the result, it will be worth whatever it costs.

Vince Gonillo, "The Grouse Dog"

2. Work! Save! Build! he does. Swabian diligence constantly tries to improve its inheritance—by evolution, not revolution. Though hard-pressed to give up his individuality and tradition, the Swabian is beginning to enjoy life in a more comfortable way than did his ancestors. But the industrious Swabian continues to be the motor of Stuttgart. A visitor drinking some local wine in one of Stuttgart's comfortable taverns and listening to the sad songs which Swabians sing has a sensation of being transferred to a different time and place. But he need only step outside to the hustle and bustle of the modern city to realize the polarity between tradition and progress.

Monica Rossi, "Work! Save! Build!"

3. There is every indication that the number and variety of options available to television viewers is increasing and will continue to do so for the near future. Correspondingly, audiences for network programs are likely to shrink. Attracting and retaining sizable audiences under these conditions will require greater insight into audience needs and wants. The networks may gradually find it more profitable to target specific audiences for advertisers and design the programs for their interests and tastes. Ultimately, the public will benefit from more diversified programming.

Ronald E. Frank and Marshall G. Greenberg, "Zooming in on TV Audiences," Psychology Today. The opening of this essay appears in Apply Yourself 1 in the preceding chapter.

4. Why study Saturn? Because it emits a tremulous C in the mezzo range every evening at seven o'clock. Because you know it is always there when you need it. Because its name helps you remember the word "saturnine" in the middle of the night. Because it bears down on a high-magnification telescope like a cement truck. Because it has something that looks like a watch stem sticking out of its north pole. Because if you were big enough to try to pin it under your thumb it looks as if it would slip away from you like a globule of quicksilver. Because it is the best at what it does. Because of the rings!

Daniel Menaker, "Saturnian," The New Yorker

5. What can we do to short-circuit the spread of smoking in the Third World? We can't stop governments in poor countries faced with immediate financial problems from mortgaging their future for cash today. We can't stop the multinational tobacco companies from profiting from the sale of legal commodities.

But we can insist that our government stop giving away tobacco as a form of bilateral aid. We can demand that our politicians help tobacco farmers kick the crop without suffering economic penalties. And we can make it clear to our leaders that we taxpayers refuse to be made accomplices in their international barter of people's health for money.

Walter S. Ross, "Let's Stop Exporting the Smoking Epidemic,"
Reader's Digest

APPLY YOURSELF 2. Revising one of your essays. Look through the essays that you've written and find one with an ending that doesn't satisfy you. Applying the principles set forth in this chapter, write a new conclusion.

Chapter Fourteen
The whole—from idea to essay

*P*rewriting, drafting, revising—each step of the writing process demands dozens, perhaps hundreds of decisions. That's why learning to write is infinitely harder than learning to drive a car, operate a computer, or fly a plane. Yet somehow all those decisions come together in a finished piece of writing.

The purpose of this chapter is to exemplify the major steps of the writing process. Although these steps are treated separately throughout this book, you might find it useful to see how one student put them together. Sarah Buntenbah was in a writing class of mine when she turned in an essay on controversies surrounding genetic research. Along with a revised draft of the essay, her writing folder contained notes, outlines, and early drafts of the piece. Arranged chronologically, these materials illustrate step by step the process of moving from an idea to a revised essay. Fortunately, she agreed to assemble and present her materials for this book. Except for this introduction and the Apply Yourself sections at the end, the rest of the chapter is hers.

If you read Sarah's materials from beginning to end, you will see the writing process in action, perhaps as you've never perceived it before. Each step is no longer isolated, but a moment frozen, a frame in a motion picture. What one writer has done here with her topic is similar to what we all do when we write an extended piece of exposition.

But you may also use this chapter in another way—as a reference to be consulted from time to time. Thus, these materials become a supplement to the rest of this book. Here is what you will find in the pages that follow:

Comments on the acts of prewriting   (Chapters 2 and 3)
From notes to outline   (Chapter 2)

The chapter numbers indicate where the topic is treated in the text.

Sarah's essay isn't perfect. Along with its strengths, you'll find weaknesses too. My purpose in including it here is to illustrate for you the process one student writer followed in composing a fairly long (ten-page) paper. If reading her essay and commentary helps you to understand better some of the steps of this complex process, its place in this book will be justified. At the end of the chapter are some questions to focus your analytical and editorial skills on problems in the essay.

THE MAKING OF AN ESSAY

Sarah Buntenbah

THE ACTS OF PREWRITING. From conception of the idea to the informal outline.

1. Finding a subject

This was more a question of the subject presenting itself to me rather than my seeking it out. At the time of writing, there was extensive media coverage on the latest developments in the branch of genetic engineering known as gene recombination. New and often dangerous forms of life were seemingly being created in test tubes at the whim of the scientist, and a recent Supreme Court decision had given patent rights to the creators. The media, often resorting to sensationalism, seemed to be doing a great deal to spread alarm and trepidation and very little to inform the public of both sides of the issue in understandable terms that would enable them to make sound judgments.

This was highlighted when in a three-day period the same newspaper published an article and cartoon dwelling on the sensational aspects of this issue, closely followed by a very small, objective article reporting the birth of the world's fourth test-tube baby (quoted in essay). When I recalled the uproar on all fronts that had followed the birth of the first such baby, many questions sprang into mind, the most obvious being—What is going on here?

If the fears expressed in the media are well founded, how can they be so quickly forgotten? downplayed?

Are the media expressing a general fear or are they feeding one?

Is fear necessary? What are we afraid of?

What are *cloning* and *test-tube babies* anyway?

Can we create monsters?

How is all this related to my existence, to future life as we know it?

Is this our entry into a "Brave New World," "1984"?

Are we thinking and making decisions for ourselves or letting others do the thinking for us?

Do we have the information necessary to make any judgments on genetic engineering? Why not?

Since genetic engineering is such a vast and complex subject, I clearly had to reduce my scope to bring it into manageable proportions. I decided to focus on the two areas that had come to my attention, namely, gene recombination and reproductive engineering.

2. Defining an audience

My audience was defined by the way in which the subject presented itself. I wanted to address the same audience as that reached by the newspaper articles: the "average reader" who has no special scientific knowledge.

3. Determining a purpose

Why am I writing this?

To see if there were any clues that might point toward the answers to my questions.

To present both sides of the issue to my audience in terms they can understand.

To help them to gain some perspective from which to make judgments and to perceive their role in this issue.

4. Selecting a point of view

5. Choosing a form

These occurred simultaneously and concurrently with the preceding three stages. My concern was not to advance one point of view on genetic engineering but rather to present both sides of specific issues while at the same time remaining within the context of the general problem, that being the tendency of the media and the general public to overreact rather than make responsible decisions based on understanding. The form that arose from this is a combination of definition, comparison and contrast, and argumentation and persuasion.

6. Collecting specifics

It became clear that for my audience to understand the issue I must build for them the world within which the genetic scientist moves. This required several steps. To begin with, I had to give them some understanding of the language of the scientific world. This necessitated research into the definition of certain terms. I also had to research into the movement of current experimentation, into the demonstrated dangers and benefits of research in my selected areas, and also into the awareness of the scientist himself and the guidelines within which he works. The methods I employed included list making and brainstorming to discover that which I already knew, as well as observation and library research.

7. Making a plan

Having gathered together the results of my research and already having a sense of the form the essay would take, I had to find a way to present the issue in a coherent manner. I had to pull all the parts together into a cohesive whole. Making a plan allowed me to do this.

Beginning with a very informal plan, I was able to arrange and rearrange the subtopics until the shape of the whole essay emerged. The movement of the essay needed to be from the general to the specific: from a general entry into and grasp of the issue, to the specific areas of study and the pros and cons of their related controversies. In the conclusion, the movement was from the specific examples back out to the general problem, now seen with the benefit of a broader perspective.

Through a series of stages, I was then able to develop the first plan into a more formal outline. The details of this procedure can be seen in the following documentation.

STATE I OUTLINE

Genetic Engineering | not always
Research | a bad/good thing? MUST look at both sides.

INTRO Attitude of general public – curiosity and fear of unknown
Much media coverage – sensational – feeds fears?
↓ thru   reflects fears?
↓ time
matter-of-fact – why?
Why "panic" over each new step?
Does it have to be that way?

Definition of terms – to understand the problem
Brief description – DNA division etc.
How do we get from eye color to gene splicing?

Body – Applications and Arguments

Against – Dangers – Biological warfare   Brave
Cloning "superman"   New
Controlling destiny   World?

For – Plants – food production
Disease – viral and genetic
Future – genetic counseling

Asilomar Conference and early experiments –
(shows awareness)
Present watchdogs
ongoing research.   corn
sickle cell anemia
foot and mouth disease

General
Intro
↑ lead
Body
Specific
Specific
Conclusion
General

Conclusion – 1. Louise Brown – test tube baby
2. Genetic recombination – conquers disease
and defects

"panic not necessary – can deal with problem rationally – think
for ourselves – needn't tie scientists down but should watch
them: guide them: don't let them lose sight of priority –
good of mankind over knowledge for its own sake. – (that's
the danger!)

STATE II OUTLINE

More details

Body

A. *Against* – Moral
           Ethical
           Religious
           Legal

   Dangers → Biological warfare, epidemic – (gene recombination)
             ↘ Clones, ectogenesis – (reproductive engineering)

B. *For* – 1. Asilomar Conference – already aware of dangers
          2. Present watchdogs – RAC, NIH, Genetic Diseases Act etc.
          3. Proteins, hormones – sickle cell
                                insulin etc.   (Gene recombination)
                     F.M.D. – Plumb Island
          4. Plants – corn etc.
          5. Answer dangers above?
             Mapping – quality of life?
             Genetic counseling? } future trend (Reproductive engineering)
                 screening?
             (what about our "rights"?)

Conclusion – Summary of evidence, reproductive and gene
             recombination call to action – to assume
             responsibilty to think

   [invert funnel – ⌐‾‾‾⌐ – action of RAC
                              ↘ "panic" not necessary } close the
                                 but watch them!   } circle]

MAKING THE FINAL OUTLINE. Major steps taken to develop states I and II of the outline into that shown at state III.

The first step was to combine the additional details of the body of the essay shown in the state II outline with the state I outline. Then I had to regroup the details of the body into two separate subtopics. From that point I could deal with reproductive engineering and gene recombination separately. Each term would have to be defined and then divided into the arguments for and against, current developments and problems, and the guidelines acting upon them.

The second step involved the development and clarification of the plan of the introduction and lead.

Step 3 was the writing of the billboard which would state clearly what was going to be covered in the body of the essay. It had to make two points: one, that the essay would explore the two areas of genetic engineering (reproductive engineering and gene recombination) and two, that it would examine the controversies surrounding both areas in order to show the risks and benefits involved.

The most satisfactory place for the definitions of terms seemed to fall directly after the billboard where they might act as a point of entry for the reader into the body of the essay.

STATE III OUTLINE

Title

    Modern and Huxley?
    Genes and future?

I. Lead
   A. Public opinion
     1. Fear, threat, scare, dread
     2. Sensation, fascination, relish
   B. Media coverage
     1. Amount
     2. Tone—plays on fears
   C. Latest controversies
     1. Test-tube babies
     2. Clones
     3. Gene splicing

II. Billboard
   A. Two types of genetic engineering
     1. Reproductive
     2. Investigative—gene recombination
   B. Examine controversies to show benefits and risks

III. Definition of terms
   A. Genetic engineering
   B. Genes
   C. DNA
   D. Chromosome

IV. The start of life
   A. DNA action
   B. "Reasons" for panic
      1. Moral
      2. Ethical
      3. Religious
V. Gene recombination
   A. Dangers
      1. Epidemic
      2. Biological warfare
   B. Asilomar Conference—awareness of dangers
   C. Benefits and applications
      1. Gene mapping
      2. Mass production of hormones
      3. Genetic defects, e.g., sickle cell anemia case
      4. World hunger, e.g., corn, nitrogen fixing
   D. Modern guidelines
      1. RAC
      2. NIH
      3. Example in work on F.M.D. vaccine
         a. Phase I Plum Island
         b. Phase II California
         c. Problems arising
VI. Reproductive engineering
   A. Branches
      1. Cloning
         a. What is it?
         b. Arguments against: fears
         c. Arguments for
            (1) Study cell development
            (2) Clues to defects
      2. Ectogenesis
         a. What is it?
         b. Arguments against: fears
         c. Arguments for
            (1) Study cell development
            (2) Birth defects
   B. Both representative of future trend in genetic awareness
      1. Counseling
      2. Screening
      3. New possibilities
      4. Genetic Diseases Act—our protection

VII. Conclusion
    A. Summary of benefits (specific)
        1. Louise Brown
        2. Genetic defects
        3. Genetic disease
        4. Food crops
        5. Food animals
        6. Danger versus benefits
    B. Relationship 'us' and science (general)
        1. Hysteria unnecessary
        2. Watch and guide scientists
        3. We must not let them lose sight of the fact that mankind comes before knowledge for its own sake.

DRAFT   **DRAFT**

Gene ~~living~~ *Juggling*

Our way ~~into tomorrow~~ *to a Brave New World.*

Clones, Test-tube babies, ~~superman~~ *BEINGS,* selective breeding. What images do these words conjure up for you? Do you feel threatened or afraid? *THE UNKNOWN FASCINATES US* ~~We are fascinated by the unknown~~ and the more unlikely the better. We devour with relish anything ~~concerning~~ *RESEMBLING* horror or science fiction. ~~and~~ *And the* media ~~knowing~~ this *AND CONSEQUENTLY* publicizes many things out of all proportion. *And* that is how a scare starts. How often have you ~~been filled with dread~~ *READ AN ARTICLE ABOUT G.E. WITHOUT A SENSE OF DREAD CREEPING OVER YOU - EVEN IF YOU DIDN'T.* ~~after reading about genetic engineering?~~ ~~Did you~~ understand it all? ~~Genetic engineering balances~~ *THE SCIENCE OF LIFE CONSTANTLY TEETERS* on the edge of new discoveries which ~~we~~ *MANY OF US* cannot understand. Almost every week something appears in the media. The ~~attached~~ *ATTACHED* newspaper clippings were taken over a three day span. ~~They~~ *THE CARBON AND ARTICLE* refer to a recent Supreme Court ruling that new life forms can be patented ~~and show~~ *THEY PORTRAY EXACTLY* the general attitude to *WARD* all forms of genetic experimentation. ~~Consider Louise Brown.~~ The news of the birth of the fourth test-tube baby was greeted calmy ~~but~~ *ALTHOUGH* only a short time ago *THE NEWS OF* the first occasion created near panic. When Louise Brown was born in Bristol, England, uproar was ~~head~~ *HEARD AROUND THE* world ~~wide~~. Moral, legal and ethical opinions abounded. But time ~~tempers~~ *HAS* *ED* ideas and the threat to our civilization does not seem so great any more. ~~But~~ *the* controversy goes on. *GENETIC RESEARCH HAS NOT STOPPED THERE* The thought of a world ~~populated~~ with countless replicas of ~~themselves~~ *OUR* jumps into our minds ~~when we hear~~ *AT THE MENTION OF* *THE WORD OF* "clones", *One* misguided charlatan convinced many people that it was possible and *A VERY REAL* *ILITY* the book and movie "Boys from Brazil" ~~was very~~ *ENJOYED HUGE* successful. When the voice of science was finally heard, the truth that this procedure had a long way to go in humans allowed everyone to relax. The term "gene splicing" *ALSO* causes alarm bells to ~~clang~~ *SOUND* in the minds of many. This procedure *ANOTHER ASPECT OF G.E.* allows the transference of genetic material from one living cell to another. (When isolated one gene can be spliced

THEREBY   *DIFFERENT BENEFICIAL POSSIBILITIES OF THIS DISCOVERY*
onto another cell's chromosome, creating a ~~new~~ organism. The ~~benefits~~ are staggering e.g. mass *THEY COULD LEAD TO*

ASPECTS
production of hormones and vaccines. Gene splicing and (clones) represent two areas of genetic en-

HAVE INHERENT
gineering, reproductive engineering and gene recombination. Both ~~are~~ dangers but both have

great benefits ~~that outweigh the risks.~~

EXAMINING   SPECIFIC
    Before ~~turning to~~ the ~~two~~ areas of genetic engineering and their related controversies, ~~we~~
SHOULD BE CLARIFIED
~~should clarify~~ some basic terms. Genetic engineering itself is "the art or science of making practical

application of the knowledge of the pure science of genetics as employed in attempts to modify

OUR INHERITED
the structure, transmission, expression or effects of genes."[1] Genes are ~~the~~ blue prints ~~which we~~

~~inherit,~~ making us what we are. They consist of specific lengths of deoxyribonucleic acid (DNA)
ED   *EXISTING*
in (double strands) DNA has a complex ladder-like structure ~~and exists~~ as an interlocking double
HAS A CODE WHICH
helix. (Fig 1) Each rung of the ladder links together in a predetermined way. Each gene ~~is coded~~

~~and~~ directs the production of a protein or part of a protein. [The DNA makes up the gene as words
EFFECT
make up a sentence.] The visible ~~action~~ of a gene is called a trait e.g, blue eyes. ~~The gene itself cannot~~
EXIST
~~be seen, however chromosomes can.~~ Genes ~~are found~~ on a chromosome like beads on a string. ~~and~~
MAY   OF GENES   ARE FOUND   EVERY LIVING THING HAS
There ~~can~~ be millions on each chromosome. Chromosomes ~~lie~~ in the nucleus of cells and ~~are found in~~
OF THE PAIR
a specific number. Man has 46 or 23 pairs. One part comes from the mother and one from the
GENES CANNOT BE SEEN BUT CHROMOSOMES CAN, SO
father. ~~We can grasp~~ the function of genes from the study of chromosomes. The cells are burst open,
CAN BE INFERRED
the chromosomes are stained, photographed and grouped [22 of the chromosome pairs are identical.]
THE ONLY DIFFERENCE BETWEEN A
Male and female cells ~~are different~~ in one chromosome pair. Females are all XX while males have

one XY pair.
AT THE START OF LIFE   WHETHER
A new cell receives 23 chromosomes from each parent. ~~when life begins.~~ ~~If~~ the fertilizing
OR Y   DETERMINES THE SEX OF THE OFFSPRING.
sperm carries an X chromosome ~~then the offspring is female, if it carries a Y the offspring is male.~~
WHEN   AT THIS POINT
As the egg and sperm unite the two groups of chromosomes merge. ~~Then~~ three things happen.
SEPARATE
First, the DNA of the chromosomes replicates itself. The double strands in each ~~spearate~~ rather

like a zipper opening] and each serves as a template onto which a new strand is built. (Fig 2) The
CONSISTING OF
result is double the number of chromosomes. ~~Each has~~ one strand of "old" DNA and one of "new".
AND
Secondly, the double complement lines up in the middle of the cell. It divides into two groups ~~and~~
FINALLY
Each group moves to opposite ends of the cell. ~~Thirdly,~~ the cell divides creating a two-cell embryo
THIS PROCESS, KNOWN AS
with the normal number of chromosomes in each cell. Mitosis ~~is repeated~~ to form all the cells of the

body. The kind of cell created is governed by selective gene activation and inactivation . . . .
                        [MIOTIC CELL DIVISION REPLACES WORN CELLS]
                        [ALL THROUGH LIFE.]

This represents the opening paragraphs of the essay only.

FROM DRAFT TO FINISHED ESSAY. Major changes made between the second draft and the completed essay in its final form.

The preceding pages show a first draft of the initial section of the essay with revisions inked in. This draft extends to the end of topic IV of the state III outline.

The major changes between this revised draft and the finished essay that follows occurred in the section leading up to the body of the essay. As they appeared in the second draft, the first paragraphs were too long and lacking in unity. To counter this I reorganized and divided them into several more cohesive paragraphs, enabling me to make my points more clearly. Particular attention was paid to sentence structure and the order and choice of words.

During this stage I incorporated the text of the newspaper articles into the writing of the essay, rather than merely pointing to them. The passage on clones was moved from the introduction into the section of the essay dealing specifically with reproductive engineering.

The billboard of the second draft seemed to me to be lost in the lead of the essay. In order to highlight it as a pointer to the movement of the essay and to emphasize the two essential points, I included it as a separate paragraph, rearranging the wording and sentence order.

The definitions of terms constituted the second paragraph of the draft. I did not feel that the relationships between the terms were made fully clear. So, this section was reworked with this goal in mind. I also felt that the link between the terms and the rest of the essay should be made more distinguishable for, when understood, the terms show how the subject of genetic engineering might lead to a "panic" reaction.

FINAL FORM OF ESSAY

Gene Juggling—
Our Way to a Brave New World?

Clones! Superbeings! Test-tube babies! Selective breeding! What emotions do these words conjure up for you? Do you feel threatened or afraid? The unknown fascinates us, and we devour with relish any news hinting at horror or science fiction, even if we do not fully understand it. The media know our preference for the sensational and often resort to that style to inform us of the latest breakthrough in the science of genetics.

Genetic engineering or the application of genetic knowledge always creates controversy making it a very newsworthy topic. Currently, it attracts almost weekly media coverage. A very recent Supreme Court ruling allowing new forms of life to be patented drew many articles and commentaries, some dwelling on the possibilities of creating monsters and uncontrollable, lethal microorganisms. Science is thus portrayed as concerned only with the act of creating new organisms rather than as solutions to specific human problems. In fact, the court decision refers to the results of the gene splicing procedure. This method of genetic engineering allows the transference of genetic material from one living cell to another. One gene, when isolated, can be spliced onto the chromosome of another cell thereby creating a different organism. The beneficial possibilities of this discovery are many, including the mass production of hormones and vaccines.

In contrast, recently there appeared a short, concise article concerning the birth of the world's fourth test-tube baby.

> *A 24-year-old Australian nurse gave birth early Monday to the world's fourth "test-tube baby," a spokesman at Melbourne's Royal Women's Hospital said.*
>
> *Mrs. Linda Reed of Churchill, a small coal-mining town in eastern Victoria, gave birth to 7-pound 14-ounce Candice Elizabeth after 12 hours in labor, according to Dr. Geoffrey Westwood, acting medical director of the Melbourne hospital. He said the mother and baby were doing well after a normal delivery ("Australian Has World's Fourth Test-Tube Baby," 1.A).*

This objective piece of reporting belies the fact that only a short time ago news of the first such birth created near panic. When Louise Brown was born in Bristol, England, the uproar was heard around the world. Moral, ethical, and legal opinions abounded. But time has tempered emotions, opening the way to acceptance. Test-tube babies no longer make front page news, and the threat to our civilization does not seem so enormous anymore.

Each time a new process is discovered, arguments will rage. By studying the specific areas of genetic engineering represented by gene splicing and test-tube babies, we can examine these related controversies. Known as gene recombination and reproductive engineering, both areas have inherent dangers, but both have benefits that could, perhaps, outweigh the risks.

Before examining those specific areas of genetic engineering, some basic terms should be clarified. Genetic engineering is "the art or science of making practical application of the knowledge of the pure science of genetics, as employed in attempts to modify the structure, transmission, expression or effects of genes" (Karp, 219). Genes are our inherited blueprints determining our physical and mental characteristics. They consist of specific lengths of double-stranded, deoxyribonucleic acid (DNA). DNA has a tiny, complex ladderlike structure, existing as an interlocking double helix (Fig. 1). Each rung of the ladder links together in a predetermined way. The DNA makes up the gene as words make up a sentence. Like a sentence, each gene is a code that transmits a message. In this case, the chemical message is sent to all parts of the body where it directs body growth and essential biochemical functions (Milunsky, 49).

Figure 1

Strand of DNA
representing many genes

Figure 2

Unzipping of the
double helix

The visible expression of a gene is called a trait (e.g., blue eyes) but the gene itself is invisible. However, gene function can be inferred from the study of chromosomes. Genes are described as lying on a chromosome like beads on a string, and each chromosome may carry millions of genes. Chromosomes are found in the nucleus of the cell. To facilitate their study, the cells are burst open and the chromosomes stained, photographed, and grouped. Every living thing has a specific number of chromosomes in each of its cells. Man has 23 pairs, one unit of the pair donated by each parent.

Study shows that the difference between a male and female cell lies in one chromosome pair, the others appearing as identical. In human females this pair is characterized as XX while in males as XY. The fertilizing sperm cell contains only one unit of the pair. Whether it holds the X or the Y chromosome determines the sexual identity of the offspring, for when the male and female cells unite, the two groups of chromosomes merge forming an XX or an XY individual.

The moment of uniting initiates a sequence of events. First, the DNA of the chromosomes replicates itself. The double strands in each separate, rather like a zipper opening and each serves as a template ont) which a new strand is built (Fig. 2). The result is a doubling in the number of chromosomes, each now consisting of one strand of "old" DNA and one of "new." Secondly, the double complement lines up in the middle of the cell and divides into two groups. Each group moves to opposite ends of the cell. Finally, the cell divides creating a two-cell embryo with the normal number of chromosomes in each cell. This process, known as mitosis, repeats to form all the cells of the body. Through mitotic cell division, worn cells are replaced constantly. The kind of cell created is governed by selective gene activation and inactivation.

Now that we have a deeper appreciation of how genes govern our existence, it becomes easier to understand how panic is generated from any thought of genetic engineering. Many moral, ethical, and religious objections have been heard. Biologist Leon Kass sees reproductive engineering as unethical experiments on the unborn. He believes that we are not "wise" enough to predict the outcome, and any attempt to "remake ourselves" is the "folly of arrogance." Theologian Paul Ramsey believes that any conceptus of any age is a human being and should be treated as such. Any attempt to alter basic genetic makeup or create life by novel techniques is "an unacceptable effort to defy divine mandates and usurp divine prerogatives" (Cited in Karp, xiv).

We probably come very close to usurping "divine prerogatives" by our experiments in gene recombination. This form of genetic engineering gives us the ability to intervene in a process that is regulated by natural forces. The phrase "like begets like" no longer holds true. After splitting during replication, the DNA of a gene can be recombined with DNA from a different origin. The result is a new species.

The danger of experimentation along these lines is obvious and has been expounded by many. New diseases could evolve presenting major health hazards. By our manipulation we could unleash a catastrophe. Politically, an awesome power might be grabbed by a few who could threaten mankind. Many believe that if scientists continue this research, "they may disturb essential relations and balances, either unwittingly or malevolently, to gain private ends or to achieve irrational objectives" (Grobstein, 51).

The scientists involved in this frontier work appear to be aware of the danger of biological warfare and horrible epidemics. In February 1975, 150 scientists met in California to discuss the necessity of controlling their genetic research experiments. This conference at Asilomar was the first of its kind. After passionate debate, they agreed to recommend that their own freedom of action as researchers be limited. For scientists to make that commitment illustrates their acute awareness of the problems. The activities leading up to this momentous conference explain why they felt restriction necessary.

Scientists were beginning to realize the potential of gene recombination, and much research was being performed on the bacteria Escherichia coli (E. coli).

This organism inhabits the lower intestine of animals and humans. Scientifically, it has many uses because its one large chromosome can be removed and broken open. The DNA can be recombined with DNA from another source and returned to the cell to replicate itself. In one instance, it was suggested that DNA from a virus known to cause cancerlike conditions in human cells be used and allowed to propagate. The danger was obvious. If an infected bacterium escaped, humans could be infected, and a lethal epidemic would result. The scientists tried to control the perceived dangers by requesting their fellow researchers not to combine the bacterium with any tumor virus or antibiotic resistant strains. But the system failed; stronger measures were needed. In response to these concerns, the Asilomar conference took place (Grobstein, 16–18).

Despite the dangers, recombinant DNA research represents a new and powerful way to explore the function and structure of genes. Learning the location of each gene will mean that it can be excised and replaced if defective. Perhaps 2½ million genes exist on a chromosome, and the site of only a handful is known. Combining human and animal genes helps in this research. Work is underway on combining human and bacterial DNA to be reinserted into the bacterium for mass production. By this method the manufacture of large supplies of insulin, human growth hormones, and other hormones will be possible.

Someday, DNA recombination will be directly used to cure genetic defects in patients. For example, sickle cell anemia, a genetic disease common among Afro-Americans, manifests itself as abnormal red blood cells. It cripples and kills many before age 20. The patient has received a defective gene from each of his or her parents; however, only one good gene is needed to prevent the symptoms. The normal gene could be mass produced by the recombinant DNA method in bacteria and combined with harmless viral DNA to act as a transporter into the human cells. If this were done, the immature red blood cells from the bone marrow of the patient could be infected by the virus. These would then be innoculated into the patient's bone marrow where they would develop and produce normal red blood cells. So the theory goes!

Gene recombination will also play a role in the world of plants and food production. Corn, one of the most important food crops worldwide, needs much nitrogen fertilizer. Legumes, on the other hand, do not. Through symbiosis with bacteria living in the root nodules, legumes can fix nitrogen. The bacteria, or Rhizobia, carry the "nif" gene. Scientists hope to transfer the "nif" genes into the cells of the corn plant. The result will be corn that can fix nitrogen (Sprague, et al., 20). Many problems lie along the path, but the benefits in these times of world hunger may well justify the research.

Genetic engineering has to follow strict guidelines. The Recombinant DNA Advisory Committee (RAC) was specifically set up to follow the progress of gene recombination. This watchdog of the National Institute of Health meets quarterly to consider any revisions to the guidelines for recombinant DNA research. Bio

Science magazine reported that in December 1979 the RAC approved limited experimentation on the Foot and Mouth Disease (FMD) virus. Work in this area had previously been prohibited (Henig, 81).

FMD rampages everywhere in the world except North America, Australia, and New Zealand. The ban on the import of animals and fresh meat from countries where it is endemic controls the disease in this country. But since the present vaccine offers very little protection, America remains a likely site for an epidemic. At Plum Island, New York, the only place where the virus is permitted to be, safety precautions are stringent. Here the RAC has approved work on the cloning of Foot and Mouth virus in E. coli. This step represents phase I in the effort to develop a safer and more effective vaccine.

Phase I of the FMD research will provide a bank of chromosome parts of the virus. These components alone cannot trigger the disease but in combination they could. Phase II would isolate the specific gene which causes an immune response in animals. That gene could be recombined in the E. coli and replicated to give a good supply. A vaccine could then be developed. But this phase would have to be worked on in the more advanced research facilities of California, which means transporting the infected E. coli across the country. The committee is worried by the obvious risks involved and awaits some results on phase I before reaching a decision. They have to decide whether the benefits justify the risks.

Reproductive engineering, another branch of genetic engineering, can be defined as any attempt to produce individuals by means other than heterosexual intercourse. This subject invites great controversy. The infamous cloning process is just one aspect of research being conducted in this field.

To the unscientific mind, the term cloning evokes visions of a world populated with countless identical replicas. The words of a misguided few have convinced many of that possibility. In the wake of this, the book and movie "Boys from Brazil" (about clones of Hitler) enjoyed huge success. But the tension eased when scientists were allowed to explain that the procedure, although achieving some success with frog eggs, had many problems to overcome before humans could be involved. Clones are the descendents of a single cell arising by asexual reproduction. The offspring is identical to the single parent. Cloning does exist in nature, the amoeba being an example. In the future, this method of reproduction could be used to study the way human cells develop, giving clues to the causes of birth defects, cancer, and chromosomal abnormalities. An infeasible suggestion has been made that we should all freeze a clone of ourselves to use as spare parts!

More popularly known as the test-tube baby procedure, ectogenesis is another form of reproductive engineering which has created as much stir as cloning. Ectogenesis occurs when the egg or embryo is permitted to complete part or all prenatal development outside the female body. Theologians have called this practice immoral and a threat to society. Fears that this method could become government controlled bring us back under the shadow of "Brave New World." Fears that *monsters might be created by using irradiated sperm or drug damaged eggs beset some people. In practice, ectogenesis is helping infertile women and aiding scientific research. It is hoped that the ability to watch cells developing will give clues to the origins of cancer, birth defects, miscarriages and chromosomal errors.*

These methods of reproductive engineering represent the future trend of genetic awareness. Genetic counseling and screening will someday be routine procedures for all of us. We can use our knowledge to improve the health of future generations. Genetic diseases can be treated or avoided by new options being discovered every day. As we explore these new fields, action has been taken to protect our rights and welfare. The National Genetic Diseases Act passed in 1976 provides for a program of health services and education programs in genetic diseases (Omenn, 123). On the recommendation of the National Commission on Protection of Human Subjects active between 1974 and 1978, the Ethics Advisory Board was established. In 1978 the President's Commission for the Study of Ethical Problems in Medicine and Biomedical and Behavioral Research came into being to reexamine the "ethical, moral, social and legal implications of voluntary testing, counseling and information and education programs with respect to genetic diseases and conditions" (124).

Genetic engineering helped to make life possible for Louise Brown. In the future, it could allow people with defective genes to have healthy children, provide pure, cheap insulin for diabetics, and ease the pain of those afflicted with sickle cell anemia and countless other genetic diseases. On the world food scene, corn crops could expand and food animals would be healthier. The danger involved in tampering with natural forces is very real, but these examples illustrate some of the benefits to be gained. Genetic engineering should not evoke hysteria; we are not under the control of madmen. Scientists have seen the warning light. We should watch them and guide them while still giving them freedom to move. We must not let them lose sight of the fact that the good of mankind has priority over the pursuit of knowledge for its own sake.

WORKS CITED

"Australian Has World's Fourth Test-Tube Baby." *The Burlington Free Press*, 23 June 1980, 1.A.

Grobstein, Clifford. *A Double Image of the Double Helix*. San Francisco: W. H. Freeman and Company, 1979.

Henig, Robin Marantz. "Foot and Mouth Disease Virus May Be Cloned in *E. coli*, RAC says." *BioScience*, February 1980, 81–82.

Karp, L. E. *Genetic Engineering: Threat or Promise?* Chicago: Nelson-Hall, 1976.

Milunsky, Aubrey, M.D. *Know Your Genes*. New York: Avon Books, 1979.

Omenn, Gilbert S. "Genetics and Epidemiology: Medical Interventions and Public Policy." *Social Biology*, 26 (Summer 1979):117–125.

Sprague, G. F., *et al*. "Plant Breeding and Genetic Engineering: A Perspective." *BioScience*, January 1980, 17–21.

APPLY YOURSELF 1. Revising. Pages 223 to 224 show two drafts of Sarah's introduction. Let's call them versions 1 and 2. Version 3, shown on pages 225 and 226, provides more details, is organized differently, etc.

A. Set up a list of changes Sarah made in going from version 1 to version 2, using a format like the one below. Examine each change—why do you think she made it? What is the effect of the change? Was it a real improvement? (If not, what would you have done instead?)

SARAH'S CHANGE	REASON OR EFFECT	MY COMMENTS
1. Title: *Jiving* to *Juggling*	Eliminate slang?	Keeps color without frivolity
2. Subtitle: *Tomorrow* to *Brave New World*	Much more specific	Good! but assumes readers know B. N. W. reference

B. Now write a similar commentary for the transition from version 2 to version 3. Consider especially the decisions Sarah made to reorganize and to add clarification and explanation. Has she provided enough or too much detail, for example? Has her introduction captured your interest and clarified the scope and rationale of her essay?

APPLY YOURSELF 2. The writer as critic. Reflecting on the topics and advice in earlier chapters of this book, consider the strengths and weaknesses of Sarah's final draft. I've listed some of the topics on page 215, but you might also want to refresh your memory by skimming the table of contents. Write notes for a class discussion of Sarah's essay. To get you started, here are some questions to think about. Does Sarah resolve all her writing problems satisfactorily? How well does she fulfill her stated purpose? How well has she handled specific writing tasks like comparison and contrast, argumentation, integration of secondary sources? Has she presented sufficient evidence for her conclusions, and are these conclusions the only ones possible from the evidence at hand? Has she reached her intended audience and kept the "so what?" principle in mind? Is the structure of her paper clear, and are transitions effectively handled? Can you suggest ways in which the essay can be improved?

Acknowledgments

Copyright works are printed by permission of the following:

NELSON W. ALDRICH, JR., "Preppies: The Last Upper Class?" Copyright © 1978 by The Atlantic Monthly Company, Boston, Mass. Reprinted with permission.

WILLIAM R. ALLEN, "Mouse Wisdom: The Terrible Costs of Choice," from *The Midnight Economist: Broadcast Essays IV*. © 1982, International Institute for Economic Research.

DAVID M. ALPERN with Phyllis Malamud and Ron Labrecque, "Boston: A City of Two Tales." © 1980 by Newsweek, Inc. All rights reserved. Reprinted by permission.

"Another Bailout?" *The Wall Street Journal*, May 20, 1983. Reprinted by permission of *The Wall Street Journal*. © Dow Jones Company, Inc., 1983. All Rights Reserved.

PAUL S. APPELBAUM, "Can Mental Patients Say No to Drugs?" © 1982 by The New York Times Company. Reprinted by permission.

STEPHEN BARLAS interview with Estelle Ramey, "My Turn." Reprinted with permission from *Working Woman*. Copyright © 1983 by HAL Publications, Inc.

WALTER BERNS, "For Capital Punishment," *Harper's Magazine*, April 1979. © 1979 by Walter Berns, Basic Books, Inc., Publishers.

ARTHUR W. BIDDLE and PAUL A. ESCHHOLZ, editors, *The Literature of Vermont: A Sampler*. Reprinted by permission of the University Press of New England. Copyright 1973 by Trustees of Dartmouth College.

CAROLINE BIRD with SARA WELLES BRILLER, *Born Female*. © 1970 by David McKay Company, Inc.

JULIE CANDLER, "Woman at the Wheel: Secrets of Defensive Driving." © February 12, 1980, by *Woman's Day*.

CAROL CARTAINO and HOWARD WELLS, "Checklist for Action." © 1979 by Writer's Digest Publications.

JOHN H. CLARKE, "The Learning Cycle" in *The Leaflet*, LXXIX (Fall, 1980). © by *The Leaflet*.

EDWIN H. COLBERT, "Mammoths and Men", in *Ants, Indians and Little Dinosaurs*, edited by Alan Ternes, Charles Scribner's Sons, 1975. Reprinted with permission from *Natural History*, Vol. 46, No. 2. Copyright the American Museum of Natural History, 1940.

"Conservation alone is not an energy policy." Advertisement. © 1977, Mobil Corporation. Reprinted with permission of Mobil Corporation.

DAVID CUSHMAN COYLE, *The United States Political System and How It Works*, The New American Library, Inc. © 1954 by David Cushman Coyle.

JOEL DREYFUSS, "Our Violent Children." © 1980 by Family Circle, Inc. All rights reserved. Reprinted by permission.

"Electric Drills." Copyright 1979 by Consumers Union of United States, Inc., Mount Vernon, N.Y. 10553. Reprinted by permission from *Consumer Reports*, March 1979.

Emergency Handbook/Directory. © 1979 by Bridge Publishers.

PETER FARB, *Word Play: What Happens When People Talk*. © 1973 by Peter Farb. Reprinted by permission of Alfred A. Knopf, Inc.

ROSWELL FARNHAM, unpublished student journal, 1848. From original in the Roswell Farnham Papers, Special Collections, University of Vermont Library, carton 20, vol. 1.

LINDA BIRD FRANCKE, "The Sons of Divorce." © 1983 by The New York Times Company. Reprinted by permission.

RONALD E. FRANK and MARSHALL G. GREENBERG, "Zooming in on T.V. Audiences." Reprinted from *Psychology Today* Magazine. Copyright 1979 by American Psychological Association.

NICHOLAS GAGE, "The Paradoxical Papandreou." © 1982 by The New York Times Company. Reprinted by permission.

RUTH MEHRTENS GALVIN, "Probing the Mysteries of Sleep," published in *The Atlantic Monthly*, February 1979. © 1979 by Ruth Mehrtens Galvin.

BOB GLOVER and JACK SHEPHERD, *Runner's Handbook*. Copyright © 1977, 1978 by Jack Shepherd and Robert Glover. Reprinted by permission of Viking Penguin Inc.

BARTLETT GOULD, "New England's First (and only) Manned Satellite." © 1979 by Yankee, Inc.

PAUL GRIMES, "Changing Money Abroad." © 1983 by The New York Times Company. Reprinted by permission.

TED A. GROSSBART, "Bringing Peace to Embattled Skin." Reprinted from *Psychology Today* Magazine, February 1982. Copyright 1982 by the American Psychological Association.

CALVIN S. HALL, *A Primer of Freudian Psychology*. © 1954 by The World Publishing Company. Reprinted with permission of Harper & Row, Publishers, Inc.

FRED HAPGOOD, "Risk-Benefit Analysis." Copyright © 1978, by the Atlantic Monthly Company, Boston, Mass. Reprinted with permission.

RALPH M. HATTERSLEY, "Basic black-and-white printing: Photograms Teach You How." Courtesy *Popular Photography*. © 1978 by Ziff-Davis Publishing Co.

YOUSSEF M. IBRAHIM, "Treasury Aide Suggests Pressure Builds For Oil Price Cut, but He Avoids a Forecast" in *The Wall Street Journal*, May 18, 1983. Reprinted by permission of *The Wall Street Journal*. © Dow Jones Company, Inc., 1983. All Rights Reserved.

"It can run a mile cheaper than you." © advertisement for Volkswagen. Reprinted by permission of Volkswagen of America, Inc., Troy, Michigan.

CHARLES W. JOHNSON, *The Nature of Vermont: Introduction and Guide to a New England Environment*. Reprinted by permission of University Press of New England. Copyright 1980 by State of Vermont.

LYNN LANGWAY, "The Superwoman Squeeze." © 1980 by Newsweek, Inc. All rights reserved. Reprinted by permission.

KAREN BURKE LEFEVRE and MARY JANE DICKERSON, *Until I See What I Say*. © 1981 by I.D.C. Publications, University of Vermont.

DAVID LUDLUM, "Almanac." Reprinted by permission from *Blair & Ketchum's Country Journal*. Copyright June 1983, Country Journal Publishing Co., Inc.

ANGUS MADDISON, *Economic Growth in Japan and the USSR*, published by W. W. Norton and Company, Inc. © 1969 by Angus Maddison.

ANTHONY S. MAGISTRALE, "For Writing Teachers Only! Suggestions for Student Writing Assignments." © 1983 by *Exercise Exchange*.

ALFRED L. MALABRE, JR. "Brisker Rebound" in *The Wall Street Journal*, May 18, 1983. Reprinted by permission of *The Wall Steet Journal*. © Dow Jones Company, Inc., 1983. All Rights Reserved.

ROGER MANN, "You Can Work Your Way Through Southern France!" Excerpted with permission from *The Mother Earth News*®. Copyright 1977 by The Mother Earth News, Inc.

JANE MAYER, "Screen Test: T.V. Anchorwomen Never Die, They Get Replaced by the Young" in *The Wall Street Journal*, May 25, 1983. Reprinted by permission of *The Wall Street Journal*. © Dow Jones Company, Inc., 1983. All Rights Reserved.

DANIEL MENAKER, "Saturnian" in *The New Yorker*. © 1979 The New Yorker Magazine, Inc.

H. L. MENCKEN, "The Incomparable Buzz-Saw," from *A Mencken Chrestomathy*. © 1949 by Alfred A. Knopf.

CAMPBELL R. McCONNELL, *Economics: Principles, Problems, and Policies*. © 1981 by McGraw-Hill, Inc.

"Microstereos: Great sound in tiny packages" condensed. Reprinted with permission from *CHANGING TIMES* Magazine. © 1980 Kiplinger Washington Editors, Inc., February 1980. This reprint is not to be altered in any way, except with permission from *CHANGING TIMES*.

DAVID MORRIS and KARL HESS, *Neighborhood Power*, Beacon Press. Copyright © 1975 by the Institute for Policy Studies.

WILLIAM A. NOLEN, M.D., "Organ Transplants: What We Know Now." © 1979 by McCall Publishing Company, February 1979.

"Nutrition Information" for DORITOS® tortilla chips is used with the permission of Frito-Lay, Inc. The information is current as of November 1983. DORITOS® tortilla chips is a registered trademark of Frito-Lay.

GEORGE ORWELL, "Politics and the English Language" from *Shooting an Elephant and Other Essays*, published by Harcourt, Brace, and Co. © 1945 by Sonia Brownell Orwell. Reprinted by permission of Harcourt Brace Jovanovich, Inc.

WENDALL RAWLS, JR., "The TVA at 50." © 1983 by The New York Times Company. Reprinted by permission.

RICHARD RHODES, "A Bean to Feed the World." Copyright © 1974 by The Atlantic Monthly Company, Boston, Mass. Reprinted with permission.

CAROL RICHARDS, "Local Boards Should Hold the Reins of Education," May 25, 1983, in the Burlington *Free Press*. Reprinted by permission of the Gannett News Service.

WALTER S. ROSS, "Let's Stop Exporting the Smoking Epidemic." *Reader's Digest*, May 1980. © by Reader's Digest, May 1980.

JOHN RUSSELL, "Tumble of Tiny Specks." © 1982 by The New York Times Company. Reprinted by permission.

MERLE SEVERY, "The Celts." © 1977 by the National Geographic Society.

CLAIRE STERLING, "The Terrorist Network," published in *The Atlantic Monthly*, November 1978. © 1978 by Claire Sterling.

CASKIE STINNETT, "Travel Writing: It Don't Mean a Thing If It Ain't Got That Sting," published in *The Atlantic Monthly*, June 1978. Copyright © by The Atlantic Monthly Company, Boston, Mass. Reprinted with permission.

EDWIN WAY TEALE, *The Junior Book of Insects.* © 1953 by E. P. Dutton and Company, Inc.

PAUL THEROUX, "A Circuit of Corsica" published in *The Atlantic Monthly,* November 1978. Reprinted by permission of the author and his agent Blanche Gregory, Inc. © 1979 by Paul Theroux.

LEWIS THOMAS, "On Natural Death," published in *The Medusa and the Snail.* © 1979 by the Viking Press.

PAUL TILLICH, *Dynamics of Faith,* Volume X of the World Perspectives Series planned and edited by Ruth Nanda Anshen. Copyright © 1957 by Paul Tillich.

NIKOLAAS TINBERGEN, "In the Life of a Herring Gull." With permission from *Natural History,* Vol. 43, No. 4. Copyright the American Museum of Natural History, 1939.

NATHANIEL TRIPP, "Summer Storm." Reprinted by permission from *Blair & Ketchum's Country Journal.* Copyright June 1980, Country Journal Publishing Co., Inc.

BRIAN VACHON, "Be a Billboard Artist," in *Writer's Digest,* April 1977. © 1977 by Brian Vachon.

KENNETH F. WEAVER, "The Promise and Peril of Nuclear Energy." © 1979 by the National Geographic Society.

"We found the engineer we needed with his nose stuck in *The Wall Street Journal's* classified pages." Reprinted by permission of *The Wall Street Journal.* © Dow Jones Company, Inc., 1983. All Rights Reserved.

Index

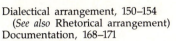